Conservation in Florida:

Its History and Heroes

Gary L. White

Conservation in Florida:
Its History and Heroes

Author: Gary White

Copyright 2010 by Gary L. White

Cover arwork by
• John James Audubon. Hooping Crane (whooping Crane) handcolored lithograph, 1834.
• Everglades photograph from Wikimedia Commons.
• Tomahs Meehan. Epidendrum Venosum. The Native Flowers and Ferns of the United States, 1879-80.

ISBN 10: 1-886104-44-1
ISBN 13: 978-1-886104-44-0

The Florida Historical Society Press
435 Brevard Avenue
Cocoa, FL 32922
www.myfloridahistory.org/fhspress

P•R•E•S•S

For my parents.

Table of Contents

INTRODUCTION

Since the arrival of the first Europeans, the peninsula now known as Florida has inspired expectations of an exotic Eden. Yet explorers have often found the place in reality to be inhospitable and forbidding.

Florida is both paradise and paradox. People have come to the state for its strange and distinctive beauty, yet they have almost inevitably sought to alter or improve upon the natural wonders, jeopardizing the source of the state's allure. In some cases, the environmental degradation has resulted from a relatively innocent misjudging of the finitude of nature, as in the ornithologists who traveled to Florida in the 19th century and returned to their northern universities with crates full of bird carcasses or the wealthy tourists aboard steamships on Florida rivers who wantonly hunted every living creature within range of their guns.

In other cases, the plunder arose from more venal motives. The plume hunters whose depredations of Florida's wading bird colonies supplied the feathers for hat-makers knew they would be handsomely compensated for their slaughter.

In more recent decades, the tension has largely arisen from competing visions of what Florida is and should be in the future. Conservationists hoping to preserve Florida's natural essence have clashed with those whose economic goals depended on incessant paving, building and population growth. The compulsion to alter is in constant competition with the yearning to preserve.

While many saw Florida around the turn of the 20th century as a place to be subdued and transformed, a few regarded the state differently. The tension between the urge to exploit and the need to protect is essentially the conflict between short-term thinking and long-term thinking, between viewing Florida's environment as a fungible commodity or a fragile ecosystem.

As we will see in the following chapters, the reaction against heedless plunder, in particular the violent decimation of wading-bird rookeries by the plume hunters, spurred nature advocates to cohere and press political leaders for more enlightened laws and policies. The impulse to unite in opposition to environmental threats has fueled the conservation movement in Florida for more than a century.

A reflection on the history of Florida's conservation movement must reach back even further than that and acknowledge the native tribes in the peninsula, whose ethos of sustainable interaction with nature was eventually displaced by the more exploitive philosophy of the Europeans who displaced them.

One man of European descent, though, served as an early exemplar of ecological awareness. William Bartram supplied the foundation for what became the conservation movement in Florida with his vivid and ardent descriptions of the bewildering beauty he encountered during his travels deep into the peninsula in the 1770s.

The impetus for collective action to protect Florida's environment came from a small group of amateur naturalists, many of them part-time residents, alarmed to learn that demand for feathers used in the fashion trade was fueling the massacre of wading bird colonies in the Everglades and elsewhere in Florida. A meeting of 15 people in Maitland in 1900, yielding the creation of what is now Audubon of Florida, offers a dramatic marker for the advent of environmental activism in the state.

In those early days of conservation, when authorities couldn't be counted on to protect wildlife from human predators, a few wildlife wardens put themselves at risk to stem the bloodshed in Florida's rookeries. Two of those wardens hired by the state Audubon Society paid with their lives for opposing the rapacious plume hunters.

As governments slowly adopted laws that halted the most egregious offenses against nature, conservationists began to concentrate on protecting not just animals but also the habitats that harbored them. Conservation groups acquired crucial lands to serve as wildlife sanctuaries and prodded government officials to set aside large tracts of Florida for the same purpose. In probably the most notable such achievement, nature advocates played a crucial role in the establishment of Everglades National Park, ensuring preservation of one of the world's ecological treasures.

As the conservation movement matured, advocates relied more on science and less on sentiment to pursue their aims. In Florida, professors and scientists provided crucial, empirical arguments against projects that threatened massive environmental harm. The science-based approach helped to persuade a president to halt construction of the Cross-Florida Barge Canal and to scuttle such proposals as a major airport sited in Big Cypress Swamp.

While conservationists sometimes seem to be a ragged band of outsiders battling much more powerful interests, by the early 1970s the excesses of industry turned public sentiment toward the need for more rigorous environmental protection. Just as the federal government was adopting landmark laws, Florida created programs for the acquisition and preservation of natural lands. Conservationists discovered that the state's voters, when asked to set aside public funds to protect important natural areas, responded in overwhelmingly positive fashion.

As Florida's population surged upward in the second half of the 20th century, conservation advocates played frantic defense against the seemingly unstoppable spread of urban enclaves into previously wild and lightly populated areas. Ecologists pushed the concept of growth management, prodding state and local governments to establish checks against the tendency of elected officials to regard all development as welcome. The effort led to the passage of important laws, though it also became clear that those who benefited economically from relentless development would not be easily deterred and would find ways to evade and overcome the measures.

By the late 20th century, ecologists could point to obvious examples of environmentally destructive projects and policies undertaken in decades past, such as the "channelizing" of the Kissimmee River. The transfor-

3

mation of one section of the wild and meandering river into a straight canal had disastrous ecological consequences, and by the start of a new century millions of dollars in public money were being spent to return the Kissimmee River to its natural, winding course. That complicated and ambitious endeavor, though, seemed relatively minor compared to the monumental Comprehensive Everglades Restoration Project, a federal-state initiative with an initial price tag of $7.8 billion. The decades-long undertaking sought to reverse much of the damage done by previous decades of water diversion projects opposed by conservation groups.

From the founding of the Florida Audubon Society in 1900 onward, successes in conservation have generally resulted from collective efforts. Certain individuals, though, have provided crucial leadership and persuasive abilities. A final chapter introduces a few Floridians, some long dead and others still quite active, whose contributions toward preserving the state's natural heritage have been particularly important.

The legacy of Florida's environmental advocates lies not only in what is to be found today — natural areas preserved and animal and plant species thriving or at least saved from extinction — but also in what does not exist.

Consider what Florida might look like today if not for the successes of those in the conservation movement. It's not an exaggeration to envision a state in which the Everglades is mostly drained and radically shrunken; a canal bisects the northern part of the peninsula, with a series of dams interrupting the natural flow of two major rivers; a massive airport sprawls in the Big Cypress Swamp; and snowy egrets, roseate spoonbills and other species of wading birds are extinct.

Environmental protection is often a lonely and difficult pursuit waged by citizens whose only potential reward is the knowledge that they will have done something to benefit their fellow citizens and future generations. The effort is particularly challenging in Florida, a state whose economy is predicated on a steady influx of new residents and a subsequent demand for new housing that stokes the construction industry. Roughly two-thirds of Floridians were born elsewhere, and as a result many lack a sense of personal attachment to the state, making it easier for them to shrug off the environmental losses that others feel so keenly.

Native-born status, though, is not an essential attribute of Florida's ecological warriors. Many of the most notable conservationists, from the early days of the movement to the present, have been people who arrived in Florida from somewhere else and realized that this was a place not only in need of protection but also profoundly worth protecting. That Florida's peculiar beauty continues to beckon visitors and new inhabitants is, in large measure, a testament to their commitment and successes.

1

Precursors of Ecological Awareness

For at least 14,000 years, humans inhabited what is now the state of Florida with little detrimental effect on the peninsula's wildlife and plants. Historians believe the first humans to occupy Florida descended from people who had migrated to North America from eastern Asia during the Pleistocene Epoch—the most recent ice age.

Hunter-gatherers called Paleoindians entered Florida around 12,000 B.C., when lower sea levels made the peninsula much wider than it is now. By 3,000 B.C., the seas had adjusted to roughly modern levels, and expanding populations had settled into most regions of Florida. The various cultures that flourished and faded over subsequent centuries relied on the natural elements that would later impress the first European explorers—the sustaining waters of powerful spring systems, the rich range of edible plants and the abundance of animals, both on land and in the region's varied forms of water. There were the freshwater lakes and rivers of the peninsula's interior, the salty and brackish marshes and estuaries near the coasts and the open waters off the coastline.

The sources of food available to Florida's native inhabitants must have seemed virtually limitless. They drew sustenance from oaks and hickories, coontie, spatterdock, greenbriar, arrowhead, maypop, buckthorn and palmetto. They munched on cattail roots and harvested hog plums, blueberries, elderberries, huckleberries, blackberries, red mulberries, persimmons, wild grapes and sea grapes. They ate the inner bark and young shoots of pine trees as well as the seeds from their cones. And around 750 A.D., some groups began cultivating corn and other crops.

There were no fewer choices of meat available to the hunters. Favored prey ranged from the large (black bears and loggerhead turtles) to the small (snails) and included much in between: oysters, rabbits, squirrels, deer, rats, alligators, snakes, freshwater mussels, crabs, dolphins, shrimp, freshwater turtles, bobcats, panthers, otters, foxes, wolves, raccoon, opossum and, of course, all manner of fish and birds.

In recognition of their dependence upon the natural world, the early cultures bred into their people a reverence toward all aspects of the environment that surrounded them. Southeast Muscogulges, for example, developed a concept of a three-tiered universe, with humans and most animals occupying the earth. Because they associated certain deities with the bottoms of lakes and the bowels of the earth, alligators, frogs, turtles, snakes and other reptiles and amphibians held exalted significance for them. The honored status of shaman or prophet went to a man who was believed to visit the bottoms of rivers and to converse with serpents. Finally, the Muscogulges venerated birds—especially high-flying eagles and buzzards—for their proximity to the heavenly gods.

Cultures rose and fell, but the state's natural architecture changed little for centuries. It proved a particularly enchanting place for the Europeans who began their explorations in the 16th century A.D. and who, of course, gave the peninsula the name that, in Anglicized form, has lasted into the present.

Two and a half centuries after the arrival of Juan Ponce de Leon, Florida remained lightly inhabited by Europeans when John Bartram, the official botanist to King George III, left his Philadelphia home and traveled to the region known as East Florida with his son William in 1765. John Bartram completed a scientific survey of the territory in nine months and returned north, but William, a somewhat aimless 26-year-old who had earlier declined a chance to learn the printing trade from Benjamin Franklin, decided to remain behind. William Bartram spent two years at Picolata, on the east bank of the St. Johns River near St. Augustine, where he attempted to cultivate an indigo plantation, but the effort failed perhaps in part because the young man spent much of his time wandering the wilderness of the peninsula's interior in pursuit of flowers, plants and glimpses of animals.

Though William Bartram eventually went home to Philadelphia, the experience in the wilds of Florida made a lasting impression on him. His botanical drawings based on observations made in Florida gained the attention of Dr. John Fothergill, a London botanist and fellow Quaker. In 1773, Fothergill granted Bartram's bold request that he sponsor a botanical exploration of the southeastern region. Fothergill provided 50 pounds a year and asked that the young naturalist collect seeds and plant specimens during his travels and send them to England. Bartram's journey lasted four years, covering the Carolinas and Georgia in addition to the Florida territories, and yielded writings that would establish the genre of naturalist reporting in American and fix Florida in the imaginations of Europeans as a paradisial land.

Bartram arrived by sail at Amelia Island in 1774 and soon began his travels down the St. Johns River into the state's interior. From the beginning, he sketched the flora and fauna around him and kept a lovingly detailed journal that reflected not only a scientific interest in the region's plants and animals but also his deistic brand of Quaker theology. Though a gentle fellow, Bartram was no dandy. He conducted much of his traveling alone by sailboat and canoe or on foot, camping among alligators and mosquitoes along the St. Johns River with no tent and few provisions. But only rarely in his journal did he seem bothered by the deprivations of wilderness life. An early journal entry is typical:

"I sailed in the morning on a fair wind. ... my chief happiness consisted in tracing and admiring the infinite majesty, power, and perfection of the Great Almighty Creator; and in contemplation, that through divine aid and permission, I might be instrumental in discovering and introducing into my native country some original productions of nature which might become useful to society."

Bartram found wonder all around him, filling his journal with rhapsodies to the grandeur of the towering magnolia trees along the river, the grace of sandhill cranes in the Alachua Savanna and the brute efficiency of the uncountable alligators he saw. Even in the midst of describing a harrowing ordeal among alligators that nearly cost him his life,

Bartram displayed an admiration for the natural order.

Through his patient observations, Bartram shaped a rudimentary understanding of bird migrations at a time when it was commonly believed that birds flew to the moon in winter (taking 60 days in each direction) or hid in the mud under ponds. He also observed that many species of animals in Florida were smaller than their counterparts elsewhere. In short, he combined a romantic gaze with a scientific one.

It would be inaccurate to call Bartram an environmentalist. The word wouldn't come into regular use until a century after his death, and he did not make a habit of advocating the protection of plants and wildlife, which after all still seemed invulnerably abundant during the time of his travels. But Bartram's writings established him as a precursor to modern environmentalists, displaying a sensitivity to the natural world around him that was lacking in most of his contemporaries. The naturalist carried a gun during his solo journeys but used it only when he felt truly threatened or when necessary to capture food.

Bartram's words serve as a prelude for the lamentations about Florida's wounded landscape that would become common in the 20th century. Upon seeing a village near Palatka that had been cleared for the planting of crops, Bartram wrote: "About 15 years ago, I visited this place, at which time there were no settlements of white people, but all appeared wild and savage; yet in that uncultivated state it possessed an almost inexpressible air of grandeur, which was now entirely changed."

One of the most poignant moments in Bartram's journal comes during a digression in which he remembers an incident from his previous period in the territory as an unsuccessful indigo farmer. He had made a trip to the New Smyrna Beach area with a hunter, and while boating (probably on Mosquito Lagoon) they came upon a group of bears near the water. The hunter shot one, and Bartram describes the aftermath:

"Whilst our boat approached very near, the hunter was loading his rifle in order to shoot the survivor, which was a young cub, and the slain appeared to be the dam. The continued cries of this afflicted child, bereft of its parents, affected me very sensibly. I was moved with compassion, and charged myself as if accessory to what now appeared a cruel murder, endeavored to prevail on the hunter to save its life, but to no effect!

For by habit he had become insensible to compassion toward the brute creation. Being now within a few yards of the harmless devoted victim, he fired and laid it dead upon the body of the dam."

Bartram also writes of an experience at one of his favorite Florida locales, the Alachua Savanna (now Paynes Prairie State Preserve), where deer, horses, turkeys and sandhill cranes "mix together, appearing happy and contented in the enjoyment of peace, till disturbed and affrighted by the warrior man." Coming upon a herd of deer with a companion who quickly drew his gun, "I endeavored to plead for their lives. But my old friend, though he was a sensible rational and good sort of man, would not yield to my philosophy."

At the time Bartram explored Florida, the few settlers treated the region's supply of wildlife as an inexhaustible resource. Bartram, though, despaired at the excesses of those around him. After describing a meal near Alachua Savanna that included a sandhill crane, the naturalist wrote: "... it made excellent soup. Nevertheless, as long as I can get any other necessary food, I shall prefer their seraphic music in the ethereal skies, and my eyes understanding gratified in observing their economy and social communities in the expansive green savannas of Florida."

And in a journal entry from Halfway Pond in what is now Putnam County, Bartram follows a long and precise description of a soft-shelled turtle with these lines: "We had a large and fat one served up for our supper, which I at first apprehended we had made a very extravagant waste of, not being able to consume one half of its flesh, though excellently well cooked. My companions, however, seemed regardless, being in the midst of plenty and variety at any time within our reach, and to be obtained with little or no fatigue or trouble on our part ..."

Bartram even writes of his regret after killing a rattlesnake, as unlikely a source of sympathy in his time as in ours.

Some of Bartram's most reverent passages capture his impressions of the many freshwater springs in Florida's interior. His description of Manatee Springs is typical: "This charming nymphaeum is the product of primitive nature, not to be imitated, much less equalled, by the united effort of human power and ingenuity."

11

Bartram could not have imagined the lengths to which people in subsequent centuries would go in attempts to improve upon Florida's "primitive nature." The naturalist returned to Philadelphia in 1777 and unhurriedly began the long process of winnowing his journal into a manuscript.

William Bartram's *Travels Through North and South Carolina, Georgia, East and West Florida, the Cherokee Country, the Extensive Territories of the Muscogulges, or Creek Confederacy, and the Country of the Choctaws* was published in 1791 and created an immediate sensation, especially in Europe. Some of England's Romantic poets, including Wordsworth and Shelley, drew inspiration from the naturalist's stirring descriptions of the alien geography of this new land. Samuel Taylor Coleridge was known to have devoured the book, and there seems little doubt that his poem "Kubla Khan"—with its "sacred river," "caverns measureless to man" and "sunless sea"—drew on Bartram's accounts of the ethereal springs of East Florida.

In addition to his Quaker gentleness toward the natural world, Bartram imbued his writings with a level of respect for the state's native inhabitants that differed from the official government policies that would eventually lead to the Seminole Wars and other conflicts. Bartram earned the trust of the natives in the peninsula, going so far as to attend the councils of the Seminoles and partake of the "black drink," a purifying emetic brewed from the leaves of the yaupon holly. The native people rewarded Bartram not only with assistance in his botanical pursuits but also with the affectionate nickname of "Puc Puggy," or Flower Hunter.

A few years after William Bartram completed the travels that would establish Florida as a place of enchantment, the man whose name eventually became synonymous with birds in Florida and elsewhere was born. Like Bartram, John James Audubon struggled through career disappointments before finding the purpose of his life—exploring the wilderness of America and capturing what he saw.

Audubon was an unknown bird painter aboard the cargo ship *Delos* when he first glimpsed the Florida coast in 1826. He made his first trip to the region (not yet a state) five years later, and his expectations derived largely from the writings of Bartram. It is clear from Audubon's writings that at first he found Florida undeserving of the glory Bartram had given it in his "flowery writings."

In correspondence with G.W. Featherstonhaugh, editor of *The Monthly American Journal of Geology and Natural Science*, Audubon made no attempt to hide his initial disappointment. Audubon was interested in animals, not plants, and unlike the botanist Bartram he viewed the land itself with an eye toward its agricultural potential: "The land, if land it can be called, is generally so very sandy that nothing can be raised upon it. The swamps are the only spots that afford a fair chance for cultivation; the swamps then, are positively the only places where plantations are to be found. ... Sugar cane will prosper, and doubtless do well; but the labour necessary to produce a good crop, is great! great! great!! ... Game and fish, it is true, are abundant; but the body of valuable tillable land is too small to enable the peninsula ever to become a rich state ..."

In a passage written about an island he named for himself in the St. Johns River, Audubon disputed the judgments of America's best-known naturalist: "Mr. Bartram was the first to call this a garden, but he is to be forgiven; he was an enthusiastic botanist, and rare plants, in the eyes of such a man, convert a wilderness at once into a garden."

In some ways it seems odd that the name of Audubon — rather than that of Bartram — came to be identified with the protection of wildlife in Florida and the entire nation. Unlike the gentle "Flower Hunter," who used his gun sparingly, Audubon had no reservations about killing the birds he encountered in Florida and elsewhere. In fact, some of the most emotional passages in Audubon's journal from Florida record his frustration at failing to shoot an animal he had targeted.

In a letter to Featherstonhaugh from the plantation of John J. Bulow near what is now Ormond Beach, Audubon wrote that he had come upon a massive flock of brown pelicans and shot two before he had trouble with his gun. "I really believe I would have shot one hundred of these reverend sirs, had not a mistake taken place in the reloading of my gun. A mistake, however, did take place, and to my utmost disappointment, I saw each pelecan (sic), young and old, leave his perch, and take to wing, soaring off, well pleased, I dare say, at making so good an escape from so dangerous a foe..."

Audubon's complacence toward the killing of birds arose in part from the abundance of wildlife he saw around him in Florida. If he were to shoot 25 pelicans at one spot, a bend in the river might bring him to another 25 or more. In addition, he sought a greater degree of precision than Bartram in his drawings. In the days before binoculars and cameras, detailed depictions of animals depended upon dead specimens.

Alexander "Sandy" Sprunt IV, a longtime officer in the wildlife protection society that adopted Audubon's name, summed up the matter this way: "Audubon's popularization of nature and particularly birds through his books and paintings has probably done more to preserve birds than any other single action. It can well be said that the birds that he collected died in an excellent cause."

Benefiting from greater resources, Audubon explored parts of Florida that Bartram never saw. He spent more than a month in the Keys and the Dry Tortugas before sailing for Charleston on May 31, 1832. At least 29 of the plates that later appeared in Audubon's landmark book *Birds of America* originated with birds he observed in Florida. These include such significant specimens as the Florida Jay (Florida scrub jay), Wood Ibis (wood stork), Caracara Eagle (crested caracara), Florida Cormorant, American Flamingo and Roseate Spoonbill.

Audubon supplemented his peerless drawings with unprecedented details about the lives of each species of bird, as well as accounts of where he had seen them. In the process, he amply expanded Bartram's record of the natural significance of Florida.

John James Audubon died in 1851, decades before the conservation movement took shape in America. He made no explicit pleas for the protection of wildlife, but in his meticulous drawings and his evocative writings he did more than any single person before him to foster an awareness of the uniqueness and value of birds. It was only logical that conservationists would realize the value of his name to their cause—first on a national level and eventually in the state that provided the subject matter for many of his famous drawings.

Members of the Florida Audubon Society touring the Everglades in 1962.
State Library and Archives of Florida

2

RECOGNIZING THE THREATS TO "EDEN"

In 1880, the state of Florida contained fewer than 200,000 residents—a figure below the current population of the city of Hialeah. Miami, not yet incorporated and still sometimes referred to as "Fort Dallas," was not even the Dade County seat (the honor belonged to a town called Juno), and the 1880 census for the county found only 257 souls sufficiently adventurous to withstand isolation, heat, humidity and mosquitoes. Railroad tracks had not yet been extended south of Jacksonville, and the steamboats that traveled down the St. Johns River ended their southward journeys at Lake Poinsett, near Cocoa.

Despite its relative lack of occupation, however, the state of Florida had achieved a certain renown arising in large part from the reports of wealthy northerners who had discovered the vast panoply of water and land known as the Everglades. Writers for the national magazines also ventured deep into the state's mysterious, swampy realms and filed dispatches in which the words "Eden" and "paradise" appeared without fail. Biologists, meanwhile, had come to regard Florida as something of an American Galapagos, worthy of annual treks yielding reports that sometimes tested the credulity of readers. Ornithologists, in particular, established Florida as a preeminent winter destination. Roaming from the pinelands of the Big Scrub region in the north to the mangrove tangles at the state's southern extremities, the bird specialists found an apparently inexhaustible supply of specimens to collect and haul back to the laboratories of the northern universities.

Ornithologists were not alone in being lured to Florida by the startling abundance of avian life. In fact, the men who traversed the state's lakes, rivers, swamps, saltwater marshes and coastal islands, gathering birds in the name of scientific advancement, often encountered members of an unofficial cadre whose quarry was the same but whose methods and motivation diverged from those of the men bearing Ph.D.'s. Though the majority of the birds harvested by this other group also were shipped to the Northeast, they wound up not on dissection tables at Princeton or on display at museums but rather on the heads of the nation's wealthy and fashionable women.

In the second half of the 19th century, the presence of birds — sometimes in their entirety but more often in the form of a few boldly draped feathers — became commonplace on the hats and dresses of ladies living far from Florida. Occupying the foremost position in the avian fashion hierarchy were "aigrettes," the term specifically denoting the elegant white breeding plumage from the backs of snowy egrets but often applied more generally to the long feathers of any wading birds. As the millinery shops of New York and Europe fed the sartorial appetites of the era, the demand grew for reliable supplies of bird plumes. In confirmation of the tenets of capitalism, men of an entrepreneurial bent emerged to provide that supply, and though Florida was not the only place in which wading birds could be found, its seemingly limitless bird populations combined with the freedoms available in remoteness made it the primary source of the milliners' stocks. With no wildlife protection laws in place to impede them, the commercial bird hunters found Florida most hospitable to their pursuits. They offered their contractors prices ranging from 20 cents to $2.50 per "skin," a considerable sum for the time and place.

By the 1880s, a fairly sophisticated network had arisen that connected the swamps of southern Florida with the haberdashers of Manhattan. Plume suppliers in Florida, sometimes employing vast crews of contracted hunters, shipped their crateloads of birds to northern agents, who sold the merchandise to millinery companies that then turned out feathered hats for the clothing stores. One of the plume entrepreneurs in Florida, a former New York taxidermist named J.H. Batty, was said to employ dozens of men ranging from Cedar Key to Key West. A plume hunter who often sold his harvest to Batty reported that the man would buy "almost anything that wore feathers." If Batty was not the preeminent commercial bird hunter in Florida during the late 1800s, then the distinction probably belonged to a man named Alfred Lechevalier and commonly referred to as "the Old Frenchman." Lechevalier (sometimes called Chevalier), an eccentric character from Montreal, mixed an interest in science with a pronounced commercial instinct. He and a band of assistants traversed the state in search of birds, but the Frenchman established a hunting base during the 1880s in the Pinellas Point area of St. Petersburg along the Boca Ciega Bay — now the campus of Eckerd College. Chevalier treated the nearby rookery islands — including Indian Key (also called Bird Key), now part of the Pinellas National Wildlife Refuge — as a personal fiefdom, chasing away other hunters who ventured too close. According to John A. Bethell's *History of Pinellas Peninsular*, two of Lechevalier's agents bragged that during one nesting season they gathered 11,000 skins and plumes and 30,000 bird eggs from the islands of Boca Ciega Bay. The early local historian offered a gruesome image of the wasteful bird hunters leaving spoiled eggs strewn across the earth for the ants to devour. He also tells of one of Lechevalier's assistants coming across a devastated rookery several days after the slaughter and being so repulsed by the smell and by the sight of starved young birds drooping out of nests that he gave up plume hunting — but only temporarily.

"The worst scourge that ever came to Pinellas Point was one Chevalier, a Frenchman ..." Bethell wrote. "I don't know how many birds Chevalier and his ruthless gang slaughtered during the three years he remained on the Point; for he brought a gang with him with a complete outfit for the murderous business. I know it was well into the thousands. Even the harmless pelicans came in for a share of powder and lead. ... Chevalier would not have remained here in the Point had not some of our settlers aided him in his nefarious work, from the fact that the hirelings he brought with him were ignorant of the bird rookeries on the land, and as they knew nothing about boats, could not hunt on the islands. But as some of the settlers enlisted in his hellish cause, then the war of extermination was waged on everything that had hide or feathers."

Lechevalier—ironically memorialized by the name of Frenchman's Creek, a tributary to Boca Ciega Bay—later lost two fingers and part of one hand in a shooting accident but taught himself to shoot again. He moved on to the Keys and the Ten Thousand Islands after decimating bird populations at Pinellas Point. At the height of his career, he told an acquaintance that his market for "skins" in Paris paid $10 for a great egret and an astounding $25 for a flamingo.

Batty, Lechevalier and the other plume hunters of Florida showed little discrimination in their pursuit of feathers. Though the milliners preferred the white plumes of egrets and herons—the exotic pink of roseate spoonbills would fade, and brown and gray feathers of other birds were regarded as dull—the hunters tended to shoot liberally and sort out the results later, especially as the competition increased and the supply waned. In Florida, the hunters turned their guns on everything from the smallest songbird to the largest owl, while on the streets of Manhattan in 1886 ornithologist Frank M. Chapman counted 40 different species of native American birds—or their remnants—in flightless display atop the heads of women. That same year, the American Ornithologists Union estimated that 5 million North American birds were being killed annually to supply the fashion trade.

Florida's wildlife populations received virtually no legal protection throughout most of the 19th century. The state legislature passed its first significant law in 1877, declaring a brief closed season on deer, wild turkeys, quail and mockingbirds, though loopholes weakened even that modest protection. Two years later, the legislature repealed the wildlife laws, restoring legality to wholesale animal slaughter, a condition lawmakers would leave unchanged for another 12 years.

It can be said with certainty that the plight of birds in Florida provided the emotional source for the American conservation movement of the late nineteenth century. The movement itself, however, did not originate in the state, which lacked the population—and especially the leisure class—to launch any such crusade of compassion. The drive to end the slaughter of Florida's birds began in the North, sparked by a small group of men who were in many ways unlikely catalysts, men whose backgrounds generally made them both tolerant of animal harvesting and aloof from social activism.

The American Ornithologists Union, founded in 1883 at the American Museum of Natural History, where Chapman served as bird curator, included the bird specialists at the nation's leading universities, among them W.E.D. Scott of Princeton University. Like many of his fellow ornithologists, Scott regarded Florida as an essential destination for research, and upon making his first trip to the state in 1876 he found it to be as bountiful in avian life as his colleagues had suggested. Without even venturing to the fabled Everglades and instead traveling along the Ocklawaha River and surrounding lakes in North-Central Florida, Scott recorded sightings of a plenitude of birds, including roseate spoonbills, snail kites, limpkins and now-extinct Carolina parakeets. Actually, Scott did more than simply report his observations. Like virtually all ornithologists of his day (and like John James Audubon before them), Scott engaged in the practice of specimen collection—a necessity for detailed observation in the era before binoculars and cameras became common. Scott reportedly left Florida after that first trip with a trove of specimens so large that he hired a six-ox team to carry it out of the woods.

By the early 1880s, however, Scott and his fellow ornithologists began to notice significant declines in Florida's bird populations—the cause of which was no mystery to the academics, who had become familiar with the tactics of the plume hunters. Scott, Chapman and other ornithologists were not inclined toward activism, and their first reports of the effects of commercial hunting on bird populations in *The Auk*, the journal of the American Ornithologists Union, bore a scientifically dispassionate tone. Yet the scientists had become sufficiently concerned about the depredation of birds, particularly in Florida, that some members of the AOU—including a magazine publisher named George Bird Grinnell—sought an activist role for the association. Despite opposition from some members, Grinnell and likeminded colleagues succeeded in creating a Committee on the Protection of North American Birds inside the AOU, and in 1886 the committee produced a document it said could serve as the basis for bird-protection legislation in every state. The guidelines in the document came to be known collectively as the "Model Law."

Not content to stop there, Grinnell decided to thrust his own national magazine, *Forest and Stream*, into a role of advocacy. In his editorial for the issue of February 11, 1886, Grinnell proposed forming an organization that would oppose "the killing of any wild birds not used for food; the destruction of nests or eggs of any wild bird; and the wearing of feathers as ornaments or trimming for dress." The organization, christened by Grinnell as The Audubon Society, collected no dues and planned to do no specific lobbying.

Grinnell debuted *The Audubon Magazine* in 1887, warning in the first issue that plume hunting "takes place on such a large scale as to seriously threaten the existence of a number of our most useful species." Noting the lack of adequate laws protecting wildlife in the United States, the magazine declared: "A war of extermination on these birds is a war against God and Nature, and reflects no less discredit on the government which tolerates it supinely, than on the individuals who prosecute it for gain." The sixth issue of the magazine featured a letter from J. Summerlin of Pinecastle, just south of Orlando—presumably Jacob Summerlin, a one-time mayor of Orlando known as the "cattle king of Florida." Summerlin decried the absence of bird protection in the state and the staggering recent decline in bird populations. He told of a trip to Brevard County in which he encountered plume hunters laden with feathers, estimating they had killed 1,200 birds in the area during a month of nesting season. Upon reaching a favorite rookery, Summerlin heard the shrieks of young herons and egrets that had been left to starve after plume hunters decimated the adult population. "I cannot describe the horror it gave me to hear the pitiful screams of the dying little birds," Summerlin wrote.

Such dispatches from the state where, as Summerlin put it, "no law (or) sentiment protects the birds," brought a response that proved to be more than Grinnell had expected or could manage. The monthly magazine lasted only two years, and the society itself soon crumbled under the weight of its own popularity. Grinnell lacked the staff to manage either the organization or its fledgling magazine, and no one emerged to sustain either endeavor.

For the next decade, advocacy for bird protection fell largely to the nation's academics. *The Auk*, which noted and applauded in its pages the brief life of Grinnell's Audubon Society, became a regular source of detailed reporting on the effects of plume hunting in Florida, with Princeton's Scott serving as the primary correspondent. Making regular visits to the previously vibrant bird territories of Florida, Scott filed a series of articles that sometimes departed from the detached, clinical tone that was customary for the magazine.

A decade after collecting his trunkloads of specimens around the Ocklawaha River, Scott arrived at Tarpon Springs in 1886 for a cruise of several weeks along the state's west coast. He had been in the area six years earlier, coming across a rookery in the Anclote Keys that supported "literally thousands" of herons, cormorants, pelicans and frigatebirds. Scott reported in *The Auk*: "This morning in passing these islands I saw but four Pelicans, two or three frightened Herons, and a few Gulls and Terns." Traveling on to Charlotte Harbor, an area that during Scott's previous visit had contained hundreds of rookeries, he found it virtually devoid of birds. In talking to local residents, including some who worked as plume hunters, Scott learned that Fort Myers served as the hub for the feather trade, with buyers for the millinery companies always on hand and ready to offer cash. Anchored in Charlotte Harbor, Scott and his party received separate solicitations from two hunters seeking to dispose of egret plumes, and Scott's unwillingness to buy the feathers left the men dumbfounded.

The mournful dispatches continued. Farther south, near Cape Haze, Scott encountered "a huge pile of dead, half decayed birds, lying on the ground which had apparently been killed for a day or two. All of them had the 'plumes' taken with a patch of the skin from the back, and some had the wings cut off ... I count over two hundred birds treated in this way. ... I do not know of a more horrible and brutal exhibition of wanton destruction than that which I witnessed here." One plume hunter, a man named Abe Wilkerson, cheerfully described his methods to Scott. Upon finding a rookery with snowy egrets, the man would enter as stealthily as possible and hide himself among the vegetation. Using a 22-caliber

Winchester rifle, whose report was no louder than the snapping of a twig, the man patiently hunted until he had cleaned out the rookery. He bragged to Scott of taking 400 birds in four days.

Scott continued to make regular visits to Florida, with his skills of observation increasingly put to use not in recording bird sightings but in documenting the ravages of the plume trade. Recalling that in 1880 he had found roseate spoonbills astoundingly plentiful at St. John's Pass near Tampa, he wrote in 1889: "All this is changed. ... My old hunting grounds have all been carefully traversed, some of them many times, and the Roseate Spoonbill is almost as great a stranger to me as to my fellow workers who live the year round in Massachusetts." And a year later Scott reported, "The 'plume hunter' is in greater numbers and more active than ever in South Florida, and there are absolutely *no Heron rookeries* on the salt water bayous or on the outlying keys of the Gulf coast of Florida, from Anclote Keys to Cape Sable."

Though birds occupied his scientific interest, Scott became aware that other animals in Florida were similarly treated as resources to be hunted without restraint. A ship captain at Little Gasparilla Pass told him that the intensive harvesting of loggerhead turtles had so reduced their numbers that before long it would be impossible to find a turtle in an area where a few years earlier "they had come to breed by the hundreds."

Other ornithologists joined Scott in drawing attention to the effects of plume hunting. Chapman, writing in *The Auk* in 1888, reported on the "merciless persecution" of herons in Paynes Prairie near Gainesville (William Bartram's beloved "Alachua Savannah"). And T. Gilbert Pearson, who had grown up in rural North Florida, also wrote about bird plunder for national magazines.

It's not clear which magazines were in the parlor of Harriett Lawrence Hemenway's Boston home during the winter of 1896, but the socialite and wife of a former state legislator read an account of bird slaughter in Florida that spurred her to do something. Hemenway, a member in good standing of the Massachusetts aristocracy, seized her copy of The Boston Blue Book, a social register, and scoured its pages with her cousin, Minna B. Hall, for the names of women whose wardrobes were likely to include ornamental feathers. The pair sent letters to these ladies of fashion, asking them to join a society dedicated to the protection of wild birds. Some of the recipients of the letters responded warmly, while others were too fond of their "aigrettes" to denounce the practice of plume hunting.

On February 10, 1896, Hemenway convened in her house a meeting that included not just fellow Boston socialites but also some ornithologists and naturalists to lend credence to the organization inaugurated that day—the Massachusetts Audubon Society. By 1900, Audubon societies had formed in 24 other states, with the groups helping to generate momentum for the AOU's "Model Law" and a related measure being pushed by Congressman John F. Lacey of Iowa that would prohibit shipment from one state to another of animals killed in violation of state laws. After the Lacey Act passed in 1900, 11 states—including Florida—either passed new animal-protection laws or strengthened existing ones.

As a century turned, the state whose wildlife had provided inspiration for the nascent conservation movement still relied almost entirely on outsiders to safeguard that wildlife. The situation was changing, however, as members of the Audubon societies of northern states carried their advocacy to Florida, either as winter visitors or year-round dwellers. Fortunately for the animal-friendly Florida residents, a culture of conservation had gained ground, its outlook encapsulated in the motto of *Bird-Lore* magazine, debuted by Frank M. Chapman in 1899: "A bird in the bush is worth two in the hand."

3

THE BEGINNINGS OF A MOVEMENT

On the afternoon of Friday, March 2, 1900, Louis F. Dommerich, a German-born businessman who had made his fortune as a silk merchant in New York, and his wife, Clara, hosted a gathering of neighbors at their winter home in Maitland, a few miles north of Orlando. The sweet waft of orange blossoms no doubt greeted the guests as they arrived at "Hiawatha," a 30-room, turreted, wooden frame house on the eastern shore of Lake Minnehaha, amid a spacious tract the owner had filled with citrus groves.

The 15 people present—10 women and five men—shared not only prominent status in the area (several were connected with nearby Rollins College) but also a fondness for birds, and their actions that day provided a convenient beginning point for the conservation movement in Florida. By enthusiastic consensus, they agreed to form an organization that would align Florida with the existing Audubon Society chapters in 24 other states, and the group adopted the bylaws of the New York Audubon Society, of which several in attendance were members. Though the gathering was small that afternoon, those present had reason to expect that a Florida Audubon Society would prosper. Some in the group carried letters from others interested in forming such an alliance as well as written pledges of both financial and moral support. Clara Dommerich, who had discussed the possibility with friends and neighbors, noted that "liberal subscriptions" had already arrived in her mailbox—seed money to support the venture. The group agreed to set the membership rates at $1 for regular members, $5 for sustaining members, $25 for patrons and 25 cents for junior members, and they decided to waive fees for any teachers who would join.

An executive committee appointed Rt. Rev. Henry B. Whipple, the retired first Episcopal Bishop of Minnesota and a winter resident of Maitland, as its inaugural president. Early honorary vice presidents included Florida Governor William D. Bloxham (who in a previous term had set in motion the draining of the Everglades), New York Governor Theodore Roosevelt (soon to be president), American Museum of Natural History ornithologist Frank M. Chapman, former president Grover Cleveland, state senator William S. Jennings (soon to be governor) and the editors of the state's major newspapers.

The group set its sights primarily on education, and to that end the committee voted to buy pamphlets on bird protection from the New York Audubon Society. It also agreed to draft a bill calling for greater protection of wading birds that would be presented to the state legislature in its next session.

Three weeks after that first meeting, Whipple sent a letter to Chapman, publisher of the fledgling *Bird-Lore* magazine (later to become *Audubon*), the national voice of the burgeoning conservation movement. After crediting Clara Dommerich as the force behind the new organization, Whipple lamented the decline of birds in Florida, noting that less than 20 years earlier he had seen a flock of some 2,000 Carolina parakeets around Lake Jesup near the town of Sanford.

"Our best work will be through the teachers of the public schools, for they can reach the hearts of the children, who wantonly destroy both birds and eggs," Whipple wrote. "We have been delighted with the enthusiasm and interest exhibited by the people of Florida in this blessed work. Our Saviour taught us that these feathered friends and companions of men are a special object of our Heavenly Father's care. And should He not have His children's help in their protection?"

The Florida Audubon Society grew to 450 members within three years. One of the first to gain "patron" status was Henry M. Flagler, the tycoon whose quest to develop South Florida commenced a cycle of devastation to the habitat in which so many of the Audubon Society's beloved plume birds lived.

Whipple died shortly after the chapter's first anniversary meeting at Hiawatha, and Louis Dommerich—whose wife, Clara, the secretary-treasurer and by all accounts the group's primary founder, also had recently died—took over as president. Within that first year, the state organization had spawned active chapters in Daytona Beach and West Palm Beach.

Though handicapped by the intermittent residence of many of its officers, the new Florida chapter possessed feistiness, especially in the person of Mary Munroe, wife of prominent nature writer Kirk Munroe. Lucy Worthington Blackman, a longtime Florida Audubon officer, summed up her colleague in an early history of the chapter:

"Wheresoe'er Mrs. Munroe's keen eye saw an aigrette waving, there she followed, and cornering the wearer—be it on the street, in the crowded hotel lobby, on the beach, at church or entertainment or party—there compelled her to listen to the story of cruelty and murder of which her vanity was the contributing cause. And Mrs. Munroe was eloquent. It was not unusual for women to be reduced to tears, whether of anger or humiliation or repentance, and several were known to have taken off their hats and destroyed their aigrettes as a result of their encounter with Mrs. Monroe (sic)."

But the Florida Audubon Society did not limit its lobbying to the individual level. In May of 1901, William Dutcher, president of the newly formed National Committee of the Audubon Societies, came to Florida to join the state group in pressing the legislature to adopt The Audubon Model Law drawn up by the American Ornithologists Union (AOU). The law would prohibit the killing of all birds not designated as game. Despite considerable opposition, the Florida Legislature passed a bill weakened by the inclusion of hawks, crows, owls, shore birds, ducks, pigeons, meadowlarks, robins, "butcher birds" (shrikes) and "rice-birds" (bobolinks) on the unprotected game list. The law also exempted any citizen who killed a bird "found injuring grapes, fruits, garden or farm products on his premises," and it sanctioned the keeping of cardinals and mockingbirds as pets. Still, the state law—setting a penalty of a $5 fine for each offense—afforded Florida birds additional protection under the federal Lacey Act, which barred interstate commerce in birds killed illegally.

The Florida chapter also achieved success closer to home when the Orange County School Committee agreed to set aside half an hour each week for bird study in its public schools. Florida Audubon supplied drawings of common birds as well as coloring books and crayons, all bought from the Massachusetts chapter. In addition, the society introduced an essay contest on bird protection for students. And the chapter accepted opportunities to give bird lectures at Hungerford School in Eatonville, a predominantly black town just north of Orlando and the home of future Harlem Renaissance writer Zora Neale Hurston.

By the time of its official incorporation on June 27, 1902, Florida Audubon succeeded in having a flyer listing Florida laws on bird protection displayed in post offices throughout the state and in the offices of the Southern Express Company. The chapter drew up a pamphlet called "An Appeal to Sportsmen" and persuaded several newspapers to publish it on occasion. And the new Audubon branch printed seven leaflets of its own with text written by members, including "Florida Birds Worth Their Weight in Gold," by Kirk Munroe, "John James Audubon," by Laura Norcross Marrs, and "The Rights of the Man Versus the Bird," by Miss Rose E. Cleveland, a board member and the sister of former president Grover Cleveland. Munroe, a well-known writer of children's adventure stories, wrote in his pamphlet: "We take every precaution to prevent a thief from stealing even the most trifling of our possessions, and at the same time make no effort to dissuade the gunner from shooting the birds upon whose existence depends our very livelihood. Queer, isn't it?" Despite the organization's continued growth, its directors decided at the second annual meeting to hire professional solicitors in an attempt to boost the membership.

The efforts of the fledgling Florida Audubon Society soon were rewarded through the action of one of its honorary vice presidents, Theodore Roosevelt, who had risen from governor of New York to the national presidency. Word reached Roosevelt that a German immigrant and boat-builder named Paul Kroegel had for several years been voluntarily guarding Pelican Island, a three-acre rookery in the Indian River near Melbourne thought to be the only brown pelican breeding site on Florida's east coast. Because of easy accessibility, the rookery had been subject to hunting since the mid-1800s. National Audubon members had raised money in a quest to buy the island from the federal government, but the offer had gotten bogged down in the General Land Office. Responding to warnings from Chapman and Dutcher about the rookery's vulnerability to the plume hunters, Roosevelt on March 14, 1903 designated Pelican Island as the first Federal Bird Reservation.

The executive order brought legal protection for the island's birds — but no money for enforcement because the act lacked congressional approval. National Audubon now hired Kroegel as the island's official warden, using money from a fund established by the wealthy painter Abbott H. Thayer. Kroegel erected a large sign proclaiming Pelican Island's birds "wards of the government."

Roosevelt would establish nine other bird reservations in Florida over the next six years, creating a network that gave rise to the current system of national wildlife refuges.

There was no shortage of issues to draw the attention of Florida's early conservationists. Florida Audubon loudly condemned the practice of "trap shooting," in which restrained birds (usually pigeons) were offered to shooters at point-blank range. Lobbying for a law against the practice prevailed, though it took five years.

Florida Audubon was the dominant force in state conservation during the first two decades of the 20th century, but it wasn't alone. The Florida Federation of Women's Clubs, a sustaining contributor to FAS almost from its inception, shared many officers with its affiliate and played an important role in the drive for bird protection. And the Audubon movement drew scientific credibility from its association with the American Ornithologists Union, many of whose members traveled to the state regularly for bird studies.

While establishing itself as a political entity, the Florida Audubon Society also made forays into the realm of conservation education. In 1904, when the membership list stood at 656, the group distributed 6,000 leaflets for children, 600 letters to legislators, agricultural officials, teachers and prominent citizens and 500 cards listing state game and bird laws to hotels, train stations, shops and other public places. Some churches also agreed to include Audubon pamphlets in their bulletins. And at Audubon's suggestion, many schools and women's clubs in the state had begun observing "Bird Days." Meanwhile, those 25-cent memberships from children led to a network of Junior Audubon Clubs, which gave conservationists a chance to reach youngsters outside the schools. At the state level, however, Florida Audubon for years failed to persuade the board of education to approve wildlife education in public schools.

While the state's only major conservation group worked to instill an appreciation for nature in Florida's children, it found that persuasion alone was not enough to protect the wading birds of Florida from the continuing menace of the plume hunters. Working with the AOU, Florida Audubon supported the hiring of four game wardens in the southern part of the state. Upon learning the wardens relied upon plodding rowboats, the FAS executive committee presented one of its wardens with a naphtha launch—an early form of motorboat.

One of the first wardens hired was a South Florida native named Guy Morrell Bradley, a reformed plume hunter and knowledgeable guide who had impressed writer and Florida Audubon member Kirk Munroe during an extended cruise in the Keys in 1902. Munroe wrote to Laura Marrs, a Florida Audubon officer, and urged the hiring of Bradley as a bird warden, saying Bradley was "fearless and brave and had an extensive knowledge of the country and the birds that lived there ... (was) always alert and faithful in the performance of his duty, and was willing to undergo any hardship to protect the birds." Mrs. Marrs relayed the suggestion to the AOU's Dutcher, and Bradley soon received an offer of $35 a month to guard the vulnerable rookeries ranging from Chokoloskee to Key Largo, a 140-mile band of coastline that included his home at Flamingo on the state's southern tip. After a few months, his official employer shifted from the AOU to the newly incorporated National Committee of the Audubon Societies.

Bradley—an excellent shot who could have made substantially more money as a plume hunter—proved a diligent and energetic warden, gathering the names not only of South Florida poachers but also of the

New York companies with which they did business. Bradley's direct approach toward apprehending plume hunters earned him many enemies during his first three years on the job, including a Civil War veteran named Walter Smith. Not only had Bradley become game warden of Monroe County—a job Smith was said to have coveted—he had reportedly arrested Smith's son twice for killing birds. Smith told neighbors that if Bradley tried again to arrest one of his family members, the warden would pay for it with his life. The threat must have reached Bradley, who early in 1905 told ornithologist Frank M. Chapman that he expected an eventual attempt on his life.

Walter Smith proved true to his word. On the afternoon of July 8, 1905, Bradley was at his cottage in Flamingo when he noticed a schooner on Florida Bay anchored near the Oyster Key rookery. Bradley promptly rowed two miles toward the suspicious boat, arriving in time to find Smith's son and another man returning from the island laden with dead birds. When Bradley asserted his right to arrest the two men, Smith brandished a shotgun and fired at the warden. Bradley fell back into his boat, which drifted slowly across the bay, eventually drawing the attention of two neighboring boys who saw vultures circling above it.

Smith, soon jailed and charged with murder, offered a story of firing at Bradley in self-defense, a claim contradicted by physical evidence and witness testimony. Nevertheless, a grand jury declined to indict the poacher. Bradley, 35, left behind a 25-year-old widow named Sophronia and two children. When news of the warden's killing spread outside South Florida, the Florida Audubon chapter organized a donation drive that yielded nearly $2,000, most of which was used to buy the widow a six-room cottage in Key West. Guy Bradley was buried near Flamingo, and National Audubon eventually placed a bronze marker at his grave reading: "Faithful unto death as game warden of Monroe County he gave his life for the cause to which he was pledged."

Three years later, another Audubon warden met a violent death. Columbus G. MacLeod's boat was discovered weighted by sandbags in Charlotte Harbor, near one of the rookeries he protected. Authorities never found his body, and no one was ever charged in the killing. After another warden was slain in South Carolina the same year, National

Audubon's Dutcher withdrew all wardens from south of the Caloosa-hatchee River in South Florida, though they were eventually reinstated.

"We meet in this bird-land of Florida obstacles that require Herculean strength to overthrow, yet the state which should listen to our suggestions for its benefit turns us a deaf ear," Florida Audubon's Laura Marrs lamented in a dispatch to *Bird-Lore* magazine.

As devastating as the presumed murders of Bradley and MacLeod were for Florida's conservation community, they benefited the movement in its campaign against the wearing of "aigrettes." Dutcher noted the moral effect when writing about Bradley's killing in *Bird-Lore*: "... A home broken up, children left fatherless, a woman widowed and sorrowing, a faithful and devoted warden, who was a young and sturdy man, cut off in a moment, for what? That a few more plume birds might be secured to adorn heartless women's bonnets. Heretofore the price has been the life of birds, now is added human blood." Florida Audubon printed pledges of abstinence from plume wearing and distributed them to women's clubs throughout the state, and the group persuaded Miami officials to halt the public trade in plumes that flourished during the winter (although many northern ladies simply began buying their feathers more secretly).

In its quest to shrink the market for bird plumes, Florida Audubon enlisted Dr. Herbert K. Job, a prominent ornithologist from Connecticut, to give a series of lectures in Central Florida and along the Atlantic coast. Job's slide show effectively juxtaposed images of birds in breeding plumage and on nests with masses of birds, stripped of their feathers and dead or dying.

While the list of Florida's Federal Bird Reservations continued to swell, the state's conservationists took a first step toward supplementing the program in 1911 when Florida Audubon member Oscar Baynard persuaded the national organization to buy an island in Orange Lake, just south of William Bartram's beloved Alachua Savanna. Baynard became the warden of the first National Audubon refuge in Florida. The national leadership soon added the Micanopy Rookery and San Sebastian Rookery to its protective program.

Emboldened by Florida's growing list of federal reservations, the

Florida Federation of Women's Clubs revived an issue that South Florida botanists had unsuccessfully pursued since 1893—the preservation of a hammock in the eastern Everglades containing the state's largest natural grove of royal palms (the tallest native palm in Florida). Known variously as Paradise Key and Royal Palm Hammock, the upland tract had been surveyed as early as 1847, and by 1914 developers were drawing up plans for the area that included a highway cutting through the hammock. May Mann Jennings, wife of a former governor who had endorsed draining the Everglades, became president of the women's federation in 1914 and made a priority of saving Paradise Key—an issue fellow members Mary Munroe and Edith Gifford had raised at the federation's annual meeting nine years earlier. Munroe persuaded James Ingraham, the late Henry Flagler's partner in the Model Land Company, and Flagler's widow, Mary Lily Flagler, to donate 960 acres of Paradise Key and surrounding land to the federation, and Jennings convinced the state to set aside a matching parcel of land after hosting a delegation from the Internal Improvement Board in what was her first visit to the hammock she had been lobbying to save.

As publicity about the hammock spread, vandals and orchid thieves increasingly ventured into the Everglades to gather what they could. Jennings, feeling the sense of urgency, personally lobbied Gov. Park Trammell for state protection, and the legislature in 1915 passed a bill designating the hammock as a state park—but failed to provide any funding for managing the tract. Jennings began writing to newspapers, civic organizations and wealthy Floridians in a largely fruitless search for money, and when Florida held a dedication ceremony for Royal Palm State Park on November 23, 1916, it remained a park in name only. Jennings managed to drum up enough private donations to hire a caretaker, Charles Mosier, who lived in a tent with his family for three years until a lodge was built at the park. Jennings continued her tireless pursuit of a state operating endowment for the next four years but nearly abandoned the effort after the death of her husband. Perhaps out of sympathy, the legislature finally granted annual funding of $2,500 in 1921, and the state also added 2,080 acres to the park. Having succeeded in an exhausting crusade, Jennings made it known publicly that her organization would donate Paradise Key to the federal government if a national park were created in the Everglades.

National Audubon for years had paid close attention to Florida, and in 1910 the connection grew stronger when T. Gilbert Pearson succeeded Dutcher as the organization's president. Pearson, who spent his childhood in the rural town of Archer near Gainesville, would hold the position for 24 years. Perhaps because of his provincial ties, Pearson made no secret of his disappointment with the slow growth of Florida's conservation community, as compared to other states. Writing in *Bird-Lore* magazine in 1916, Pearson lamented (in a considerable exaggeration): "I can count on the fingers of one hand the names of all the men and women in [Florida] who contribute a dollar to this work. And so we cannot look there for the sinews of war for our Egret campaign in 1916, but, as usual, must turn to the New England school teacher, the New York businessman, and others of our friends who dwell north of the Potomac River."

The Florida Audubon Society underwent a change of leadership when failing health prompted Louis Dommerich to resign as president at the 1912 annual meeting, held at his Maitland home. William Fremont Blackman, the president of Rollins College in the wealthy neighboring town of Winter Park, succeeded him and would serve for nine years. Dommerich died a few months after his resignation, and his four children donated $5,000 to Florida Audubon in a memorial to the man whose home had given birth to the organization. Dommerich's daughter, Paula W. Siedenburg, would become a mainstay of Florida Audubon, serving for several years as vice president.

During its second decade, Florida Audubon continued to devote much of its energy to education. In 1913, the state and national organizations jointly hired Katherine H. Stuart of Virginia for a two-month series of lectures at schools and Junior Audubon Clubs throughout the state. By the time Stuart finished her assignment, Florida Audubon had passed out 20,000 leaflets to children in the state. The organization continued the program in subsequent years, enlisting Isabelle Goodhue to continue the series of lectures and to display her range of bird songs and calls. Florida Audubon also brought in ornithologists Eugene Swope and Henry Oldys, who appeared before groups of both adults and children and spoke about birds from a scientific perspective.

While Florida's budding conservation community relied largely on wardens to protect birds, there were other means of combating the slaughter. In 1905, National Audubon officials learned that a poacher named J.R. Jack, operating out of Punta Gorda on the state's west coast, had sent the skins of the endangered ivory-billed woodpecker to dealers in New England and Canada who claimed to have "scientific" interests. Audubon anonymously offered to buy two skins from Jack, who promptly mailed them. Audubon officials forwarded the evidence to the Department of Agriculture, and Jack eventually pled guilty in Tampa to violating the Lacey Act and was fined.

Not all of the wildlife slaughter in Florida at the time involved profiteers motivated by greed. The growing tide of tourism gave rise to "motorboat hunting," which had become rampant in rivers and lakes and along the Atlantic coastline by the turn of the century. Conservationists reacted with alarm to the stories of all manner of birds and mammals blasted from boats merely for the amusement of northern "sportsmen," who rarely even bothered to retrieve the carcasses. In some cases, the "shoots" were organized competitions, with gunners earning points for each animal they shot. While National Audubon lobbied Congress to ban the practice, the Florida chapter pressed the legislature to establish a game commissioner who would administer existing laws for wildlife protections. Those efforts eventually succeeded when state lawmakers created the Department of Game and Fish in 1913 and established an Office of State Game Commissioner, with the commissioner and his wardens authorized to make arrests and issue fines. The legislature also instituted a system for issuing licenses to hunters, and it passed a measure that gave legal protection to a new category of game and birds, including the previously neglected robin. At the same time, Florida Audubon's Laura Marrs—who had been contributing annual state reports to Audubon's *Bird-Lore* magazine (as Mrs. Kingsmill Marrs)—took part in a lobbying effort in the nation's capital that yielded the Federal Migratory Bird Law and the Non-Importation Bill. The passage of the latter led to significant drops in the overseas markets for bird feathers from Florida.

The first state game commissioner, E.Z. Jones, seemed to take his job more seriously than some legislators intended. During his first year in office, Jones collected $42,177 from a combination of hunting licenses and fines. Jones angered some of the state's prominent citizens by daring to enforce the laws on not just "Negroes and crackers," and the legislature responded in its next session by abolishing the Department of Game and Fish and the commissioner's office. (For good measure, the state assembly also passed an act encouraging the extermination of turkey vultures and black vultures.) The repeal of the progressive wildlife protection laws provoked, as Florida Audubon Society historian Lucy Worthington Blackman put it, "an orgy of lawless hunting."

As a substitute for state protection, lawmakers decreed that birds and game animals were the property of the counties in which they were found and substituted a system of wardens appointed by county commissions. The Florida Supreme Court later ruled the county warden system unconstitutional and effectively ended any government wildlife protection program. A few federal wardens enforcing the Migratory Bird Act joined those hired by the state and national Audubon organizations to protect as many rookeries and bird reservations as they could.

But the limits of that network became apparent in 1916, when hunters decimated the Alligator Bay rookery in the southwestern Everglades. The area had been a tense battleground between Audubon wardens and plume hunters for years, with warden Charles Allen resorting to gunfire in 1913 to repel and eventually arrest a poacher named Haynor Whidden and his two brothers. Three Audubon wardens had kept approximately 800 egrets safe at Alligator Bay through the 1915 nesting season, but the organization ran short of money to retain the wardens. In their absence, bird hunters harvested the entire colony and then burned out the rookery so that birds wouldn't return to a place so remote and difficult for the poachers to reach. Long after the deaths of Guy Bradley and Columbus MacLeod, protecting birds remained a dangerous prospect. National Audubon retained a network of anonymous informants who watched important bird colonies, and one of them filed a report published by Frank M. Chapman's *Bird-Lore* magazine in 1912. To protect the "unpaid agent," the magazine avoided identifying the rookery he protected, saying only that it was in South Florida.

The incident at Alligator Bay showed that despite increased public support for the protection of wildlife, Florida conservationists remained disadvantaged in many ways. While the coalition of naturalists focused on saving birds from unchecked slaughter during the second decade of the century, Florida's change from a mere winter playground for the wealthy to a place that growing numbers of people called home brought changes that would soon compete for their attention.

An unidentified man kneels by a monument for Guy M. Bradley in the Everglades. The photograph was taken in 1957. The monument reads: Guy M. Bradley (1870-1905) Faithful unto death as game warden of Monroe County. He gave his life for the cause to which he was pledged. State Library and Archives of Florida.

4

PROTECTING MORE THAN MERELY ANIMALS

The national conservation movement and the one that followed in Florida arose from the same birthing grounds—the swamps of South Florida, the vast area known as the Everglades. The galvanizing concern in those first decades of the movement involved protection of the region's birds from slaughter at the hands of plume hunters. Eventually, though, conservationists began to recognize an overarching need. It was not merely the birds of the Everglades that faced dire threats but the existence of the Everglades system itself.

From the earliest days of southward movement into the newly established state of Florida, speculators and developers regarded the Everglades as a problem to be solved—as worthless swampland in need of draining. The southern end of the peninsula formed a wide and shallow delta flowing south from Lake Okeechobee—a "river of grass," in the lasting phrase of writer Marjory Stoneman Douglas—that in its natural condition was inhospitable to either settlement or agriculture. The wealthy and powerful men who set their sights on South Florida envisioned a paradise, if only something could be done about all that water.

As early as the mid-19th century, people inside and outside Florida mulled the possibility of drying up the Everglades. In 1847, two years after Florida's admittance to the union, a Harvard-educated attorney living in St. Augustine made the first known drainage analysis of the Everglades. Buckingham Smith estimated the land could be reclaimed at a cost of no more than $500,000. A few years later, Florida's first senator,

J.D. Westcott, suggested that the entire region would drain so quickly that the biggest problem would be the health hazard resulting from dead fish and plants.

An 1850 act of Congress gave states ownership of swamps and "overflowed lands" for the purposes of drainage and reclamation. The state of Florida took possession of 10 million acres so defined, and in 1851 the state's general assembly created the Internal Improvement Board to manage those lands.

The "reclamation" of the Everglades became an official state objective under Governor William Bloxham. In 1876, Bloxham began negotiating with Philadelphia manufacturing magnate Hamilton Disston to have Disston and his associates drain 12 million acres of submerged land in exchange for half of what they reclaimed. After some legal wrangling, the state sold Disston 4 million acres for $1 million—one-fifth of its assessed value. Disston's crews almost immediately began dredging work designed to funnel water from Lake Okeechobee east to the Atlantic Ocean and west to the Gulf of Mexico. Disston also envisioned a canal bisecting the peninsula in its middle, an idea that would persist well into the next century.

Disston's dredging ended in 1894, when his company held title to 1.6 million acres. Despite Disston's efforts, including the digging of 11 miles of canals and the transformation of the Caloosahatchee River into a straightened ditch that diverted water into the Gulf of Mexico, the Everglades remained quite wet.

Such was the situation when William S. Jennings, a former judge from Brooksville, mounted a run for governor on a platform that prominently featured plans to drain the Everglades. Jennings said the feat could be accomplished by cutting natural rock dams in the south-flowing rivers and allowing the water to run to sea—downhill, as he envisioned it. He drew up maps and diagrammed canals, compared the Everglades to the Nile and the waters of Holland and labeled his project a simple engineering feat. After Jennings' election in 1900, the Florida Legislature created a Board of Drainage Commissioners with the right of eminent domain.

Jennings' successor, Napoleon Bonaparte Broward, campaigned on a platform of drying up the Everglades, which he called a "pestilence-ridden swamp." Broward in 1905 lifted the first shovel of dirt as a pair of dredges began churning their way up both branches of the New River near Miami. A few years later, crews blasted away the ledges of the Miami River that blocked the salt tides from reaching the freshwater Everglades system. The dynamite diverted fresh water to Henry Flagler's Royal Palm Hotel.

Drainage efforts continued in the following decade when Florida Gov. Albert Gilchrist convinced the United States Department of Agriculture to release a flawed report written by a discredited former employee, James O. Wright, that claimed a series of canals radiating from Lake Okeechobee would drain 1.8 million acres of land. Wright got a job with a company that received the state contract for the dredging work and completed it in 1913, to little effect. By then, the draining of the Everglades had become a continuing state project under the authority of the Everglades Drainage District, with its work financed by state bonds. Between 1907 and 1929, the district spent nearly $18 million, excavated nearly 79 million cubic yards of dirt and rock and built 440 miles of canals and levees. It was the first phase in a decades-long alteration of the Everglades' natural water flow.

While dredges gouged canals through the Everglades, developers raced southward along the dry lands of the state's eastern coast. Flagler, who made his fortune as a partner of John D. Rockefeller in Standard Oil, bought a 36-mile railroad in north Florida in 1888 and by 1912 had extended it to Key West. Along the way he built a series of luxury hotels that spawned the cities of Palm Beach, Fort Lauderdale and Miami.

The replumbing of the Everglades did not draw immediate or unanimous condemnation from Florida's conservation community. University of Miami botanist John C. Gifford, for example, actually favored drainage of the Everglades even as he lamented the indiscriminate harvesting of orchids and the dumping of sewage into South Florida waterways. (Gifford eventually changed his mind about the canal-digging schemes.) Others, however, recognized the dangers of the drainage plans from the beginning. Long before the establishment of Everglades National Park, conservationists were writing letters of protest about the drainage programs. Writer A.W. Dimock toured the Everglades at the height of the drainage mania and wrote in the 1908 book *Florida Enchantments*: "Their most conspicuous charm, which has departed, might be restored if the birds of Florida could secure the same protection as the beasts of the Yellowstone National Park." David Fairchild, a botanist at the University of Miami, argued that the government should buy certain hammocks in the Everglades to ensure the preservation of rare plants and animals. Alden H. Hadley, a lecturer for Florida Audubon, wrote in the organization's magazine in 1941 of the profound changes the Everglades had undergone since his first visit in 1900: "To me and many others the wholesale drainage of the Everglades is a conspicuous example (of which there are many) of greatly misdirected reclamation. A well-known scientist and long-time resident of Florida has characterized it to me as an 'infinite tragedy.' " In his 1920 book *In Lower Florida Wilds*, Charles Torrey Simpson wrote in dismay of the shrinking of Lake Okeechobee under the siphoning effect of three major canals. And Simpson repeated the call of Dimock and others for a national park in the Everglades.

The push for federal protection of the Everglades can be traced to the efforts of the Florida Federation of Women's Clubs, which in 1916 averted a proposed road from Homestead to Paradise Key and created Royal Palm State Park. Emboldened by that success, the women's clubs and their allies—including botanist David Fairchild and former government biologist Harold Bailey—formed the Florida Society of Natural History in 1922 to lobby for a considerably larger goal: Everglades National Park.

The fledgling movement received a boost in 1923, when Stephen Mather, director of the National Park Service, wrote in a report to the Secretary of the Interior: "There should be an untouched example of the Everglades of Florida established as a national park." That conviction soon took hold among a group of conservation-minded people in South Florida, most notably a landscape architect named Ernest F. Coe, who moved to Miami from his native Connecticut in 1925 at the height of the South Florida real-estate boom. Coe, impatient with the deliberate pace of the existing group, in 1928 formed the Tropical Everglades National

Park Association, prompting the Florida legislature the following year to establish a similarly named commission with Coe as executive chairman.

Coe spent nine months surveying the Everglades—sometimes through plane rides he cadged from Coast Guard aviators—in order to craft a precise map of the region. He made the first of many trips (at his own expense) to Washington in 1929, lobbying for protection of the Everglades through the creation of a national park. Coe knew the odds were not in his favor: Only 26 of the previous 500 proposals for national parks had gained congressional acceptance. Yet his presentation persuaded the Senate to approve funding for a study of the proposal—the last official document signed by President Calvin Coolidge. Coe cultivated federal support by hosting trips of senators to the Everglades, by both boat and blimp, and in 1934 Congress passed and President Franklin D. Roosevelt signed a bill authorizing the creation of an Everglades National Park in theory. A problem remained, however: The procedure for establishing national parks required land to be bought by a state and donated to the federal government. Congress declined to provide money for land acquisition, and Florida lawmakers showed no inclination to approve funding for the purchase of what was still commonly regarded as worthless swampland.

While Coe served as point man for the Everglades, others played equally active roles in the crusade. May Mann Jennings, widow of the former governor and longtime president of the Florida Federation of Women's Clubs, used her Tallahassee connections to help ensure passage of bills for the acquisition of 325,000 acres of land and the creation of the Everglades National Park Commission. Jennings' distant relative by marriage, Ruth Bryan Owen, in 1928 became the first woman elected to Congress from Florida, and Owen soon sponsored a House bill promoting an Everglades park. In an anecdote that came to symbolize the resolve of park supporters, an opponent dumped a snake on the table before Owen during a hearing to emphasize his description of the Glades as a reptilian wasteland. In response, Owen reportedly draped the snake around her neck and said, "That's how afraid we are of snakes in the Everglades."

45

Gary White

The Florida legislature finally voted in 1937 to designate $2 million for buying privately owned lands, but the momentum stalled and a series of governors cut funding for Everglades studies. Coe used a meager pot of private contributions to continue his push in the face of statewide apathy and the economic pressures of a continued Depression and then the advent of World War II. A further obstacle arose when the Humble Oil and Refining Company drilled Florida's first producing oil well in 1943 at Sunniland, 30 miles from Florida's southwest coast. The discovery of oil just outside the proposed park boundaries not only drove up the cost of nearby land but also caused state officials to reconsider the wisdom of giving to the federal government acreage that might hold considerable value. Complicating matters, the state had sold mineral leases on hundreds of thousands of acres of land, and many of those leases had been subdivided into small parcels and resold, often to distant buyers. Speculators also had capitalized on a recent state law to snatch up properties on which tax payments were in arrears.

Such was the situation in 1944, when Florida's lame-duck governor, Spessard L. Holland, decided to make good on a campaign pledge to establish an Everglades park during his term. In December, the state of Florida officially transferred approximately 850,000 acres of land to the U.S. Fish and Wildlife Service. Holland and his elected successor, Millard F. Caldwell, met with representatives of the oil and real-estate industries and produced a plan that reduced the park from its original 2 million acres to 1,355,000 acres, a seemingly unavoidable compromise. That still left the problem of convincing a conservative state legislature dominated by rural North Floridians to approve the state's obligation of $2 million for land acquisition as a condition for the establishment of the park. At that point John Pennekamp, associate editor of the *Miami Herald* and a member of the Everglades National Park Commission, took over Coe's former role as the project's chief advocate and went to work lobbying the legislators who held the state's purse strings. Pennekamp, drawing on the help of Florida Power and Light chairman McGregor Smith, arranged a weekend retreat with the lawmakers at FP&L's fishing camp on Horseshoe Lake near Ocala. Decades later, Pennekamp described the scene of a post-dinner poker gathering in which he

46

uncharacteristically claimed one pot after another. The editor's accompanying jibes prompted one of the senators to offer the $2 million for the park if Pennekamp would ease up on them. The Florida Legislature delivered the money in its next session, and Secretary of the Interior Julius A. Krug declared the park established on June 20, 1947.

Though most people involved with the push for a national park accepted the necessity of political trading and concessions, the man who would be described in the *Saturday Evening Post* as "Papa of the Everglades National Park" could not abide any departure from the ideal. In Coe's original vision, the park would have included part of the Big Cypress Swamp to the north and the upper part of Key Largo to the east, as well as the surrounding coral reef. On top of the whittling of the proposed park's size, congressional action modified the original plan by allowing the federal government to take title of the land but reserving mineral rights to the state and to private landowners. When Coe learned of the compromises, he announced his withdrawal from the project that had been his obsession for nearly two decades.

The official dedication ceremony of the 28th national park took place on December 6, 1947 in Everglades City on the park's western edge. A gathering of 4,500 people heard speeches by President Harry Truman, Gov. Caldwell and former governor Holland (then a senator). Those taking part in the ceremony included May Mann Jennings, perhaps second only to Coe in her efforts to preserve the "swamp" her late husband as governor had endeavored to drain. Marjory Stoneman Douglas, the former reporter turned environmental advocate, also witnessed the historic moment. She had written in her epic book, *Everglades: River of Grass*, published earlier that year: "It will be the only national park in which the wild-life, the crocodiles, the trees, the orchids, will be more important than the sheer geology of the country."

Chief William McKinley Osceola attended the dedication ceremony, presenting Truman with a flag of the Seminole Indian Nation, some of whose members still lived within the boundaries of the new park. The National Park Commission served up one ton of mullet for the historic gathering, but it wasn't clear until just before the event whether the man often referred to as the father of Everglades National Park would join in

47

the festivities. Coe, after having noisily withdrawn his support in anger over the park's compromised dimensions, was persuaded by his fellow activists to attend and sat with the president on the platform that day, wearing his ubiquitous white suit and bow tie. A half century later, most of the 1.1 million people who visit Everglades National Park each year pass through the Ernest F. Coe Visitor Center, the main entrance to the park on the eastern edge of the remaining Glades.

Even with the official designation of the national park, battles remained. The park's boundaries of 1947 were hardly absolute, with a notable block of 30,000 acres forming what was known as "the hole in the donut"—an interior section of farmland considered too valuable by its owners to relinquish. Decades after the creation of the park, government officials would still be acquiring land designated as part of the protected Everglades. And the state's environmental community soon realized that federal protection would not end threats to the health of the Everglades ecosystem. In the coming decades, the actions of the federal government itself—through the U.S. Army Corps of Engineers—would become the chief source of concern for environmentalists. The Corps had already been at work on flood-control plans when overflows caused by a 1947 hurricane added urgency to the project, spurring Sen. Holland to push for a permanent solution. Within a year of the ceremony at Everglades City, Congress established a public-works project devoted to controlling the water flow of the Everglades. The Central and South Florida Project for Flood Control launched the Corps of Engineers on a decades-long mission of digging canals and building pumping stations, culverts and spillways that divided the massive ecosystem into manageable sections, transforming the Everglades from a single, enormous ecosystem into something entirely different. It soon became clear to conservationists that the happy day in Everglades City by no means marked the salvation of the River of Grass.

While the campaign for Everglades National Park kept segments of the environmental community occupied from the mid-1920s through the 1940s, the conservation movement continued its broader endeavors. From its first emboldening victory in 1901 with the passage of the Audubon Model Law in the Florida Legislature, Florida Audubon recognized the necessity of legislative advocacy. The organization established an official legislative committee to focus its attentions on Tallahassee, setting a list of goals before each of the biannual lawmaking sessions and devoting equal zeal to battling the inevitable worrisome bill that would, say, place a bounty on hawks and owls. In part to pursue its legislative agenda, the Florida Audubon Society established its first regular publication in 1919, a four-page, theoretically quarterly journal called the *Florida Audubon Bulletin*, co-edited by William F. Blackman, the former Rollins College president who would later become the leader of Florida Audubon. The journal published just 13 editions before ceasing in 1925. Two years later, the state organization debuted *The Florida Naturalist*, a quarterly magazine edited by Rubert J. Longstreet, a trained ornithologist who solicited scientific articles during more than two decades of running the magazine. Longstreet also served as Florida Audubon's president from 1930 to 1936.

The mid-1920s proved a fertile period for environmental legislation, perhaps because Florida's real-estate boom had lawmakers in an indulgent mood. The legislature in 1923 passed a bill making bird study compulsory in public schools, and Audubon lobbyists for more than a decade helped ward off attempts in each subsequent session to rescind the law. During the same period, the state and national Audubon organizations collaborated on a program to present credit courses in ornithology at colleges and universities. While Florida Audubon remained the most prominent conservation body, the Chicago-based Izaak Walton League expanded into Florida in the early 1920s, quickly forming chapters throughout the state. The "Ikes," as they called themselves, played an assertive role in the resurrection of a state wildlife authority a decade after lawmakers had abandoned the idea. In 1925, the legislature again created a Department of Game and Fresh Water Fish and established a State Game Commissioner, ending Florida's ignominious status as one of only three states without such an authority. In an indication of the prevailing good will of the era, J.B. Royall, the appointed commissioner, served as keynote speaker at Florida Audubon's annual meeting shortly after being appointed. This time the commissioner's office didn't vanish in the next legislative session, and the first issue of *The Florida Naturalist* of October 1927 led with an article by Royall, in which he noted that his office had prosecuted 1,200 cases of wildlife violations in its first two years, with a high conviction rate. Royall also stressed the importance of a recent statewide game and fish law that superseded a passel of often contradictory local regulations and included a provision for establishing state wildlife refuges.

Legislative successes, however, proved to be more anomaly than custom, especially after the collapse of the land boom and the stock market crash ushered in a more conservative era. In a typical example of the fate of environmental initiatives, Florida Audubon in 1931 adopted a resolution urging the state to ban the hunting of alligators, whose value to the garment trade was fueling population declines reminiscent of those inflicted on wading birds five decades earlier. Not only did the legislature reject the idea in that session, it would delay the protection of alligators for nearly 40 years, until the situation had become inescapably dire.

The state's population continued to swell even amid the Great Depression, and bulldozers steadily made their way into sections of Florida that had previously remained untouched. In the late 1920s, a group of winter residents in South Florida became alarmed about the potential loss of a forest containing nearly every major plant community known to exist in Florida. Following the example of the private purchase that had saved Paradise Key in the Everglades, Margaret S. Roebling, the granddaughter-in-law of the builder of the Brooklyn Bridge, organized her winter neighbors to buy a 3,800-acre tract in the state's southern interior near the town of Sebring. The group established Highlands Hammock as a public sanctuary in 1931 and donated it to the state four years later.

Though the creation of Everglades National Park tended to dwarf other land-acquisition efforts, both the state and federal governments found funds to purchase other lands during the first half of the 20th century. President Theodore Roosevelt, in the most ambitious of many conservation actions affecting Florida, designated the "Big Scrub" area in the northern center of the peninsula as the Ocala National Forest in 1908, a protected area originally comprising 207,285 acres (it has since swelled to 366,000 acres). Roosevelt established the Choctawhatchee National

Forest in the Panhandle three days later, but that forest was eventually transferred to the Army and became Elgin Air Force Base.

Despite the state's relatively low population of humans, Florida was hardly a virgin landscape in the early 20th century. Lumber companies established themselves in Florida around 1830, lured by vast tracts of longleaf and slash pines, durable live oaks in the uplands and rich swaths of valuable cypress in the wet areas. The United States Navy became dependent on live oaks for shipbuilding until the advent of the steel era. The timber companies harvested pines for lumber, and the naval stores industry extracted pine sap — originally used for caulking in wooden ships and by the mid-1800s distilled into turpentine, an ingredient in soap and patent medicines, among other products. And lumber crews ventured deep into Florida's swamps to fell cypress trees, the largest of them well over a thousand years old, which became shingles, shipping crates, barrels and paneling. Exporting to Spain, England and the Caribbean as well as northern states, Florida's timber industry thrived during the late 19th century as companies (commanded mostly by out-of-state owners) purchased more than 1 million acres of federal land in the state from 1877 to 1888. By 1910, annual production in Florida exceeded one billion board feet, and Florida's naval stores industry led the nation in output.

Like the plume hunters, though, the timber companies showed little interest in perpetuating the source of their profits. Starting in the western Panhandle and moving east and then south, the companies made virtually no attempt to replant on the lands they swept through, and by 1932 the native pine forests of northern Florida were gone. (Farmers also contributed to the devastation in the late 19th century, employing a practice of using uncontrolled fires to clear massive stretches of land.) The naval stores industry — which relied almost exclusively on a brutal system of forced convict labor — proved equally short-sighted, using sloppy techniques that unnecessarily killed a high percentage of their trees. Even when the trees weren't ruined outright, the gashes in their trunks made them susceptible to destruction by fires — part of a natural cycle that healthy pines could survive. By 1928, only 6 million acres of the state's original 27 million acres of virgin timber remained, and it was fast disappearing.

The devastation of Florida's trees created an outcry among conservation groups, including the Izaak Walton League, which had formed several local chapters by the late 1920s. Another organization emerged specifically out of concern over the rape of the trees and quickly established itself as a political force. The Florida Forestry Association formed in 1923 to advocate protection of forests, and as with most major environmental issues of the day, May Mann Jennings played an energetic role. Her organization, the Florida Federation of Women's Clubs, had drafted resolutions as early as 1905 calling for a state forestry authority, and in a speech to the Florida Audubon Society Jennings suggested that timber should be taxed as a crop, with surplus funds used to acquire land for preservation. Jennings' son, Bryan, composed a bill that won legislative approval in 1927 after fervid lobbying by the woman who came to be called Florida's "Mother of Forestry." The bill created the Florida Board of Forestry (now called the Division of Forestry), which during the Depression engaged workers from the Civilian Conservation Corps in a campaign of replanting forests devastated by intensive timbering.

The lumber industry's indiscriminate practices actually created an opportunity for the federal government to expand its national forests by reclaiming territory it had previously sold, either from the timber companies themselves or, in some cases, from the state, which assumed control of land after its owners stopped paying taxes on it. The National Forest Reservation Commission established a purchasing unit in 1929 to begin acquiring land between Lake City and Jacksonville for the creation of a third national forest in the state. With 145,000 acres in federal possession, President Herbert Hoover unveiled the Osceola National Forest on July 10, 1931. The Apalachicola National Forest, mostly pine hardwood habitat covering nearly four times the area of the Osceola, came into existence five years later. The state embarked on its own land acquisition program, with thousands of acres of Florida land bought by the federal government during the Depression and originally designated for reclamation and resettlement projects becoming the basis of the state forest system. Starting with 7,000-acre Pine Log State Forest in the Panhandle in 1936, the holdings grew by the century's end to include 30 forests totaling 830,000 acres.

With environmental education comfortably established in the state, the National Audubon Society and the University of Florida worked out an arrangement in 1936 that placed nature writer and Stetson University graduate Alden H. Hadley in the state's public schools. Given the charge of acquainting the people of Florida with "the economic and esthetic value of the State's wild-life resources," Hadley was assigned to the staff of UF's General Extension Division. He toured the state, regularly reporting on his travels in *The Florida Naturalist*. During his first year, Hadley visited every public school in Alachua, Orange, Brevard, Volusia and Seminole counties as well as some in Duval, Hillsborough, Pinellas and Manatee counties. He also gave lectures at colleges, spoke to civic groups, women's organizations, garden clubs and tourist clubs and offered lectures on the radio. Despite annual funding crises, Audubon and the Federation of Garden Clubs managed to keep the educational program alive until 1941, at which point Hadley had delivered more than 1,700 lectures and accumulated more than 80,000 miles on his car without mishap. (An automobile accident in his home state of Indiana claimed his life in 1951.)

Despite the passage of wildlife protection laws, the state and national Audubon groups found ample cause to continue their warden programs amid the financial challenges of the lingering Depression. Hunting remained commonplace in the remote reaches of South Florida throughout the 1930s. Locals reported that when mackerel season ended each year, Cuban fishermen would embark for the Everglades and kill thousands of birds for the return trip to Havana. A black market in bird feathers persisted in Key West as well.

Katherine Bell Tippetts, a wealthy businesswoman from St. Petersburg, rose to the presidency of Florida Audubon in 1920, a position she would hold for four years. During her time as leader of the St. Petersburg chapter, she had helped popularize the idea of bird sanctuaries, convincing Pinellas County to establish such protected areas. The notion reached the state legislature, which in 1921 designated Volusia County in its entirety as a bird sanctuary. While the protections afforded by a proclamation and a hand-painted sign may have been effective in residential areas, environmentalists knew that stronger measures were still needed in less civilized settings.

Audubon wardens continued to guard the state's most important and vulnerable rookeries, with nine wardens working in the state in 1927. Two years later, National Audubon Society president T. Gilbert Pearson, who had spent his childhood years in the rural town of Archer, near Gainesville, increased the warden force on the state's southwest coast. Audubon soon installed wardens in new, interior locations of the Kissimmee Prairie and the marshes of the St. Johns River. In the 1930s, the organization enlisted the aid of the U.S. Coast Guard, U.S. Navy and Goodyear Rubber Company to conduct aerial surveys of bird populations in remote areas.

Florida Audubon Society steadily expanded even in the midst of the Depression. At its annual meeting in 1937, the group reported 708 members, a gain of 102 percent from the previous year. Though Florida Audubon remained the state's dominant conservation entity, it was not alone. On August 22, 1931, a consortium of environmental groups held an unprecedented gathering in Daytona Beach. Representatives of Florida Audubon, the Federation of Garden Clubs and Women's Clubs, the Izaak Walton League, the Committee on Conservation of the State Chamber of Commerce, the Game and Fish Protective Association, the Field and Trail Association, the Forestry Association and several other groups agreed on the need for a statewide collective of conservationists. The assembly voted to install Florida Audubon president Rubert J. Longstreet as chairman of the State Chamber of Commerce's Committee on Conservation, which served as a clearinghouse for environmental information. The well-intended confederation was barely heard from again, and eventually the Chamber of Commerce group adopted an unabashedly pro-business outlook that regularly put it at odds with its former allies in the environmental movement. That was not unusual. As the conservation forces grew in both number and influence, they found themselves facing increasing—and increasingly aggressive—adversaries.

5

A STRUGGLING MOVEMENT FACES WIDENING CHALLENGES

Thomas Barbour, a naturalist and writer, first visited Florida as a youth in 1898, spending an extended vacation with relatives near Melbourne as he explored the nearby woods and the marshes of the upper St. Johns River. Barbour made annual trips to Florida for the next four decades, and in 1944 he published a book whose title encapsulated the changes he had witnessed: *That Vanishing Eden*. (The title echoed one another naturalist, John Kunkel Small, had used for his Florida book of 1929, *From Eden To Sahara – Florida's Tragedy*.)

"The speed with which the world is changing," Barbour wrote, "indeed with which the world is being ruined from the naturalist's point of view, is accelerating so that what is left for the naturalist of the future will be a poor imitation of the country which we have seen and loved."

Florida may have changed more than any other state during the first half of the 20th century, as its population jumped from 228,000 in 1900 to 2.7 million in 1950. In addition to the transformation of the Everglades through government-funded drainage programs, several industries—timber, turpentine, sugar and phosphate—altered the state's landscape in dramatic ways. The influx of people lured southward by cheap land and a hospitable climate wrought other changes, particularly in the thriving Miami area, where as early as the 1920s giant dredging machines were scooping tons of dirt from the bottom of the Atlantic

Ocean and extending coastlines or creating islands. All along the state's edges, machines carved out precise canals around which exclusive neighborhoods could be built.

During the first decades of the century, the conservation movement in Florida had largely concentrated its attention on two big issues—bird protection and the saving of the Everglades. By mid-century, the challenges increasingly splintered into other areas, as it became clear that the state's continuing growth in itself threatened the health of Florida's natural resources.

Phosphate, a naturally occurring form of rock used in the production of fertilizer, was discovered in Florida in 1879, giving rise to the state's third major industry (after timber and turpentine). A successful dig for phosphate at Dunnellon in the late 1880s prompted the *New York Republic* to compare the find to California's gold and Pennsylvania's oil and touched off an era of "phosphate fever," with 400 companies at work in 1895. Phosphate mining proved even more invasive and environmentally damaging than timbering. Mining operations left behind barren craters in the earth and generated toxic by-products that lasted for centuries. Jet drills came into use around the turn of the century, and within another two decades the mining companies relied on draglines—machines weighing as much as 320 tons that chomped out similarly enormous chunks of earth. With taxpayer-funded assistance from the Florida Development Council, the phosphate industry flourished after World War II, and in 1952 annual production had reached 8.6 million tons. While companies such as American Cyanamid were transforming phosphate into healthy profits, however, conservation-minded citizens became increasingly concerned about the consequences, including a by-product known as "slime," a thick, yellow liquid that sometimes escaped containment structures and leaked into groundwater supplies, causing fish kills. In an early example of grassroots activism, residents in West-Central Florida in 1919 began protesting the effects of phosphate mining on waterways. A labor strike in that year stopped production at a plant near Arcadia, allowing the Peace River to regain its natural clarity, and a coalition of towns along the river told the phosphate operators that they wanted the river to remain clean. With profits to be made and government regulations virtually nonexistent, however, the company soon resumed operations and the river again became polluted.

By the 1940s, concerns about air pollution from phosphate mining spurred a campaign for legislative action against the industry, but powerful supporters of the industry in Tallahassee squashed any meaningful legislation. In 1948, Armour Agricultural Chemical Company opened the first of many chemical fertilizer plants in Polk County, and the effects soon became apparent in major declines in local crops and the mysterious deaths of area cattle. Researchers traced the problems to fluorosis, a by-product of the new phosphate plants, and years of legislative wrangling over emission standards ensued. Florida Audubon began focusing its attention on the issue, seizing on a State Board of Health Report that blamed the phosphate industry for the pollution of the Alafia River near Sarasota. In 1955, the state legislature responded by passing a law setting limits for industrial discharge into the river.

While environmentalists' concerns about phosphate mining originally centered on the industry's unwanted additions to waterways, activists soon became equally alarmed at what the companies were taking out. Phosphate mining and processing relied on vast quantities of water (approximately 32 billion gallons in 1950), and companies drilled gigantic wells to ensure steady supplies. In reporting that industrial wells had caused a major artesian spring—Kissingen Spring near Bartow—to go completely dry, Florida Audubon argued for laws protecting both underground and surface water supplies. The relentless scrutiny that environmental groups applied to phosphate mining eventually overcame the industry's legislative clout and yielded attempts at public-relations repair. By the early 1960s, some companies began turning over reclaimed land for public parks, and in 1963 American Cyanamid donated 315 acres near Tampa to Florida Audubon for use as a wildlife sanctuary.

The Florida Audubon Society survived the Depression only to waste away during the following decade—just as the drive for Everglades National Park intensified. In 1949, the organization had only 900 members, not significantly higher than during the mid-30s, despite annual membership dues that remained at a mere two dollars. A half century after its formation, Florida Audubon had no headquarters, no paid staff and virtually no budget. The organization did little on a unified basis other than publish *The Florida Naturalist*, and that was done from the New Smyrna Beach home of its editor, former FAS president Rubert J. Longstreet. When H.S. Newins resigned after two years as the chapter's president in 1949, Florida Audubon had difficulty finding anyone to accept the presidency. Finally John Storer, who had turned down a first offer, agreed to take over under certain conditions. Storer, a Harvard graduate, longtime farmer and documentary filmmaker, demanded a change of charter that would give Florida Audubon a broader mandate and he also requested the hiring of a full-time, professional naturalist. As a result, the organization created the new office of executive director, which had three short-lived occupants until Storer in 1957 hired C. Russell Mason away from the Massachusetts Audubon Society. Mason brought a stability that allowed the organization to regain its financial strength, growing to a budget of $100,000 by 1961.

The roster of wildlife sanctuaries—managed either by environmental groups or by the state or federal government—swelled during the 1950s and 1960s. Despite its financial problems, Florida Audubon Society added sanctuaries at Fort Pierce and Orange Park in 1954 and one west of Orlando in 1959, and with the acceptance of the 200-acre former Hialeah Race Course in 1962 the organization had 30 parcels under its protection. Even as conservationists set their sights on such small and regionally important preserves, though, they continued to think big.

The creation of a national park in the Everglades still left environmentally crucial tracts in South Florida vulnerable to development. (And indeed developers tried, with little success, to slice off pieces of Everglades National Park itself for a decade until Congress finally settled its boundaries.) After the victory in the Everglades, conservationists turned their attention to Corkscrew Swamp, the last significant stand of bald cypress in southwest Florida that had not yet been decimated. Originally stretching 25 miles through Collier County, the stand had been whittled down to three miles by the early 1950s, when the National Audubon Society set its preservation as a matter of urgency. Conservationists in Tampa formed the Corkscrew Cypress Rookery Association and appointed National Audubon President John Baker as its leader.

Baker began meeting with officials from the two companies that owned the land — Lee Tidewater Cypress Company and Collier Enterprises. Marjorie Smith, president of the Florida Federation of Garden Clubs, went about raising money from her membership, but it became clear it would take more than personal donations to meet the asking price of $200,000 for Lee Tidewater's portion alone. Baker enlisted the help of Dick Pough, conservation chief of the Museum of Natural History in New York, and Pough persuaded John D. Rockefeller Jr. to pledge $90,000, the amount needed to complete the fund drive. Lee Tidewater officials responded with a "Christmas gift" of an additional 640 acres, bringing the total area to 6,080 acres. Collier Enterprises, not to be outdone in public relations, agreed to lease 3,200 acres to National Audubon for one dollar a year on the assumption that Audubon would eventually buy the land. Again conservationists made a national appeal, this time drawing a pledge from the Ford Foundation on the condition that Audubon would raise twice that amount by August 31, 1968. Soliciting donations from local chapters, women's clubs and other civic groups, as well as more than 2,000 individual contributors, Audubon reached its monetary goal with two months to spare. The National Audubon board of directors approved purchase of an additional 1,680 acres of contiguous land that served as feeding grounds for wading birds, bringing the total acreage of Corkscrew National Sanctuary to 10,400 acres. The organization eventually opened the refuge to the public, and a winding boardwalk gave visitors a glimpse of South Florida before its taming by man.

In the quest for environmental protection, the battles overlapped and there was little time to savor victories. Concurrent with the battle over Corkscrew Swamp, environmentalists strove to prevent the destruction of one of Southwest Florida's last remaining sizable stands of wild palms. As early as the 1930s, conservationists had unsuccessfully sought to establish a state park on Fakahatchee Strand, a tract also owned by Lee Tidewater. After World War II, the company relentlessly felled palms and cypress (destroying countless orchids in the process), and by the early 1960s the Florida State Road Department had begun construction of a highway from Fort Lauderdale to Naples—Alligator Alley— that would truncate the forest on its northern end. Florida Audubon Society, The Nature Conservancy and other groups formed an alliance in hopes of acquiring the threatened land, or at least convincing the state to alter the course of the road. Though unsuccessful in their immediate goals, the conservationists did manage to designate Fakahatchee Strand as an important wilderness area, creating hope that at least part of it would eventually be saved.

On the other side of the state, a less public lobbying campaign yielded similarly important results. When the military began experimenting with space flight after World War II, the government sought a lightly populated area with mild weather as a staging ground. Those in Washington decided on Cape Canaveral, an elbow of marshland on Florida's central eastern coast, and the first successful rocket launch took place there in 1950. With the acceleration of the space race in the late 1950s, the newly created National Aeronautics and Space Administration decided on the adjoining Merritt Island, a peninsula between the Banana and Indian rivers, as the site of the nation's launch operations. During 1962 and 1963, the federal government gathered land on Merritt Island that eventually totaled 140,000 acres, the majority of it serving merely as a buffer between the space center and the mainland to the west. Revered by naturalists for their wildlife, the marshlands of Merritt Island held great ecological value as a home to 150 species of animals, with winter waterfowl populations sometimes reaching 400,000. As it happened, the birdwatchers who regularly visited the area included Allan Cruickshank, a longtime lecturer and photographer for National Audubon Society, and his wife, Helen, also a nature photographer and author. The couple had moved to nearby Rockledge in 1953, and Allan often led bird-watching tours on Merritt Island. Seeing the government collect a sprawling tract of land in one of his favorite avian zones, Allan Cruickshank began calling some of the many officials in the National Park Service and the U.S. Fish and Wildlife Service—both at the state and national levels—and lobbying to have part of the burgeoning space center set aside as a wildlife refuge. The idea took hold among high-ranking officials, and in 1963 Secretary of the Interior Stewart L. Udall designated all of the federally owned land not used for space operations at Kennedy Space Center (roughly 140 square miles at the time) as the Merritt Island National Wildlife Refuge.

"It took a lot of doing to convince NASA it could tolerate another use of the land next to Kennedy Space Center," said Curtis Wilson, the first director of the refuge. "But after a while, Allan made it apparent to them there was a definite compatibility."

Bordering the biologically rich Indian River, the refuge soon acquired a worldwide reputation for its roseate spoonbills and other abundant waterfowl. The refuge's salt marshes offered habitat for some of the few remaining dusky seaside sparrows before the species went extinct in 1987.

At the same time that the federal government was protecting wildlife on Merritt Island, the state government took steps that would have greatly damaged the nation's first such refuge about 50 miles down the coast near Melbourne. In 1963, under its routine policy of raising revenue through the sale of submerged land for use in dredge-and-fill projects, the state prepared to offer river bottom around Pelican Island National Wildlife Refuge to developers. Opposition arose from local naturalists and commercial fishermen, who found an influential ally in Arthur Marshall, a biologist with a U.S. Fish and Wildlife office in nearby Vero Beach. The state relented and decided instead to lease 616 acres to the refuge, and some of the locals who had worked to derail the government's original plans later formed the Pelican Island Audubon Society.

The publication of Rachel Carson's book *Silent Spring* in 1962 brought nationwide attention to the devastating effects of chemical pesticides on birds of prey. Environmentalists in Florida, however, were pursuing the issue long before Carson's book became a bestseller. Dichloro-diphenyl-trichloroethane—a compound known by its initials, DDT—was discovered in the late 1930s to be effective as an insecticide, and during World War II a Department of Agriculture entomology research station in Orlando became the headquarters for the testing and production of DDT, seen as the solution to malaria and other mosquito-borne diseases. When the war ended, government officials began using DDT to control mosquito populations in the United States through spraying programs. Almost immediately, some environmentalists raised concerns about the widespread application of a toxic substance throughout Florida. Herbert R. Mills, a medical doctor, wrote a series of lengthy, heavily annotated articles for *The Florida Naturalist* from 1946 to 1949 questioning the safety of DDT's use, noting in one that the government had sprayed the chemical over 500 acres of the Everglades in preparation for the 1947 dedication of the park. "There never has been an urge for the wholesale aerial broadcasting of lead and arsenic, and DDT should not be an exception in this respect," Mills wrote. He added: "There is a preponderance of evidence at this time that DDT cannot be used in sufficient strength to kill mosquito larvae without, at the same time, killing fish and other valuable cold-blooded aquatic animals." By 1951, Florida Audubon was actively lobbying against the use of DDT "in certain areas that supply the key food of important wildlife," but the protests had no immediate effect. In 1959, Florida undertook a program to eradicate imported fire ants (a threat to livestock), and Harold A. Peters, a research biologist for Florida Audubon, lamented that the state had begun, without any studies on the environmental effects, to scatter chemicals 15 to 20 times as toxic as DDT.

Carson's book made DDT a national issue in 1962, but the compound's use continued in the face of growing opposition. Finally, in 1967, several national environmental organizations—including the National Audubon Society, the Environmental Defense Fund and the National Wildlife Federation—initiated court proceedings challenging the use of DDT by government agencies. Various court rulings led some states to halt DDT spraying outright, but Florida in the late 1960s only put restrictions on use of the insecticide. The United States Environmental Protection Agency gradually limited the use of DDT and finally issued an effective ban in 1972.

Two of the birds whose drastic population declines would be traced to the presence of DDT in the fish they preyed upon—bald eagles and ospreys—traditionally nested in Florida by the thousands. In 1961, Florida Audubon pushed a bill that would make it illegal to kill or maim bald eagles or to disturb the trees in which they nested, but the legislature dismissed it.

Undaunted, environmentalists took more direct steps in trying to assure the survival of the state's largest raptor. George and Dorotha Heinzman of Winter Haven took joint chairmanship of Florida Audubon's bald eagle project in 1962, when the state's population had reached a new low of 251 nests. The Heinzmans established an agreement with 66 ranchers to create the Kissimmee Cooperative Bald Eagle Sanctuary. The sanctuary, covering 713,000 acres, held 54 active bald eagle nests, or 20 percent of the statewide population. In a non-binding agreement, the ranchers pledged to protect the eagles and their nesting trees and to notify Florida Audubon in the event of a sale of the property. The program seemed to strike a chord with ranchers, and hundreds of thousands of additional acres soon came into the program, allowing the Heinzmans to compile statistics on eagle birth rates and population trends for several years. Meanwhile, Florida Audubon formed the Bald Eagle Club, reviving a program begun earlier in Massachusetts. The program offered memberships ($1 for adults and 20 cents for children) that raised money for eagle protection.

While the plight of bald eagles eventually produced a national outcry that averted possible extinction, not all of Florida's native wildlife had such luck. One of the state's most distinctive birds, the ivory-billed woodpecker, went virtually unnoticed outside the conservation community as it disappeared during the 20th century. The largest North American woodpecker at nearly two feet long, the ivory-bill was prized by hunters (Native American and European alike) for the distinctive, whitish bill that gave the bird its name. By the turn of the 20th century, ornithologists considered the ivory-billed woodpecker to be nearing extinction throughout its range, which included the swamplands of several southeastern states. The reclusive and little-understood bird, however, proved resilient enough to postpone its demise for several decades. In 1917, a pair of ivory-bills and their young were observed at Royal Palm Hammock, reviving hope of the species' survival. In 1935, ornithologist Arthur Allen brought a team from Cornell University with cameras and recording equipment to Florida in search of the birds, spending several weeks around Winter Park and Tallahassee in a fruitless quest. They later found some ivory-bills in a cypress swamp in Louisiana that continued to produce unverified sightings into the 1990s, long after the bird was considered likely extinct.

Ornithologists regarded certain locations in Florida — the area around the Chipola River in the Panhandle and the Big Cypress Swamp in the southwestern part of the state — as potential refuges for scattered groups of ivory-bills, and the National Audubon Society set aside a tract along the Chipola as a sanctuary, but as the decades passed without evidence even the most hopeful birdwatchers resigned themselves to the birds' extinction. There was a surprise in 1967, when a pair of ivory-bills were spotted near Highlands Hammock State Park in the state's southern interior. Eventually the roost tree of one of the birds blew down in a storm, and two feathers from an ivory-bill collected from the tree's cavity wound up in the Florida Museum of Natural History in Gainesville. Reports of the ivory-bills in the area continued for another year or so, but there would not be another verified sighting of the birds in Florida. In 2005, reports of sightings in a remote area of Arkansas raised hopes that ivory-billed woodpeckers might not yet be extinct.

As ivory-billed woodpeckers disappeared from bird watchers' guidebooks, they joined two other prominent birds native to Florida in the category of "presumed extinct" — the passenger pigeon and the Carolina parakeet. Remarkably, ornithologists estimate that passenger pigeons once constituted as much as 40 percent of the total land bird population in what is now the United States, with a figure of 3-5 billion at the time of European arrival. Commercial hunting of the birds began during the Colonial era, with the birds harvested for food and their feathers used for bedding. During the 1800s, "pigeon shoots" became popular as a sort of skeet shoot using birds that had been captured alive. By the late 19th century, the population of passenger pigeons had reached a dangerously low level, and the species ceased with the death in captivity of its last member in 1914.

Like ivory-billed woodpeckers, Carolina parakeets — with their green, yellow and reddish-orange plumage — presented a startling appearance that entranced both bird-lovers and hunters. As early as the 1830s, John James Audubon noted that the birds seemed to be in decline. Although the disappearance of the only parakeet native to Florida involved a complex set of factors, hunting and the loss of habitat through land clearing rank as major factors. Because of the relatively late settlement of Florida, the birds endured in the state after they had disappeared elsewhere. The bird's scarcity, however, only made it more attractive to the milliners, who placed great ornamental value on the parakeet's exotic feathers. Various reports arose in 1913 and 1914 of shootings of the last wild parakeet, including one in Brevard County and one in Orlando. The continuation of unconfirmed sightings into the 1930s probably reflected not reality but an unwillingness to accept that one of Florida's loveliest birds was gone forever.

If aesthetic appeal was not enough to save the Carolina parakeet from extinction, conservationists had to wonder if there was any hope at all for the American alligator, whose decline over the course of two centuries rivaled the dramatic (though much more rapid) collapse of the passenger pigeon. When William Bartram made his celebrated excursion into the thickets of Florida in 1774, he encountered alligators along the St. Johns River "in such incredible numbers, and so close together from shore to shore, that it would have been easy to have walked across on their heads had the animals been harmless ..." A century later, however, the market for alligator hides — used to make handbags, shoes, luggage and more — transformed the animals from feared monsters into a coveted commodity, with an estimated 2.5 million alligators killed in Florida between 1880 and 1894 alone. Once abundant throughout the Southeast, alligators had by 1900 disappeared from much of their natural range, and "alligator farms" sprouted along the major highways in Florida to display live animals for tourists who were no longer likely to see them in the wild.

Florida Audubon included alligators among the native animals needing state protection as early as the 1920s (as well as skunks and poisonous snakes, upon which legislators considered placing bounties), but lawmakers persistently refused to take action for decades. Even after Florida finally placed some restrictions on the hunting of alligators in the 1940s, the animal's population continued to shrink as illegal poaching flourished. Finally, in 1961, the Florida Department of Game and

Fresh Water Fish declared a closed season on alligators and crocodiles. The out-of-state market in hides, however, continued to lure the poachers, and decades of frustration spurred the Florida Audubon Society to organize a boycott of alligator products in 1967, a campaign with more public relations value than economic bite. As has often been the case for the environmental cause in Florida, the decisive actions came from outside the state. The adoption of the Endangered Species Act in 1967 gave alligators federal protection, and three years later an amendment to the Lacey Act—the law passed at the turn of the century in response to the depredations of Florida's plume hunters—forbade the interstate shipment of alligator hides.

The long-sought moratorium on hunting created the conditions for a recovery that proved to be as audacious as the previous decline of the species. Alligators, whose numbers in remote areas had probably been greater than estimated all along, rebounded to the point that their status was changed from endangered to threatened within a decade.

While many of Florida's mid-century environmental battles involved trying to protect animals from being killed for commercial purposes, one clash pitted the conservation community against farmers in a bid to save animals that weren't making anyone rich. As cattle ranching boomed during the early 20th century, Florida's farmers became alarmed by reports that Texas tick fever (sometimes called tropical fever) had emerged in the state's cattle population. Despite an absence of scientific proof, many ranchers became convinced that the state's population of native white-tailed deer were spreading the dreaded malady by serving as hosts for the contaminated ticks. The federal Department of Agriculture had taken action in 1906, setting up quarantine areas in 15 southern states and overseeing a program of "cattle dipping"—using cement vats to soak the animals in a solution that contained arsenic, among other toxic elements. Some Florida ranchers had built their own dipping vats around that same time, but the state didn't officially join the federal program until 1923, when the legislature passed a law requiring all cattle, horses, mules and other vulnerable farm animals to be dipped every 14 days. Ranchers generally emptied their vats each spring, not always careful about the disposal process, and environmental groups grew alarmed about the prospect of toxic liquids seeping into groundwater supplies on hundreds of ranches throughout the state.

Despite the dipping regimen, tick fever flared again in 1935, and this time agriculture officials settled on a more direct approach: the extermination of deer. The state began paying authorized poachers $80 a month, plus provisions and bounties—excellent money at the height of the Depression—and the gunmen pursued their quarry on horseback, by car and by boat, employing dogs and sometimes even spotting planes. Outraged conservationists and sporting hunters in 1937 formed a coalition, the Florida Deer Protective Association, and secured an injunction against the state, but an appeals court overturned the ruling and the slaughter resumed. Deer populations virtually disappeared in Central Florida, and only the forbidding terrain of the Everglades and Big Cypress prevented the same outcome in South Florida. When members of a Seminole Indian tribe in Hendry County refused to allow state-sponsored hunters onto their reservation, Sen. Claude Pepper of Florida pushed a bill through Congress giving the federal Department of Agriculture the authority to overrule the Seminoles' wishes. Florida Audubon stepped in as a mediator, gaining permission for its scientists to examine a limited number of deer killed by the government. When the deer proved free of infected ticks, the killing finally came to an end. It would take decades for the populations of native deer to rebound toward their previous levels. The state continued to mandate cattle dipping into the 1950s before the weight of negative publicity finally brought an end to the program—but not before an estimated 4,300 vats had been built. Half a century later, state agencies are still dealing with the consequences of the practice. High concentrations of arsenic have turned up at the sites of many old dipping pools, and state officials can only guess at how many such sites remain undiscovered.

In South Florida, a separate conservation campaign on behalf of deer took shape in the Keys. Among the species endemic to the curving array of islands, perhaps the most conspicuous is the Key deer, a distinct subspecies of Virginia white-tailed deer not found in mainland Florida. Migrated southward during the last ice age and then becoming stranded centuries ago when rising sea levels covered a land bridge from the peninsula, the Key deer serves as a paragon of environmental adaptation. The subspecies evolved in response to the snug confines of the Florida Keys, becoming a miniature version of its common mainland relative — about one-third the size of most white-tailed deer. While their diminutive stature may have endeared them to tourists traveling Henry Flagler's "Overseas Railway," which reached all the way to Key West by 1912, the Key deer's restricted range also made them easy targets for hunters. The state banned hunting of the tiny deer in 1939, but poaching continued and by the 1940s the animal's population had sunk to fewer than 50.

Members of the Miami-based Tropical Audubon Society for years had warned about the possible extinction of the Key deer, and the chapter convinced the state organization in the 1940s to include among its biannual legislative objectives a request for a wildlife refuge in the Keys specifically devoted to the preservation of the deer. The National Wildlife Federation also took up the cause, making the saving of Key deer the theme of its annual National Wildlife Week in 1952. On a more pragmatic level, the National Wildlife Federation teamed with Florida Audubon and other groups to provide funds for a warden to contend with poachers. Proposals for a Key deer sanctuary appeared in the legislature as early as 1951, and in 1957 Congress approved the creation of National Key deer Refuge on Big Pine Key and No Name Key. The population of the appealing mammals rose to an estimated 400 in subsequent years before beginning to drop again, with cars rather than hunters now the main cause of unnatural death. An original member of the endangered species list, the Key deer has never lost that status.

John Pennekamp, the *Miami Herald* editor, often sloughed off the label of "environmentalist," despite his crucial role in securing the state funds that helped make Everglades National Park a reality. Pennekamp did not go looking for environmental crusades, but he didn't hesitate to embrace and promote someone else's good idea when he learned about it. During the mid-1950s, marine biologists in South Florida grew increasingly concerned about the condition of the coral reef just off Key Largo in the Atlantic Ocean — the only hard coral reef formation in North America. Unrestricted by any laws, vendors in the burgeoning tourist trade had for years been hammering and blasting the reefs for corals, sponges and queen conch that wound up for sale in stands along U.S. 1. In a reversal of the usual process, a scientist sought the aid of conservation groups in warding off further destruction of the reef. In 1957, Dr. Gilbert Voss of the University of Miami organized a biological conference in Everglades National Park (inviting National Audubon Society scientist Charles Brookfield), during which he lamented the damage he had seen during his studies of the reef. Voss raised the hope of gaining official protection for the reef, and conservation groups embraced the concept, which reflected Ernest Coe's original vision of an Everglades National Park that extended eastward into the ocean beyond Key Largo.

Pennekamp, an associate editor at the Herald, decided to make it happen. Using his considerable clout—he had been the inaugural chairman of the Florida Board of Parks and Historic Memorials and still held a seat as a director—Pennekamp gathered an alliance of conservation figures to begin lobbying at the state and federal levels for the nation's first underwater park. In utter contrast to Pennekamp's experience with the Everglades, virtually no one opposed the idea, and the process sped quickly through the state and federal bureaucracies. In 1959, Governor Leroy Collins approved a reserve extending to the three-mile limit of Florida's jurisdiction, and the following year President Dwight Eisenhower agreed to transfer the federal property beyond the three-mile boundary to the state. At a ceremony on December 10, 1960, Gov. Collins dedicated the preserve, giving it the name "John Pennekamp Coral Reef State Park"—surprising the journalist. With the preserve itself secured, Pennekamp worked to acquire land that would yield access to it. He eventually convinced a landowner named Radford Crane to donate a tract on Key Largo for a park base, and other sales and donations yielded a 74-acre site along Largo Sound for the park's headquarters, which opened in 1963. (Crane later donated much of Largo Sound and an island to expand the park.)

Throughout the many challenges of the mid-century period, environmental groups had their greatest successes when—as with Herbert Mills' treatises on DDT—they drew upon science to make their cases. The National Audubon Society and its state organizations knew that reliance upon demonstrable facts rather than emotional appeals bolstered the credibility of their arguments and made it more difficult for politicians and industry representatives to dismiss their positions. Whereas at the beginning of the century most of National Audubon's resources in Florida went to the warden program, by mid-century the organization was also funding many scientific programs (although the need for wardens hadn't disappeared). National Audubon's Director of Audubon Sanctuaries, Robert Porter Allen, in 1938 established a research station at Tavernier in the Florida Keys, with its focus on study of the life cycles of roseate spoonbills, the distinctive wading birds native to the state. During the 1950s, the Tavernier Science Center expanded its studies to the Florida Keys environment as a whole, including corals, mangroves, crocodiles and bald eagles. As a way of passing its scientific knowledge on to the public, Florida Audubon used a donation from Alfred and Elizabeth Kay in 1961 to open the Pine Jog Conservation-Education Center, a 150-acre facility in West Palm Beach that held workshops for teachers from public schools and also hosted field trips. Audubon handed the center over to Florida Atlantic University in 1970, and it continues to serve its original role in promoting the scientific basis for conservation efforts.

The increasing emphasis on dispassionate approaches to issues about which they were passionate would soon become critical to environmentalists in Florida, for some of the most daunting fights of the century were brewing as the state and nation headed into their most turbulent decade.

Representative Bernie C. Papy speaks at the dedication of John Pennekamp State Park, the nation's first underwater park, on U.S. Highway 1,
three miles north of Key Largo. The Florida Park Service acquired the park
in 1959. State Library and Archives of Florida.

6

SENTIMENT AND SCIENCE COME TOGETHER

The sixties—whether the phrase is applied with chronological precision or used more metaphorically—evokes a period of unprecedented turmoil in American society. It was a transitional era, one in which mere citizens used the power of outrage and determination to do what seemed impossible, changing the policies of the institutional authorities on such epochal issues as civil rights and the Vietnam War. Even if the goals seemed radical at the outset of the process, their eventual achievement depended on acceptance by the mainstream.

The experience of the environmental movement in Florida during the early 1960s through the early 1970s followed much the same course. The period—in retrospect often regarded as the pinnacle of conservationism—was filled with colossal battles in which the defenders of the natural world achieved victories that seemed unthinkable just a few years earlier. As with society at large, the successful challenge of Florida's entrenched powers required a conversion of those outside the original core of activists, a process in which "ecology" became not a fringe issue but a mass concern. And while the advocates of civil rights, for example, could rely on appeals to moral law in making their arguments, Florida's environmental community learned that its best hopes for persuasion rested with the laws of nature—that is, scientific knowledge.

Of the many conservation clashes that raged during the period roughly described as the sixties, the most contentious revolved around a notion that had existed for at least 140 years: a watery bisection of Florida. In 1818, three years before the United States took possession of the territory of Florida from Spain, Secretary of War John Calhoun raised the prospect of an inland waterway cutting across the northern peninsula and making use of the Suwannee and St. Mary's rivers. The territory's legislative council made the canal idea official six years later in an address to Congress, promising that the existing waterways "would render the expense of this work an object of comparative insignificance." That pitch — perhaps the first bid for taxpayer-financed development in Florida — persuaded Congress to order a feasibility study of such a canal, with President John Quincy Adams appointing a seven-man surveying party.

For the next century, the notion of a canal that would protect ships from piracy and the dangerous coral reefs off the Keys never completely lost currency — 28 possible canal routes received consideration — but never gained government sanction. Canal proponents, led by businessmen in Jacksonville and by Florida's congressional delegation, revived the project in the 1920s, citing both military and commercial benefits. They appeared finally to have gotten their wish in the early 1930s, when President Franklin D. Roosevelt decided a ship canal would provide jobs and stimulate Florida's economy. A board appointed by Roosevelt designated a route from Jacksonville to an outlet just south of Yankeetown on the west coast, taking advantage of existing waterways, and Roosevelt earmarked $5.4 million in Works Project Administration funds for the canal. Jacksonville mayor John T. Alsop called for a week of celebration, and hundreds of Ocala residents showed up at a construction site on September 19, 1935, when FDR pressed a telegraph button to remotely detonate a charge and officially launch the project. The jubilation didn't last long. Conservatives in Congress, ever hostile to Roosevelt's "make work" projects, refused to appropriate funding for the canal, and construction went silent within a year of its noisy beginning. The project's legacy, a shallow ditch dug mostly by WPA workers with shovels and pickaxes west of Ocala, soon became overgrown with weeds.

The project remained dormant for another two decades, but the momentum swung again on the basis of two election results. John F.

Kennedy, in the midst of the bruising 1960 presidential campaign, courted Florida voters by pledging his support for the canal project. Meanwhile Farris Bryant, hailing from Ocala, a city that stood to profit from the canal, became Florida's governor in 1961 and set the project as a distinct priority. Kennedy's 1962 budget included $200,000 for final design and planning of the canal, and Bryant secured the endorsements of the two state agencies with environmental oversight authority—the Florida Game and Fresh Water Fish Commission and the Florida Board of Conservation. The Cross Florida Barge Canal, as it was officially called, would cover the same basic course as the aborted canal of the 1930s, connecting the Atlantic Ocean near Jacksonville to the Gulf of Mexico near Yankeetown. The blueprint used a combination of natural rivers—the St. Johns between Jacksonville and Palatka and the Ocklawaha between Palatka and Ocala—though the Corps of Engineers and the Canal Authority of Florida (both based in Jacksonville) released few public details about the planned canal's alteration of the existing landscape. Altogether, the canal would cover 185 miles, averaging 150 feet wide and 12 feet deep and making use of five locks and three dams, which the Corps of Engineers assured the public would prevent saltwater intrusion into the freshwater rivers. Planners estimated the cost of the project at $157.9 million.

Florida's politicians and newspapers were virtually unanimous in their support of the canal—particularly the *Ocala Star-Banner*, whose editor, Bert Dosh, had energetically lobbied for the waterway since the early 1930s. As the state's newspapers reported on the project's gathering momentum, the conservation committee of the Alachua Audubon Society in Gainesville met one night during 1962 on the University of Florida campus and mused about canal's likely effect on the Ocklawaha River, a canopied stream described by 19th-century poet Sidney Lanier as "the sweetest water lane in the world." The assignment of finding out more about the canal fell to the committee's co-chairmen—David Anthony, a professor of biochemistry at UF, and Marjorie Harris Carr, a trained biologist and the wife of Archie Carr, a renowned zoologist and author on the UF faculty. Marjorie Carr had a particular fondness for the Ocklawaha, having worked as a technician at a federal biological research station along the river 25 years earlier while pursuing a master's at UF. Anthony and Carr began writing to state officials, who forwarded their letters to the Corps of Engineers' Jacksonville office, and the Corps responded with letters that not only lacked details but were transparently misleading. "We said, 'Hey, if this project was so good why would you have to reply to an inquiry about it in this manner, with evasiveness and downright untruths?' " Anthony recalls. Further letters yielded replies uniformly lacking in either sympathy or information, including one from O.E. Frye, assistant director of the state's Department of Game and Freshwater Fish, who informed Carr the canal would be "beneficial rather than harmful to overall conservation interests." Despite the official obfuscation, Carr and Anthony did collect a few facts. The Corps of Engineers planned to eliminate 45 miles of the Ocklawaha River — more than 80 percent of its free-flowing length — by damming the river and building two large, shallow reservoirs. In addition to virtually erasing one of the most scenic rivers in Florida, the project would destroy 27,000 acres of adjacent swamp forest, a crucial portion of the ecosystem that includes the Ocala National Forest.

Alachua Audubon's point people — under the rallying cry of "Save the Ocklawaha" — changed strategies and began pushing for a public hearing. (None had been held on the major project, though state officials tried to claim that an unadvertised gathering of the Canal Authority and proponents at a Jacksonville hotel satisfied the statutory requirement for public discussion.) Finally the state sent two officials to a meeting at Gainesville High School. Though one biologist spoke openly about the details of the project — and soon lost his job as a result — the other offered a performance of scripted dissembling that further angered those in attendance. Convinced that the game was rigged at both the state and federal levels, Carr and Anthony began focusing on the official untruths about the canal's environmental effects, and they slowly gathered attention from the media and from other conservation groups. Meanwhile the canal project moved forward. President Lyndon Johnson attended a ceremony on February 27, 1964, at the Rodeheaver Boys Ranch, just south of Palatka, pulling a switch to trigger a blast and launch the first phase of the project. As work on the canal continued in 1965, Alachua Audubon sent hundreds of letters to conservation groups, newspaper editors, Corps of Engineers officers, state bureaucrats and members of Congress—even one to Claudia "Lady Bird" Johnson, the president's wife, whose polite but noncommittal response Carr interpreted as "encouraging."

The Sierra Club passed a resolution condemning the damage to the Ocklawaha, and other environmental groups fell in behind the lead of Alachua Audubon. The conservationists, recognizing political reality, avoided challenging the concept of the canal itself and instead sought only a realignment that would spare the river. Even that goal, however, seemed utterly hopeless, for the Ocklawaha's protectors faced not only institutional indifference at the state and federal levels but also the considerable influence of business leaders in Jacksonville and other cities and counties the canal would cross, who viewed it as an economic boon. Eventually, though, the growing publicity surrounding Carr's group— including a *New York Times* editorial advocating protection of the Ocklawaha—prompted Gov. Haydon Burns, a staunch supporter of the canal, to allow discussion of the route at his cabinet's water resources development conference in early 1966.

It proved to be a galvanizing event for the pro-Ocklawaha contingent. Traveling from as far away as the Keys, about 400 conservationists squeezed into the House chamber in Tallahassee, and Anthony read a 20-page statement raising specific objections to the canal route, but the only cabinet member who bothered to attend the meeting, Secretary of State Tom Adams—who had recently become chairman of a national pro-barge lobby—treated the environmentalists with contempt. "He even insulted old ladies, and that a politician doesn't do," Anthony said. Adams' barrage of hostile questions and bullying tactics was captured on film and used for years to inspire canal opponents. Allan Cruickshank, a nationally famous photographer and lecturer with the National Audubon Society, arrived late with word of a radio report saying the cabinet had secretly met earlier that day and voted full support for the canal.

"The environmentalists came there kind of hat in hand, saying, 'Have your barge canal but please don't mess up our river doing it,' and they went away from there apostles against (the canal)," Anthony said. Arthur Marshall, a biologist with the U.S. Fish and Wildlife Service and an increasingly outspoken ecologist, left the meeting so incensed he could barely make the drive home to Vero Beach.

The full cabinet held its official meeting a month later and unanimously reasserted its support for the canal route. Seeing the impossibility of derailing the institutional momentum for the canal, environmentalists turned pragmatic. Carr's group focused attention on economic factors, charging that the Corps of Engineers had used misleading figures in order to come up with a favorable benefit-to-cost ratio that would justify the project. And Anthony, a fisherman familiar with the sudden squalls of the Gulf of Mexico, learned that the risks of driving barges from New Orleans to the canal's western entrance at Yankeetown would yield prohibitive insurance rates. At his urging, the vice president of the nation's largest barge company told a state senator that his company would not use the canal if it were completed.

Proponents of the canal reacted to the environmentalists' criticisms with dismay. Business leaders offered outlandish justifications for the project, with one suggesting that the reduced cost of shipping grain would yield a huge drop in the price of eggs. Charging that the environmental groups were a front for some competing interest—perhaps the railroad companies, which had opposed the ship canal in the 1930s—some canal backers looked for a phantom benefactor. "They couldn't understand why citizens on their own would do this unless money was involved," said former Florida Audubon official Bill Partington.

Despite their fervent efforts, the canal opponents endured three discouraging years. The Corps of Engineers began excavation work in 1966 at both the eastern and western ends of the canal, and by 1969 the corridor was one-third complete, including a 10-mile channel from Palatka southwest to a dam on the Ocklawaha. Rodman Dam, one of three such structures planned along the canal path, ended the natural flow of the Ocklawaha on September 30, 1968, creating a 13,000-acre reservoir in the place of the river and surrounding forest. But the Corps' efficiency in following its plans gave the environmentalists an opportunity they were happy to exploit. In preparing to create Rodman Reservoir (Rodman

Pool to its detractors), the Corps used a 306-ton, diesel-powered "crusher-crawler" to flatten 6,445 acres of the Ocklawaha floodplain, squashing cypress, maple, ash, oak and other trees into the swampy ground. Photos of the devastated landscape—before it became covered in water—appeared in newspapers and magazines, generating a significant public-relations boon for opponents of the canal.

During the lengthy campaign to protect the Ocklawaha, Carr's contingent had drawn encouragement from several national trends. Growing mainstream indignation about decades of industrial pollution had given rise to what was being called the ecology movement, and government institutions were beginning to regard environmental groups more favorably. A member of Alachua Audubon read an article in *Sports Illustrated* about a successful suit brought by a group called the Environmental Defense Fund to halt the use of the insecticide DDT on Long Island. He brought the article to the attention of his fellow members, noting that the Environmental Defense Fund (EDF)—like Alachua Audubon—consisted largely of academics. Carr's group got in touch with EDF and learned that the New Yorkers had been seeking an opportunity to take on the Corps of Engineers. EDF officials agreed to join the canal fight on the condition that the Gainesville contingent form a group separate from any national organization, and the Floridians agreed, knowing that the national and state Audubon chapters had grown increasingly uneasy about Alachua Audubon's prominent role in the controversy. Using the EDF as a template—and making a deliberate play on its initials—Carr and Anthony in July of 1969 led the founding of the nonprofit Florida Defenders of the Environment, whose expressed purpose was not merely to alter the route of the barge canal but to halt its construction altogether. Partington, a conservation officer with Florida Audubon, accepted an offer to be FDE's president, and the organization soon unveiled a 29-member board of trustees that included 20 Ph.D.'s (Archie Carr among them). Shortly after the group's formation, the Environmental Defense Fund applied to a U.S. District Court in Washington for an immediate hearing and a preliminary injunction against the Corps of Engineers, the opening salvo in the legal phase of the canal battle.

Partington, working out of a small office in Gainesville, led a campaign that raised $65,000 in three years. FDE also gained valuable publicity by inviting reporters to inspect any of its files and talk to any of its members, contrasting that approach with the secrecy of the Corps of Engineers. In January of 1970, *Reader's Digest* published an article entitled "Rape of the Ocklawaha," drawing on information supplied by John Couse, a Lake Worth businessman and FDE member and one of the earliest opponents of the canal. James Nathan Miller's article went out to millions of subscribers, giving canal opponents priceless publicity. Facing a spiral of negative press, the Canal Authority of Florida responded by hiring a public relations consultant at $1,600 a month, distributing "Cross Florida Canal Booster" bumper stickers and arranging to take outdoors writers for tours of Rodman Pool.

Several factors benefited canal opponents in the late 1960s. The Vietnam War had cut into the federal budget, squeezing appropriations for domestic engineering projects, and had fueled mistrust of government institutions. At the same time, electoral turnover had changed Florida's political landscape. Governor Claude Kirk, a moderate Republican elected in 1966, supported the canal but didn't treat it with the religious fervor of his predecessor, Farris Bryant. Likewise, President Richard Nixon entered office in 1969 with no particular commitment to the canal—a project whose Democratic roots went back to FDR—and canal opponents drew hope when Nixon's first budget in 1969 included $6 million for the canal, significantly less than the Corps had requested.

In January of 1970, 162 environmental scientists from across the nation signed a letter asking Nixon to halt construction of the canal and order a comprehensive environmental study, and Nixon referred the issue to the newly created Council on Environmental Quality. Meanwhile, the Florida Defenders produced a 117-page document, co-authored by Arthur Marshall, a biologist with the Fish and Wildlife Service and increasingly an environmental activist as well. The report, calling for the removal of Rodman Dam and the return of the Ocklawaha River to its natural state, came to be regarded as an unofficial environmental impact statement, one of the first of a type that had just become required by law for all major federal projects. In June, Secretary of the Interior Walter Hickel asked the secretary of the army to suspend work on the canal so that an official government study could be completed, but the work continued unabated. The Council on Environmental Quality eventually advised Nixon to stop the canal project, and in January of 1971, U.S. District Judge Barrington Parker granted the temporary injunction sought by the Environmental Defense Fund against the Corps of Engineers. Adding to the momentum, *Audubon* magazine was at work on a full spread about the canal, complete with color photos of the wrecked Ocklawaha valley. (The article didn't mention the organization's previous nervousness over the role of one of its chapters in fighting the canal.) Three days after Parker's ruling, National Audubon Society President Elvis Stahr gave an advance copy to John Carroll Whitaker, Nixon's cabinet secretary. The following day, Nixon announced in a press release that he would order the Corps to abandon construction of the canal. In the release, Nixon called the Ocklawaha "a uniquely beautiful semi-tropical steam, one of very few of its kind in the United States." He added, "The step I have taken today will prevent a past mistake from causing permanent damage." The government had spent approximately $63 million and constructed roughly one third of the canal. To the disappointment of environmentalists, Nixon's executive order did not include the removal of any existing structures.

Still, nine years after beginning what seemed a hopeless undertaking, Marjorie Harris Carr and the many people across Florida who had joined in her crusade finally had a moment of unequivocal triumph. FDE members gathered in their Gainesville office on the decisive morning, taking a phone call from a White House staffer who read Nixon's statement. "We had a party that evening that was highly memorable — well, if we hadn't had so much to drink it would have been more memorable," Anthony said. "It was a hell of a party. We celebrated perhaps not wisely but quite well."

Not surprisingly, the canal's backers refused to accept Nixon's ruling as final. Adams, perhaps the most vocally anti-environmental lieutenant governor in the state's history, fumed that Nixon had thrown the canal to "phony ecologists as he would a bone to a pack of hungry dogs." Of greater significance, the Canal Authority of Florida filed the first of several lawsuits challenging the constitutionality of Nixon's decision, and in 1974 a judge ruled Nixon's order invalid but forbid further work pending further environmental impact studies that recent state laws had mandated. The injunction by the judge, however, held up against challenges in court. The matter dragged on at the state and federal levels for years, with the Corps of Engineers issuing another favorable benefit-to-cost survey that state officials lambasted. The Florida cabinet of Gov. Reubin Askew in 1976 withdrew support for the canal and authorized a state agency to make plans for restoring the Ocklawaha. At the Congressional level, authorization for the canal remained on official record through 1985, and the project wasn't officially dead until the early 1990s, when President George Bush signed a measure deauthorizing the canal and state officials ratified it. The orders, however, did not address the question of returning the Ocklawaha River to its original state — a change that required, above all, the removal of Rodman Dam. As that quest — the consuming mission of Marjorie Carr and Florida Defenders of the Environment since 1971 — continued, the war over construction of the canal would come to seem just a brief skirmish.

The barge canal was far from the only major waterworks project to occupy the Corps of Engineers during the period. Following the floods caused by Hurricane Donna in 1960, the state legislature created the Southwest Florida Water Management District, which began working with the Corps of Engineers on a flood-control plan for a 16-county region that included the Green Swamp, a crucial water recharge area between Orlando and Tampa. Using 100-year high-water marks as its guide, the Corps plotted the Four Rivers Basin Project, a reconfiguration of the area around Tampa Bay as severe as the one under way in South Florida. The project called for a panoply of canals, spillways and levees, as well as the straightening of parts of the Ocklawaha, Withlacoochee, Hillsborough and Peace rivers. Like the complicated flood-control system in South Florida, Four Basins would divert massive quantities of fresh water out to sea. Environmental groups, noting that saltwater intrusion had already forced Hillsborough County to import its drinking water from Pasco County, argued that the region could not afford to squander more water, but the Corps pushed ahead with its replumbing of the Green Swamp. The environmental groups eventually convinced the water district to request a new analysis of the project, and the Corps instead abandoned the project, which was less than one-fifth complete. A state cabinet designation of the Green Swamp as an Area of Critical State Concern in 1974 increased protection for the wetlands, though it was by no means a complete ban on development in the area.

While opposition to the barge canal radiated from North Florida, the southern part of the state had no shortage of grueling environmental fights during the 1960s. With the area between Miami and West Palm Beach growing at a dizzying rate, developers had come to take government approval of their plans for granted—a reality that spawned an opposition force among those concerned about the consequences of the rampant dredging and building. Daniel K. Ludwig, an entrepreneur from Connecticut, began buying up thousands of acres south of Miami in the late 1950s for a development project that included an industrial port and oil refinery. Local commissioners unanimously approved rezoning for the project, known as Seadade, with the only public opposition coming from a small group called the Safe Progress Association (SPA), recently formed by a Pan American Airlines employee and Izaak Walton League member named Lloyd Miller. The SPA pointed out the many dangers the huge development posed for Biscayne Bay, an ecologically fragile saltwater lagoon, and it gradually drew public attention to the project, partly through its bumper stickers, which declared: "NUTS to Dirty Industry." Larger environmental groups joined the battle, convincing state officials to deny the dredge-and-fill applications and effectively killing the project. Around the same time, however, another development was in the works that posed similar threats to South Florida's coastal ecosystem. The planners of Islandia envisioned it as a new city in lower Biscayne Bay, with a causeway from the mainland and bridges connecting Elliott Key with other small islands. The Metro-Dade Commission, perennially a rubber stamp for development, approved the project, but again the Safe Progress Association led a coalition of environmental groups in opposition. Their effort benefited from recently passed state and federal laws requiring environmental impact studies before construction of major regional projects. The protracted and bitter clash ended when Islandia's developers gave up in the face of continuing legal challenges.

The environmentalists' two monumental victories were not absolute. After being denied their plans for Seadade, developers sold a 20,000-acre tract to Florida Power and Light, which gained permission in the early 1970s to build a power-generating facility at Turkey Point on the southern shore of Biscayne Bay. Still, the derailing of two large-scale developments —an unthinkable prospect a decade earlier—emboldened environmentalists to push for a permanent shield around southern Biscayne Bay. As it happened, the 1964 Metro-Dade Commission was the first in memory with a pro-environment majority, and the council passed a proposal to offer the estuary as a national preserve. The Department of the Interior conducted a study headed by Arthur Marshall, who declared the bay to have national environmental significance. Marshall also hosted delegations from Congress and federal agencies to the bay. Secretary of the Interior Stewart L. Udall endorsed the idea, and Congress in 1968 passed a measure establishing Biscayne National Monument, a preserve of 96,000 mostly aquatic acres. As the vote loomed, angry landowners on Elliott Key plowed down the island's largest hardwood hammock in hopes that the key would no longer merit protection. Instead, they wound up having to pay for replanting of the trees.

The clashes over Seadade and Islandia, significant though they were, served as mere warmup bouts for another colossal collision between South Florida's environmentalists and government officials. In a parallel to the evolution of the barge canal struggle in North Florida, the insurgency over the Big Cypress jetport began with a handful of people unhappy about a project whose institutional support seemed truly insurmountable. In the late 1960s, the Dade County Port Authority decided that Miami International Airport could no longer support the airlines' flight training programs, and it began searching for the site of a second major airport for South Florida. After considering 17 locations, the Port Authority settled on a 39-square-mile parcel in Big Cypress Swamp, a few miles north of Everglades National Park's border, and quietly began acquiring land in 1967. The Port Authority had grand plans for the remote and lightly inhabited area—the nation's most modern airport, with up to six runways (two of them possibly six miles long) and a surrounding complex of shops and facilities. Because of its location—45 miles from Miami—the new airport would require a new highway as well. Gov. Claude Kirk attended the groundbreaking ceremony on September 18, 1968, and construction of the first runway began before environmentalists could mount any significant opposition to the project.

A month after the ceremony, Robert Padrick, chairman of the Central and Southern Florida Flood Control District, attended a state transportation meeting and glimpsed a map showing a four-lane extension of Interstate 75 from Naples to Miami cutting through the Big Cypress Swamp. Padrick relayed his concerns about the massive development to Nathaniel Reed, a conservation aide to Gov. Kirk. Reed flew over the construction site and was stunned by the magnitude of the project. "I couldn't believe my eyes," Reed said. "But there it was." Reed openly questioned the wisdom of the project, a stance that brought him vilification from South Florida business leaders.

A coalition including the state and national Audubon societies, Sierra Club, 21 other environmental groups, two labor unions and Miccosukee Indians quickly formed to oppose the "jetport," as everyone called it. Environmental leaders pointed out the role of the Big Cypress in the Everglades ecosystem, warning that the proposed highway would disrupt natural water flows into the Glades. Gary Soucie, eastern representative for the Sierra Club, wrote in *Sierra* magazine, "If the jetport isn't moved, say goodbye to the continent's only subtropical national park and to the world's only Everglades." In an indication that environmental concerns had reached the mainstream, some church groups joined the lobbying, and high school and college students distributed flyers condemning the proposed jetport. Gov. Kirk and Secretary of the Interior Water Hickel received a combined 24,000 letters in opposition to the development.

Like their counterparts in the canal fight, opponents of the jetport benefited from the publicly expressed antagonism of various public officials. Alan C. Stewart, director of the Port Authority, derided environmentalists as "butterfly chasers" and "yellow-bellied sapsuckers" and boldly declared, "A new city is going to rise up in the middle of Florida.

You are going to have one (jetport) whether you like it or not." Chuck Hall, the mayor of Metro-Dade, referred to Reed and Friends of the Earth founder Joe Browder as "white militants." Michael O'Neil, Florida's secretary of transportation, said during testimony in Washington on the jetport: "Everglades National Park is a swamp. Alligators make nice shoes and pocketbooks. I care more about people."

The authorities' arrogance extended to a disregard for recent laws mandating detailed environmental impact studies before any major development project could be carried out. Responding to the crescendo of protest, state and federal officials suspended construction on the jetport while awaiting the results of three scientific studies. The most significant, headed by Dr. Luna B. Leopold of the U.S. Geological Survey, determined that any major development in the area would threaten the health of the Everglades ecosystem. As with the canal battle, the scientific credibility of the arguments against the jetport made the difference. On January 16, 1970, Secretary of the Interior Hickel and Secretary of Transportation John Volpe announced the end of the jetport as originally envisioned. They outlined a complicated three-way agreement among federal, state and local authorities that would allow use of one completed runway for training flights under strict guidelines covering altitude levels, fueling facilities, disposal of wastes and the presence of culverts to maintain water-flow levels. Nixon, in approving the agreement, said the experience showed that decisions about massive developments cannot be left entirely to local authorities. The decision, and the one that followed a year later on the barge canal, delighted environmentalists, who had greeted a Nixon presidency with trepidation and who had lobbied against Hickel's confirmation as Secretary of the Interior.

One of the comments of the jetport proponents still resonated even after the project was shut down. Richard H. Judy, deputy director of the Port Authority, said, "The Big Cypress Swamp is just typical South Florida real estate. It's private property; eventually it's going to be put to human use." Wary of that prediction, conservationists had been urging government acquisition of Big Cypress even before the jetport issue was settled. Nat Reed, a new member of the Nixon administration, warned: "Without government control over Big Cypress, the (Everglades

National) Park and Southwest Florida will rot. I predict the destruction of the area in 50 years if Big Cypress is developed—and yet I have not found a solution short of buying it." Reed, a savvy shaper of public policy, arranged for the president's daughter Julie to visit Big Cypress while the debate over its purchase raged on. Senator Lawton Chiles, a Florida Democrat, took up the issue in Congress, and Nixon embraced it as his own in 1971, proposing federal purchase of 547,000 acres of the swamp as a national preserve. The projected cost of the acquisition would require the largest expenditure ever for a single federal park or recreation area, and it took two years for Congress to approve funding. In Florida, meanwhile, environmental lobbyists—including Johnny Jones of the Florida Wildlife Federation and Charles Lee of Florida Audubon—successfully pushed the Big Cypress Conservation Act through the legislature in 1973, authorizing a state contribution of $40 million toward the purchase. Big Cypress National Preserve came into existence, and its state designation as an area of critical concern offered protection against any adjacent development that could have an impact on the preserve.

The milestone contained one disappointment, and it involved oil. Speculators had first targeted Florida in 1901, with Humble Oil striking the first successful well in 1943 at Sunniland, just west of the eventual preserve boundaries, and energy companies had been probing Southwest Florida ever since. The state's Department of Natural Resources approved the first application to drill for oil inside Big Cypress in 1971, after which Florida Audubon's Scott and Lee gained permission from four oil companies to observe their operations. Based on what the pair saw, Audubon urged the state to deny permits for further oil exploration. DNR officials imposed restrictions based on the Audubon complaints but approved the drilling and the construction of access roads in the region. With the creation of the Big Cypress Preserve, the federal-state plan left intact the mineral rights of several oil companies, meaning drilling could continue in an otherwise protected area.

Federal money had rescued the largest sections of Florida from development, but environmental groups had long pushed the idea of a state bank account dedicated to the purchase of ecologically important properties. The legislature finally heeded the call in 1963, setting up a Land Acquisition Trust Fund to be supported by a five-percent tax on outdoor recreation clothing and equipment. The tax generated about $1.5 million a year, allowing the purchase of lands that expanded the state park system to 84 units by 1969. The legislature altered the funding mechanism in 1968, tapping funds from the sale of documentary stamps (used in public transactions)—which brought about $1 million a year—and approving a one-time bond issue that yielded $20 million. The use of bonds for land acquisition proved palatable to both politicians and environmentalists, setting the stage for more ambitious programs in later years.

Two years before lawmakers established the state's first land-acquisition program, a band of South Floridians decided the time had arrived for a state chapter of The Nature Conservancy, which had formed a decade earlier. The national organization and its chapters pursued a more specialized strategy than other conservation groups: By working to save endangered lands through either outright purchase or the brokering of government acquisition, the Conservancy tapped into the sympathy of wealthy Floridians willing to donate money but not necessarily engaged in environmental activism. The original 12 members of TNC's Florida chapter, some of them scientists, started with assets of just $25, but the group had both the backing of the national organization and connections to enough conservationists in the state to give them optimism. For its first project, the Florida chapter began a campaign to fend off development on Jack Island in St. Lucie County. A three-year fund drive resulted in the purchase of 1,000 acres, which became Jack Island State Reserve. Shortly after completing that campaign, the Florida Conservancy learned of an unrealized dream of the late Edward Bok to preserve a haven of rare biota in the state's central highlands. Bok, the former editor of the *Ladies Home Journal*, offered something of a template for the Conservancy, having used his wealth to create a botanical garden near Lake Wales that included Bok Tower, set on the highest point in peninsular Florida. Ken Morrison, director of Bok Tower Gardens, worked with Bok's son, Cary, to revive the late naturalist's goal of purchasing a tract a few miles south known as Tiger Creek. The land's owner, the Atlantic Coast Line Railroad, set a price of $260 an acre, and the Conservancy launched a "Buy An Acre" campaign, eventually drawing contributions from 3,000 people and groups, including the Florida Federation of Garden Clubs and Florida Audubon. By 1971, the Conservancy had raised enough money to begin buying land for what grew to be the 4,700-acre Tiger Creek Preserve, a home to some plants found nowhere else on earth. In the midst of that campaign, the growing reputation of the Florida Conservancy chapter yielded a donation of 73 acres on Jupiter Island from a group of local residents (including the family of Nathaniel Reed), land that became Blowing Rocks Preserve, an important nesting site for sea turtles. In less than a decade, The Nature Conservancy's Florida chapter had become an important force in protecting important areas from development.

While North and South Florida produced titanic environmental conflicts that sparked national interest, one of the most significant development projects in the state's history arose in the central part of the state during the 1960s. It all happened so stealthily, however, that environmental groups had little chance to react. Orlando remained a rather sleepy metropolis of 90,000 people in the early 1960s, when the Walt Disney Corporation began secretly acquiring an eventual 30,000 acres of land in Orange and Osceola counties, about 20 miles southwest of the city. The company employed a complex arrangement of dummy corporations to buy up the swamp, citrus groves and pasture land at low prices, with the intent of replicating its famous California theme park in another sunny locale—only this time with a sufficient buffer of land to isolate the park from its surroundings. Disney threatened to abandon the project if its plans became public, and the few locals privy to the details happily acceded to the company's wishes. Martin Andersen, then the owner and publisher of the *Orlando Sentinel,* assisted the secretive company but claimed not to know its identity until one of his reporters broke the story in 1965. Walt Disney wanted the freedom to develop the land as he chose—an "experimental absolute monarchy," as one Disney executive described it—and industry-hungry state and local officials granted him his wish.

The creation of an autonomous government, headed by the Reedy

Creek Improvement District, gave the corporation more power and immunity from regulation than any city could ever hope for. The arrangement—exempting Disney from any restrictions on land use and even giving the company the authority to build an airport or a nuclear power plant—stemmed from Disney's stated plans of developing a utopian city of 20,000 people that the company never actually intended as a reality. The extraordinary concessions shielded Disney from environmental restraints, and it took full advantage, draining a large lake on its property to remove the organic material on the bottom that gave the water a brown tint. The creation of Walt Disney World also involved digging a 200-acre lake, which was lined with four million gallons of white sand dredged out of the ground. In all, the company dug 40 miles of canals (engineered to resemble natural rivers) and built 18 miles of levees and 13 water-control structures, drastically altering a huge swath of Central Florida. Though Bill Partington, then with Florida Audubon, and other local environmentalists cringed at some of Disney's actions, they realized the project was a done deal. They also knew that a gigantic corporation with seemingly limitless assets would make the Army Corps of Engineers seem like a junior varsity opponent. Skilled in the art of public relations, Disney consulted with Florida Audubon and other environmentalists, setting aside a parcel of land as a nature preserve. Complaints from environmental groups, including the local Environmental Council of Osceola, did persuade the U.S. Army Corps of Engineers against converting Reedy Creek into a channel that would have funneled water out of the theme park. Walt Disney World opened its gates on October 1, 1971, setting up the ineluctable spread of urban sprawl through Central Florida.

The melees over the barge canal and the jetport coincided with the growth of an American "ecology" movement, and Florida fully participated in the national trend. Local chapters of formidable national organizations, notably the Sierra Club, sprouted during the 1960s, and smaller organizations such as the Florida Defenders arose to pursue a particular conservation objective. In answering its own question about the need for another environmental group in Florida when so many already existed, the inaugural bulletin of the Sierra Club's Florida

Regional Group explained that relentless growth created a multitude of challenges at the local level. Indeed, while the period of the 1960s and early 1970s produced some of the most outsized environmental gains in the state's history, it was an era in which the smallest towns could become fierce battlegrounds between the forces of "progress" and the champions of nature. While new groups were emerging, the state's most established conservation entity reinvigorated itself during the period as well. Florida Audubon Society, while maintaining interest in legislative matters, had ceased to be a powerful lobbying organization by 1960, when it comprised 1,500 people (only twice its membership in 1937). The arrival of C. Russell Mason, formerly of Massachusetts Audubon, as executive director and editor of *The Florida Naturalist* in 1957, signaled a change in emphasis toward more aggressive advocacy. Under the leadership of Mason and later Hal Scott, another tough-minded activist, Florida Audubon reasserted its influence in Tallahassee, and the group swelled to 25,000 members by 1973. Another group underwent a wholesale metamorphosis to become a conservation force during the 1960s. The Florida Wildlife Federation, an offshoot of the National Wildlife Federation, had existed since 1937, but for decades it had contented itself with the pursuit of pro-hunting policies and had even opposed an expansion of Everglades National Park in 1957. In the late 1960s, however, a plumbing contractor from West Palm Beach named John C. "Johnny" Jones rose to leadership of the group and steered it toward a true conservation agenda that made it an important agent of the Tallahassee battles for the next decade.

The period also marked the rise of conservation-minded public officials, two of whom played some role in virtually every significant environmental issue of the 1960s and 1970s. Nathaniel Reed, a wealthy Republican in the real-estate business from Hobe Sound, became a national figure largely as the result of the unexpected 1966 victory of Claude Kirk, Florida's first Republican governor since Reconstruction. Reed, well known in the environmental community for his involvement with Florida Audubon and The Nature Conservancy, served as a fundraiser for Kirk and helped draft the conservation plank of the candidate's campaign platform, which included a pledge to curtail the dredging of bay bottoms for development projects. After his election, Kirk—

who had, in Reed's words, "scant environmental credentials" — created a position for the 33-year-old Reed as the first official environmental advisor to a Florida governor and later chose him to head the newly created Department of Air and Water Pollution Control (the predecessor of the Department of Environmental Protection). Reed arrived in Tallahassee at a period that marked Florida's environmental nadir. In the mid-1960s, there was only one modern sewage-treatment facility in the state — the city of Jacksonville dumped raw sewage into the St. Johns River, and most cities in Southeast Florida piped raw sewage into the Atlantic Ocean. In addition, the state for decades had not only routinely approved dredge-and-fill projects — allowing developers to scoop dirt from the bottoms of oceans, bays and rivers and extend shorelines and build islands — but had sold state-owned submerged lands to developers.

Keeping his campaign pledge, Kirk used his influence on the board of trustees of the Internal Improvement Fund — the governor and his cabinet — to bring a virtual halt to state sales of underwater land, but that still left untold acres of privately owned submerged lands vulnerable to development. Before the arrival of Kirk and Reed in Tallahassee, such reviews had been a formality, with the state approving more than 2,000 projects a year. The practice had created a public backlash as estuaries were filled across the state, perhaps most egregiously in the case of Boca Ciega Bay in St. Petersburg. During his first year in office, Reed helped sculpt a bill under the sponsorship of state representative Ted Randell of Lee County that for the first time required a biological survey before state or local governments could approve any alterations to state-owned lands under lakes and tidal waters. When Randell himself worried that the bill seemed too bold, Reed assured him, "Ted you're going to go down in history." The legislature passed the Randell-Thomas Act in 1967 (with Jerry Thomas of Palm Beach County as Senate sponsor), making it much more difficult for developers to gain dredge-and-fill permits.

"Between the four years of Kirk and the first two years of Askew, we basically ended the sale of submerged lands and the dredge and filling," Reed said. "You just couldn't get a permit from the state any more."

At Reed's urging, Kirk also took on the state's woefully inadequate sewage systems, threatening local officials with removal from office on grounds of malfeasance if they delayed in taking steps to build sewage-treatment plants. With local officials reluctant to raise taxes to build the facilities, the situation had the potential for chaos. But a confluence of factors brought about a long-overdue solution to Florida's sewage problems. The federal government at the time offered grants that in some cases paid 90 percent of the cost for the construction of regional sewage-treatment plants, with the federal percentage scheduled to decrease in the near future. Meanwhile, local officials began feeling pressure from developers who feared a moratorium on building permits and from contractors eager to build the sewage-treatment plants. (Once cities and counties agreed to build plants, they often wildly overestimated their needed capacity to allow for unchecked future growth.)

Reed led an equally aggressive state effort to curb industrial pollution. He urged Kirk to order local governments into "enforcement conferences," during which representatives of industry were forced to share details of their companies' discharges—or, as Reed put it, "confess their sins." The public disclosures of corporate pollution yielded citizen outrage, making it easier for the state to set strict guidelines for emissions from plants and factories. The federal Clean Water Act of 1972 further strengthened the state's enforcement abilities. As head of the state's pollution-control agency, Reed had the authority to take offending companies to court. In one of his most successful challenges, Reed convinced a phosphate firm to pay the state $200,000 for cleanup efforts after a containment wall broke and allowed industrial slime to infiltrate the Peace River.

Reed's reputation as "Mr. Clean" led to his appointment by Richard Nixon in 1971 as Assistant Secretary of the Interior, a position he would hold for six years. During his decade of public service, Reed served as the insider for the conservation brigade, exerting influence on some of the weightiest environmental decisions the state has faced.

While Reed arrived at his conservation role from an unlikely background, Arthur Marshall discarded traditional taboos in becoming perhaps the state's single most influential advocate during the age of environmental enlightenment. Marshall, who grew up in South Florida, became the supervisor of a U.S. Fish and Wildlife field office in Vero Beach in 1960, and he quickly grew dismayed with the Corps of Engineers' approach to coastal dredging projects, which were causing incalculable biological damage to shallow estuaries. He decided to transform himself from an invisible government bureaucrat into a spokesman for the environment—in the process violating an unwritten code of public silence among officials with regulatory agencies. Marshall sought out speaking opportunities with local environmental groups, accepting offers even when he knew his audience would consist of just a handful of people. Though a specialist by vocation, Marshall possessed a comprehensive knowledge of Florida's major ecological issues, and he stressed the importance of the big picture — the effect of small changes on entire ecosystems, particularly the Everglades. Marshall, dubbed a "biopolitician" by a friend, formed contacts with environmental groups across the state, providing helpful information and giving them credibility by association. He supplied scientific papers for opponents of the barge canal, and he co-authored a Department of the Interior study that proved crucial in stopping the jetport project. His pronouncements on the interrelated nature of the South Florida ecosystem — codified in the "Marshall Plan," a blueprint for saving the Everglades — added urgency to the quest to save Big Cypress Swamp.

Perhaps inspired by Marshall's public advocacy for the Everglades, Marjory Stoneman Douglas assumed a new role for herself during the era. Although she gained fame with the publication in 1947 of *The Everglades: River of Grass*, both a dispassionate history and a scalding critique of human alterations to the ecosystem, Douglas had for two decades maintained the demeanor of a journalist, avoiding direct involvement with the many political issues that affected the Everglades. In 1969, at the urging of Joe Browder of the National Audubon Society, she decided to take an active role in opposing the Big Cypress jetport. Douglas formed an alliance called Friends of the Everglades, with $1 annual dues, and the group swelled to 1,000 members within two years. Thus, at the age of 80, Douglas began a new career as not just a chronicler of the Everglades' demise but a public advocate for its restoration. Like Marshall, Douglas began making frequent public appearances, traveling the state to inveigh against those she considered enemies of the Everglades — the sugar industry, the Corps of Engineers, developers and the politicians who avoided taking real action to save the ecosystem. Marjory Stoneman Douglas got a late start in activism, but she had plenty of time left in her life to plead on behalf of her cherished River of Grass.

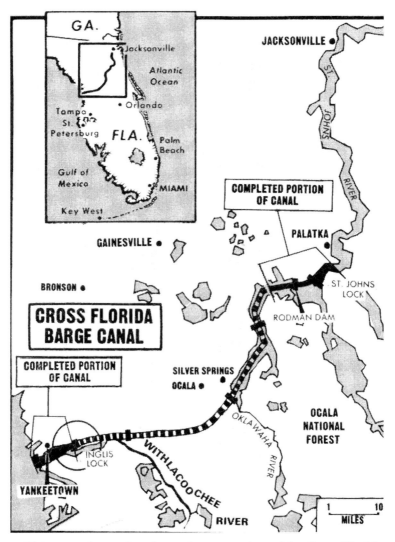

This map shows the planned construction of the Cross Florida Barge Canal. Construction was halted in January 1971. State Library and Archives of Florida.

Gov. Claude Kirk presents conservationist Marjorie Carr with an award for her environmental work in 1971. Her husband Dr. Archie Carr is on the right. State Library and Archives of Florida.

7

AN INCREASINGLY SPECIALIZED APPROACH

In the realm of conservation, as in other areas, the trends of the 1960s carried through the first years of the following decade. The convergence of many factors — the sprouting of new environmental groups, the rising popularity of conservation issues with voters, the visible effects of decades-long tolerance of corporate pollution yielded an atmosphere — during the early 1970s in which environmentalists held unprecedented sway in the state legislature, and a progressive governor responded to shepherd into law some of the most important conservation measures the state would produce during the 20th century. This relatively brief era stands — especially when viewed through the prism of the return to primacy of commercial concerns in Tallahassee — as Florida's apex of environmental achievement.

The widening affinity for the ecology movement prompted Wisconsin Sen. Gaylord Nelson to declare April 22, 1970 as "Earth Day," intended as an annual celebration of the natural world and a focal point for protests against the ongoing degradation of the nation's land, water and air. In Florida, the day drew together environmentalists of various stripes and with different ideas of the best means for commemoration. In Dade County, a small group calling itself "Eco-Commando Force 70" dumped yellow dye into water at sewage treatment plants in an attempt to demonstrate the eventual destination of polluted water. A similar mood of disenchantment prevailed in downtown Miami, where activists held a "Dead Orange Parade," in which a dozen floats bearing dour environmental messages followed the path of the annual King Orange Parade. Taking advantage of the day's expected publicity, small groups of activists picketed at a Florida Power and Light plant to protest the company's plans to discharge heated water from its Turkey Point plant into Biscayne Bay. Colleges across the state marked the day with symposiums and litter-gathering events. And in Tallahassee, Gov. Claude Kirk chose the date to sign the first two bills of the 1970 legislative session, which increased the penalties for alligator poaching.

Like Nathaniel Reed, the owner of an Ocala sporting goods business parlayed his fundraising efforts for the Republican Party into a position of prominence during the late 1960s. Lyman Rogers, the party's leader in Marion County, collaborated with Reed in articulating the environmental positions of gubernatorial candidate Claude Kirk in 1966. At the pair's urging, Kirk pledged in his campaign to create a board of environmental advisors, and upon taking office Kirk rewarded Rogers with an appointment to head the Natural Resources Council. Reed also joined the governor's staff, and before long the two recognized that the efforts of conservationists suffered from the diffusion of groups and objectives. Environmental lobbying had remained a fairly ragged effort into the late 1960s, with representatives of Florida Audubon, the Izaak Walton League and a few other groups traveling to Tallahassee for a day or two when important legislation was under debate. (A few well-informed citizens also served as informal lobbyists, most notably Virginia Forrest and John McQuigg, both of Stuart, Carl Radder of St. Petersburg, Brad Patton of Fort Myers, Jim and Polly Redford of Miami and Bill and Gwen Lund of West Palm Beach.) To get things done in the capital, Reed and Rogers decided, environmentalists needed a unified lobbying alliance, like those that represented the state's major industries. At their prompting, 52 people — including most of the Natural Resources Council and a few legislators and heads of state agencies — gathered in Orlando in July of 1969 to establish a group that called itself Conservation '70s (C-70s for short). The organizers intended for the alliance to be a lobbying force in Tallahassee and a clearinghouse for facts on legislation that would affect the environment. It hired as its executive director a young man named Loring Lovell, a former aide to Secretary of State Tom

Adams—who had proved himself a virulent foe of conservationists.

The creation of a well-connected group devoted to environmental legislation coincided with the arrival in Tallahassee of Reubin Askew, elected in 1970 as a state senator from Pensacola and little-known except as a champion of civil rights. (Strangely enough, he picked Adams as his running mate.) The moderate Republican's sympathy toward environmental matters contributed to an atmosphere of new possibility in Tallahassee, and Conservation 70s proved to be a formidable entity during its first legislative session in 1970. The group actively promoted 55 bills, 41 of which passed into law, an unprecedented success rate for environmental lobbying. Though many of the bills were uncontroversial and only vaguely environmental, the package included important measures that tightened rules on coastline construction, dredge-and-fill operations and offshore oil drilling, gave greater protections to alligators and other species and added strict requirements for sewage treatment facilities. Further gains followed in the 1971 session, including a severance tax on phosphate mining, a measure that gave individual citizens the right to sue companies over pollution or environmentally harmful development projects and another that set higher standards for wastewater-treatment facilities.

Responding to a paper by Arthur Marshall, who had become the director of the University of Miami's Center for Applied Ecology, Askew organized a Water Management Conference in 1971. Marshall, as he had been doing for years, emphasized the interrelated nature of the state's water systems, and he put forth his 14-point "Marshall Plan" for restoring the natural water passage—known as "sheet flow"—from the upper Kissimmee River basin through the Everglades. Marshall's ideas gained urgency that summer, when a drought exacerbated the man-made problems of declining water levels in the Everglades. Askew appointed Marshall to lead a water policy task force, and the panel recommended a more comprehensive approach to water management in South Florida, warning of the imminent collapse of life in Lake Okeechobee if pollution sources were not contained. In 1976, Marshall served as a consultant for a report prepared by the Division of State Planning that stressed the dangers posed by the nutrient-rich water pumped back into Lake Okeechobee by sugar growers. The original draft of the report recommended a water-use tax on farmers and said that discharges into the lake should be greatly reduced, if not stopped altogether. Agricultural interests and some state legislators objected, and the agency deleted those proposals from its final report—as well as the authors' judgment that the water management district operated as a functionary of large farming companies.

In Tallahassee, the environmental momentum continued into the 1972 legislative session, when lawmakers passed several of the most significant measures of the century. It was the year that John C. "Johnny" Jones turned his plumbing business over to his son to become the National Wildlife Federation's executive director and dedicated lobbyist, and he aligned himself with representatives of Florida Audubon and the Sierra Club in pursuing several measures that hadn't passed in the previous session. The environmental groups found an ally in Bob Graham, a state senator from Dade County who would later become governor and a congressman. Heeding the recommendations of the Marshall task force, Graham sponsored the Environmental Land and Water Management Act, which called for a combination of state and local regulation over major development projects. The act strengthened the state's role in approving projects on environmentally sensitive lands, known as "areas of critical concern," and it set definitions of projects whose potential effects merited scrutiny beyond the local level. The measure also divided the state into five water management districts, whose directors would play a role in the review of projects. The Florida Comprehensive Planning Act also passed during the session, a measure more important for its later offspring than for its own effect. The measure established the concept of the "comprehensive plan," a statement of intended growth patterns that cities and counties would be required to submit. Though hardly binding on local governments, such plans would give environmentalists another basis on which to challenge harmful projects.

The legislature passed a third measure whose symbolic significance may have overshadowed the other two. The Land Conservation Act, promoted by all the state's major environmental groups, authorized $200 million (a tenfold increase over the first such bond issue four years earlier) for the state to purchase environmentally sensitive lands, pending the approval of Florida's voters. Graham worked with the lobbyist Johnny Jones in crafting the bills, and after it passed both houses Gov. Reubin Askew formed a private corporation called Lands For You, dedicated to persuading voters to approve the bond issue. Askew appointed Graham as chairman and Jones as vice chairman of Lands For You, and they toured the state throughout the summer, meeting with civic groups and editorial boards of newspapers and television stations. In November, 74 percent of voters endorsed the idea of using public funds for land conservation—a landslide that exceeded even Jones' optimistic expectations. Environmental groups quickly offered their suggestions as state agencies drew up priority lists for the newly created Environmentally Endangered Lands program, though it soon became apparent the rankings would often be skewed more toward political desires than ecological urgencies. In addition to its tangible effect, the Land Conservation Act and the subsequent ballot result gave lawmakers a clear statement of the public sentiment on environmental matters, a mandate to protect important lands before the developers could get them. "We lobbied through 10 environmental bills," Jones said of the 1972 session. "That was more than anybody ever dreamed of." Though Jones and other environmentalists hoped the gains signaled the future for Florida politics, the reality proved otherwise. "In 1973 our enemies started fighting back," Jones said.

The 1972 legislative session—hailed by environmentalists as one of the most productive ever—followed directly from the goals of Conservation 70s, the group founded two years earlier by Lyman Rogers and Nathaniel Reed. As an entity, however, C-70s quickly faltered, disappearing long before the end of the decade for which it was named. Based in Tallahassee with a staff of two, the alliance relied on public donations for its budget—$32,000 in its first year. Within a year of its formation, the organization was nearly broke. Executive director Loring Lovell, lamenting the paucity of individual donations, glumly told a reporter, "I think the problem is the average fellow does not give a hoot about conservation." The departure of the formidable Reed for a federal position in 1971 also contributed to the demise of the alliance by 1973. During its brief existence, however, C-70s offered a model of effective, fact-based lobbying on environmental issues, and in its wake the major environmental groups realized the importance of full-time lobbyists in the capital. An unpaid volunteer for C-70s, a law school graduate named David Gluckman, would carry on the organization's work in spirit if not in name beyond the end of the century.

As a harbinger of the possible fate of Lake Okeechobee, the state's largest, environmentalists had a sad example in Lake Apopka, once the state's second-biggest lake and long renowned as a haunt of trophy largemouth bass. A series of "improvements" to the lake began in 1880 with the digging of a canal connecting it to Lake Beauclaire, a change that affected the natural filtering of water between the lakes. Beginning in the 1920s, Lake Apopka, covering 48 square miles northwest of Orlando, became a receptacle for all manner of pollution, including byproducts of citrus processing and effluent from a sewage treatment plant owned by the adjacent town of Winter Garden. The artificial control of water levels and the use of chemicals by state agencies—first to eradicate water hyacinths and later to kill gizzard shad—created an accumulation of decaying material on the lake bottom that altered its biological dynamics. The preeminent threat to Lake Apopka's health, however, arose from an act of the state legislature during World War II, when lawmakers leery of possible food shortages approved a plan to convert the marshy area along the lake's northern rim into farmland. Given the authority of their own government entity, the Zellwood Drainage and Water Control District, farmers dug canals throughout their 19,000 acres and built an earthen dike that truncated the lake (reducing it to the state's fourth largest) and removed an important filtering system for surface water. The soil of the dried marsh—rich, dark peat—proved extremely fecund, and the farmers began growing lettuce, carrots and celery, along with the corn that spawned a popular annual festival in the nearby town of Zellwood. The farmers made full use of the powers granted to their drainage district, pumping water out of Lake Apopka to irrigate their crops and allowing runoff back into the lake—water that carried the phosphates and nitrates of the fertilizers used on the crops as well as pesticides, including DDT. The first major algae bloom occurred in 1947, and by the early 1960s the steady dose of unnatural nutrients had overwhelmed the lake, causing eutrophication—a lack of oxygen at the levels needed to sustain healthy animal and plant life. The famous bass fishing was history, as was the commercial harvest of catfish. During 1966 alone, algae blooms in Lake Apopka killed one million fish. In that year, a group of people living near the lake formed the Central Florida Anti-Pollution Association, which gathered 5,000 signatures on a petition asking government and industry to halt the cycle that sent nutrient-rich runoff into the lake. Instead, the Department of Air and Water Pollution Control in 1971 began an experimental drawdown of the lake in the hope that loose sediments would settle, leading to an improvement in water quality. The plan backfired, generating tissue-destroying bacteria that began claiming turtles and alligators in addition to the fish. With the need for a more comprehensive plan obvious, the state finally halted emissions from citrus processing and the dumping of sewage from the city of Winter Garden after six decades, and officials from wildlife agencies and water management districts spent the rest of the decade debating ways to bring Lake Apopka back to life.

The moribund condition of some of Florida's largest lakes mirrored the imperiled state of some groups of animals. While several species of native birds had passed into extinction, Florida had not lost a major land-dwelling mammal (though the Caribbean monk seal, whose northern range included the Gulf of Mexico, disappeared by the 1950s). In the early 20th century, however, it was clear that the Florida panther, a reclusive member of the cougar family (also called puma), had reached dangerously low population levels. Like every animal in Florida large enough to be shot, panthers had been hunted since the arrival of the Europeans, and in 1832 the territorial legislature placed a bounty on the animals, reiterated by the state assembly 55 years later at a payment rate of $5 a scalp. In 1935, a Leesburg resident named David Newell wrote an article for the *Saturday Evening Post* that gleefully described a six-week hunting trip to Big Cypress Swamp in which his party of experienced puma hunters from Arizona and their dogs killed eight panthers, including an immature male that they roasted and ate. Newell expressed great pleasure in having proven to skeptical friends that the "varmints" still existed in Florida. In addition to such direct threats, panthers had been unintentional victims of the state-mandated frenzy of deer slaughter in the name of tick control during the first half of the century. The sudden decimation of deer, especially in Southwest Florida, decreased the panthers' main source of food, causing their numbers to shrink even further. The state game commission finally gave panthers partial protection in 1950 and full protection eight years later. At that point, biologists were uncertain whether a viable population of panthers remained in the state. The deer eventually repopulated Florida's green spaces, but the remaining panthers faced the more insidious threat of human encroachment. Like the Florida black bear, another threatened mammal, the panther requires a large tract of land on which to hunt for food (each panther has an estimated home range of 150,000 acres). As the forces of development sliced up the topography, fragmenting their habitat, panthers found fewer suitable places to live—the largest being the Everglades/Big Cypress region. When Congress passed the Endangered Species Act in 1973, the Florida panther received the dreadful honor of being on the original list. The historic act compelled federal wildlife officials to devise plans for ensuring the survival of each species, inevitably a complicated process.

Florida Audubon, following the example of its national affiliate, had become increasingly involved in scientific studies since mid-century, and one of the organization's greatest academic assets was Peter C.H. Pritchard, an Oxford-trained zoologist who had earned a doctorate under Archie Carr at the University of Florida. Though turtles were his specialty, Pritchard was also a generalist with a keen interest in all imperiled animals. While waiting for the U.S. Fish and Wildlife Service to unveil its panther protection strategy, Pritchard organized a meeting in 1976 at a Unitarian church in Orlando, inviting a mix of scientific and environmental figures to offer facts and opinions about the endangered animal. An official from Fish and Wildlife attended the seminar, and soon afterward he asked Pritchard to serve on a group in the process of being created, the Florida Panther Recovery Team, to be headed by the state Game and Freshwater Fish Commission. Pritchard joined representatives from several state agencies on the panel, which spent five years putting together a plan to increase the animal's chances of survival. One important element of the strategy, the use of radio collars to allow tracking of the panthers, provoked resistance from the public and some environmental groups, who considered the collaring process dangerously invasive. Pritchard convinced Florida Audubon's board of directors to endorse the radio collars, and that support faced a severe test in 1983, when a panther died in Big Cypress after a tranquilizer dart punctured a blood vessel in the animal's leg and delivered its drug too fast. Florida Audubon's leaders reiterated their approval of the program, trusting in the value of the information about the panthers' life cycles that the tracking would eventually produce. Around the same time, environmental groups successfully lobbied to have the panther declared the official state animal. A few years later, the state unveiled a license plate depicting the face of a curiously benign-looking panther, and the tag remained the state's most popular even as the list of specialty plates expanded into the dozens.

While the plight of the panther gained nationwide attention, the demise of another animal endemic to Florida played out more quietly. The dusky seaside sparrow, first noticed by ornithologist Charles Maynard along Florida's eastern coastal marshes in 1872, lived a highly circumscribed existence, dependent on a precise balance of water and vegetation that limited is population to a 25-square-mile patch of northern Brevard County, east of Orlando. The species comprised about 2,000 birds in the 1950s, but the combination of increased development in the area and mosquito control measures—including the use of insecticides and the building of impoundments—sent the dusky into rapid decline. In 1968, a survey found only two remaining clusters of the birds on Merritt Island and the marshes along the St. Johns River. The Fish and Wildlife Service began buying land for a sparrow refuge, a process that moved with typical bureaucratic slowness. Compounding the bird's problems, a revision by the American Ornithologists Union in 1973 changed the dusky seaside sparrow from a distinct species to a subspecies, a taxonomic adjustment whose timing couldn't have been worse. As a federally endangered species, the dusky warranted a protection plan, and Herb Kale, an ornithologist associated with Florida Audubon, joined a recovery team that lobbied unsuccessfully for immediate protection of the St. Johns habitat area. A series of fires burned much of the bird's domain along the river, presumably killing the last females. The recovery team captured a few of the remaining birds, and after lengthy bureaucratic debates, an attempt to crossbreed captive males with similar species began at Discovery Island, Walt Disney World's zoological facility. The experiment produced a few hybrids, but the captive population of pure duskies dwindled to a single aging, half-blind bird named Orange. On June 16, 1987, a door to the bird's enclosure was accidentally left open and a predator killed the last dusky seaside sparrow.

The epic fights over the barge canal and the jetport in the late 1960s taught environmentalists the importance of fact-based persuasion. When activists tried to sway government decisions with generalities about natural beauty, they had little hope of derailing development. But when they offered scientific evidence that a project would harm an ecosystem, they had at least a chance of success. That awareness led to a new emphasis on shared knowledge. One of the main functions of C-70s in its short life was to publish a newsletter, the Tallahassee Report, which went out to 2,500 supporters. Another organization that arose during the same period had the main purpose of keeping activists informed on the intricacies of environmental issues. Bill Partington, fresh from his success with Florida Defenders of the Environment in the canal war, used a grant from the Ford Foundation in 1971 to create the Florida Conservation Foundation, a nonprofit organization based out of a small office in Winter Park, near Orlando. The foundation supported the Environmental Information Center (one of a series of such centers around the country seeded by Ford money), which began publishing a roughly bimonthly bulletin called *ENFO*. The 8 to 12-page newsletter generally devoted its entire space to a single environmental issue — land laws, biological pollution, oil drilling, conservation corridors — with the articles scrupulously researched and sometimes written by academics. *ENFO* lacked color photos or slick design elements and reached a maximum circulation of only about 1,200, but it proved influential far beyond its size. Officials with state regulatory agencies subscribed, as did activists and educators, with such titans as Arthur Marshall regularly citing information from *ENFO* in their arguments. Journalists found the newsletter particularly valuable, and John Pennekamp—the *Miami Herald* editor for whom an underwater state park was named—often filled his columns with summaries of the latest issue. In 1972, the Environmental Information Center prepared the first comprehensive study of the environmental effects of the private canals that abounded in upscale neighborhoods along Florida's coasts, and the governor and cabinet cited the report in virtually halting the approval of permits for the "finger" canals. The Florida Conservation Foundation also organized frequent conferences throughout the state, and it published brochures—including a guide to building a solar water heater, a copy of which wound up in the national library of Saudi Arabia. Even before heading up the Florida Defenders, Partington had preferred temporary, single-issue environmental groups to vast, multi-purpose organizations, and he used the FCF to seed small groups whenever possible. Partington ran the foundation for 20 years before retiring, and successors kept the ENFO bulletin alive for a few more years before the endeavor finally folded.

Marshall seemed to draw on the example of Partington's small organization when he drafted a paper in 1972 entitled, "A Proposal To Establish the Florida Environmental Institute." Noting that some people "already see Florida as the 'New Jersey of the South,' " Marshall wrote, "The kinds of decisions we face cannot be made by agencies of government alone, nor by educational institutions alone. They must be made by those who are affected by the results of those decisions—the people of Florida." Based on his tenure with the U.S. Fish and Wildlife Service, Marshall had long lamented the specialization that fragmented government decisions about the environment. At the same time, he thought bureaucratic decisions would improve if informed environmentalists were given a formal and permanent voice in state government. His proposed institute would be a non-profit organization, designed to study environmental problems in an "integrated" way and then serve as an independent advisor for state government and the public, and it would also have an educational component, taking in a few carefully selected college students each year. Marshall estimated the annual cost at

$800,000, which would come from private donations, foundation grants and possibly government grants. The concept, unrealistic in its assumption of government's willingness to be advised, went nowhere, but after Marshall's death a foundation formed in his name and headed by his nephew followed the structure of his proposal.

In the public mind, the creation of a national park in 1947 meant that the Everglades would forever remain in its natural condition. The belief, of course, had little association with reality. Beginning in 1948, working under the aegis of a flood-control agency, the Army Corps of Engineers embarked on a massive water diversion project that included the digging of 1,400 miles of canals. The Corps undertook the last major element of its redesign of Central and South Florida in 1962, when it started work on a canal that would essentially replace the Kissimmee River, a meandering, 90-mile waterway running southward from Lake Kissimmee to Lake Okeechobee. Environmental groups, along with the Florida Game and Fresh Water Fish Commission and the Fish and Wildlife Service, had adamantly opposed the "channelization" of the Kissimmee River from the moment it was first proposed in 1948, but influential people—particularly cattle and dairy farmers owning land in the river's floodplain—favored the canal, which would expand their dry-land holdings. Congress approved the project in 1954.

When the Corps of Engineers completed its work in 1971, the 90 miles of the meandering Kissimmee River had given way to a 52-mile conduit, 300 feet wide and 35 feet deep, as straight in some stretches as an interstate highway, with the official designation of Canal 38 (or C-38). Environmentalists dubbed it the Kissimmee Ditch. The river's 40,000 acres of floodplain became dry pasture land, and its former oxbows became stagnant pools, clogged with exotic, invasive plants. At Gov. Askew's task force meeting in 1971, Arthur Marshall warned of the damage the channelization of the Kissimmee River would cause, and it didn't take long for Marshall to be proven correct. Historically, the river and its floodplain had served as a filtering system for water flowing toward Lake Okeechobee, but the deep and straight canal funneled all the fertilizers from the bordering pastures directly to the lake. (Sugar cane fields along Lake Okeechobee's southern rim did even greater damage to Florida's largest body of water.) Whereas the Kissimmee River had been a biologically healthy waterway, Canal 38 proved to be lacking in the dissolved oxygen needed to support aquatic life.

Marshall was far from alone in his outrage over the mutilation of the Kissimmee River. Johnny Jones of the Florida Wildlife Federation, a West Palm Beach native who became enamored of the river as a teenager, had been protesting the channelization long before it was completed, and when he became a full-time lobbyist in 1972 he set the restoration of the Kissimmee River as one of his chief priorities. The scientific credibility of Marshall and the doggedness of Jones and other activists paid off in 1976, when both houses of the state legislature unanimously passed an act (largely crafted by Jones) geared toward returning the Kissimmee River to its natural state. Though the practical effect proved to be so weak that future assemblies would have to address the issue again, the passage of such a measure just a few years after water began flowing through the "Kissimmee Ditch" signaled the respect environmental groups commanded in Florida politics. As Marshall said at the time, "The interests represented by the members of these two august assemblies are so diverse that unanimous agreement on so complex a problem is in itself some sort of precedent."

As a footnote to the Kissimmee River legislation, the legislature in 1979 finally abolished the Internal Improvement Fund—the ironically named state agency responsible for a century of draining and diking wetlands throughout Florida. Lawmakers assigned the authority over wetlands to the Department of Natural Resources, with the governor and cabinet having final approval over its decisions.

Even as environmentalists made progress in Tallahassee, relentless development throughout the state generated continuing regional fights. One of the decade's fiercest centered around the creation of a new community off the southwest coast. The Mackle brothers had made their fortune developing retirement homes in Southeast Florida, and during the early 1960s their Deltona Corporation shifted its attention to the other side of the state, deciding that the coastal islands of the Gulf of Mexico had the potential to be another Key Biscayne. Deltona Corporation bought several of the Ten Thousand Islands, an almost entirely undeveloped chain of small keys extending from near Naples down into Florida Bay. Deltona began construction in 1964 on Marco Island, the largest of the Ten Thousand Islands, and the company completed the first two of five scheduled phases through the early 1970s. When the company turned toward the northern end of the island, however, environmentalists sprang into action.

A local coalition of retirees known as the Conservancy had formed several years earlier in Naples to oppose the building of a highway from Naples to Rookery Bay, just north of Marco Island. The group collected 1,000 signatures on a petition, and their pressure swayed the Collier County Commission to reject the proposed road. Deciding the Rookery Bay islands needed permanent protection, the group organized as the Collier County Conservancy and formed an association with The Nature Conservancy, a national group dedicated to land preservation. The Collier Conservancy collected enough donations to purchase the islands, and in 1966 it gave the National Audubon Society possession of 1,600 acres to be managed as a wildlife sanctuary. Further purchases increased the preserve to 4,000 acres, with the 9,000-acre Collier-Read tract separating it from the newly developed Marco Island to the south. When Deltona bought the buffer area in 1969 and made plans to build on it, the Conservancy mounted a challenge, led by Bernie Yokel, who would later become president of Florida Audubon.

Arguing that the proposed development would threaten Rookery Bay, the Conservancy gained a series of public hearings with the Florida Department of Pollution Control and other state agencies. The state eventually approved, putting the decision in the hands of the Corps of Engineers. As the delays continued, Yokel's group drew encouragement from the passage of important national laws tightening restrictions on development, and the Conservancy also seized on academic studies that demonstrated the importance of shoreline mangrove trees to the health of Gulf waters. James Tripp of the Environmental Defense Fund organized the legal opposition to Deltona, and 19 environmental groups — including Sierra Club and Florida Audubon — joined with the Conservancy, supplying scientific experts to testify at hearings and organizing letter-writing campaigns. The process dragged on into 1976. Finally, after a last marathon hearing, the Corps of Engineers denied Deltona two of three permits for which it had applied, limiting development to a small area away from the buffer with Rookery Bay. Deltona, which had sold 3,700 homesites in the disputed areas, appealed all the way to the U.S. Supreme Court, which refused to hear the case. The company eventually sold its undeveloped holdings to the state and environmental groups for inclusion in Rookery Bay Sanctuary.

Florida Audubon Society had regained its strength, both in numbers and in political activism, by the time an Orlando insurance executive and Unitarian named Hal Scott succeeded Russell Mason as the group's president in 1971. Scott continued the approach of Mason's 13-year term, steering the organization into skirmishes big and small, all across the state. As the legal appeals of President Nixon's decision to kill the barge canal dragged on, Florida Audubon continued to work against a related project that threatened incalculable environmental harm. Though it received far less attention, a longstanding proposal to build a 35-mile water highway connecting the St. Johns River to the Indian River drew fierce opposition from local activists, including the famed nature photographer and lecturer Allan Cruickshank, who lived in Brevard County. Florida Audubon officials argued that the planned canal would have disastrous effects on both the freshwater St. Johns and the saltwater Indian River—actually a lagoon despite its name. With the barge canal itself in serious doubt, government officials dissolved the St. Johns-Indian River Canal District in 1973.

While Florida Audubon retained a name recognition factor no other group could touch, the late-arriving Florida chapter of the Sierra Club established itself during the 1970s as an equally formidable entity. Nationally, Sierra had distinctly western origins, arising in 1892 from the frustrations of John Muir and his fellow naturalists over threats to Yosemite National Park. Within a year of its official formation, the Florida Sierra chapter pushed for legal action to stop the state from its continued use of the toxic pesticide Mirex in combating fire ants. (The Environmental Defense Fund filed an unsuccessful federal suit, and the state resumed spraying in 1972.) Following the example of the national Sierra Club, the state chapter often took a more aggressive approach than Florida Audubon, which tended to focus on persuasion. The Sierra Club, led by the husband-and-wife lobbying team of David and Casey Gluckman, actively pursued its agenda in Tallahassee, but when lobbying failed the group didn't shy away from litigation.

The gasoline shortages and price spikes of the early 1970s gave rise to the phrase "energy crisis" — to which Florida Audubon responded in *The Florida Naturalist*, "We do not have an oil crisis ... we have an oil consumption crisis." Not surprisingly, Hal Scott's organization devoted much of its own energy during the period to oil-related issues. Florida had been the site of oil speculation since the turn of the century, but suddenly it seemed oil companies were seeking to drill in every area of the state, both offshore and inland. Scott led the opposition in 1971, when Phillips Petroleum filed the first application to the Florida Department of Natural Resources for permission to drill in Big Cypress. After the attorney general reluctantly ruled that the state had no authority to deny the permit on privately owned land, Scott told his membership that rather than "donning sackcloth," he would try to learn as much as possible about the process of oil drilling so that Florida Audubon could play an informed role in shaping future decisions on permits. Scott formed a committee that spent time at drilling sites in Florida, Louisiana and the Gulf of Mexico, and suggestions from Audubon and other groups shaped a list of guidelines for oil and gas drilling adopted by Gov. Askew and his cabinet in 1972. Florida Audubon eventually published a position paper that outlined in detail the safeguards required for acceptable oil drilling, with special emphasis on protecting the Floridan Aquifer, the massive underground reservoir that provides drinking water for much of the state. Florida Audubon also called for approval from the governor and cabinet and the U.S. Fish and Wildlife Service of each drilling site.

The oil companies, of course, didn't sit idly while Florida Audubon decided on its official policy toward drilling. After the failure to stop drilling in Big Cypress, environmental groups fought against the sale of oil leases in East Bay near Pensacola and gained an initial court ruling against the sales, though Getty Oil persisted and eventually won the right to drill. Other battles followed. When the federal government pushed for oil drilling off Florida's Gulf Coast in 1972, the national and state Audubon groups reviewed the plan and issued a statement of opposition. The government went forward with its lease sale, but the objections of Gov. Askew and Sen. Lawton Chiles convinced the Department of the Interior to greatly limit the drilling area. The effects of the oil embargo by Middle Eastern countries put environmental groups at an increasing disadvantage in their quest to curb oil drilling in the state. In the early 1970s, a coalition that included the Sierra Club and Florida Defenders of the Environment formed under the name Save Our Coast. Despite fervent lobbying, the group failed to block passage of a bill that limited the liability of corporations responsible for oil spills off the Florida coast. Another defeat came when the Sierra Club led the legal opposition to permits that would allow Exxon, Mobil and Chaplin Oil to drill in the northeastern Gulf of Mexico, near Fort Walton Beach. Ignoring the potential threat to tourism, let alone the environment, a judge allowed the drilling to begin.

The battles over oil drilling were not confined to offshore waters. In the case of Placid Oil Company's request to drill in the Apalachicola National Forest in North Florida, the government ordered a two-week delay so that Florida Audubon could review the plans. Following Scott's pragmatic strategy that focused on fighting the most objectionable projects, Florida Audubon told the state it could live with Placid Oil's drilling proposal, and the project went forward. Florida Audubon's accommodating approach sometimes caused rifts with other environmental groups, most notably in the case of the Ocala National Forest. Lyman Rogers, the Ocala-based founder of the Conservation 70s, discovered in 1971 that the Department of the Interior had leased 344,000 acres—nearly the entire forest—to the Amoco Production Company, which had plans to dig an exploratory well near Juniper Springs, a popular recreation area. Outraged, Rogers quickly spread the word to environmental groups and formed his own coalition specifically dedicated to keeping the forest free of oil wells. The ensuing public outcry caused the federal government to suspend its approval of drilling permits, while business groups lined up in noisy support of the oil exploration, which they presented as a solution to the long lines at gas stations. After a series of contentious hearings, the Department of the Interior released an environmental impact statement in 1973 setting guidelines for drilling operations. Rogers said the ruling would allow damage to the largest remaining water recharge area in the state, and he noted that the relatively small expected yield didn't justify its harmful effect. While some other environmental groups joined him in adamant opposition to any drilling in the forest—and blasted the federal government for selling the mineral rights at a mere 50 cents an acre—Florida Audubon offered conditional support of the government plan but recommended more and tighter rules. The hard-liners took heart when U.S. Rep. Bill Gunter of Winter Park filed legislation to ban test drilling in the forest, but Gunter failed to follow through, drawing scorn from Rogers. After the U.S. Geological Survey staff approved the drilling plans in early 1975, even Rogers conceded defeat, and Amoco sank a well near Pat's Island, the setting for Marjorie Kinnan Rawlings' Pulitzer Prize-winning novel *The Yearling*. Around the same time, the foes of oil drilling received further bad news when the U.S. Supreme Court decided that the federal government held control over offshore drilling rights beyond a three-mile border along Florida's Atlantic coast and a 10-mile border in the Gulf of Mexico. The ruling meant that fights over offshore drilling would no longer be restricted to Tallahassee, where Florida's environmental groups had their best hope of influence.

Meanwhile, Florida Audubon faced some uncomfortable internal debates that involved energy companies. In the mid-1970s, *The Florida Naturalist* began running glossy color advertisements from the likes of Exxon, Gulf Oil, Conoco, Arco and Florida Gas Corporation. A series of angry letters from Florida Audubon members prompted the magazine to run an editorial in the October 1976 issue defending the acceptance of the ads, with the promise that the *Naturalist* would not publish anything that conflicted with the "principles or standards" of Florida Audubon. Environmental battles had grown more complex, increasingly involving legal challenges, and groups such as Florida Audubon sought new sources of funding for their efforts. The debate over the magazine's choices of ads—along with the disagreements among conservation groups over where to draw the line on oil drilling—reflected the changes in the state since 1900, when the slaughter of birds presented a single dominant issue for the protectors of nature.

In addition to the concerns over oil drilling, environmental groups had to contend with the federal government's authority to sanction other forms of invasive industry. In 1971, conservationists greeted with alarm the news that the Department of the Interior was considering a proposal to allow phosphate mining on 52,000 acres of the Osceola National Forest in northern Florida. Environmental groups reacted in unanimous protest, and Gov. Askew took a public stance against the mining. U.S. Sen. Lawton Chiles, a rural Democrat who had earned a reputation as a friend of conservation, joined in the protest, and the federal government discarded its plan for mining in the forest.

Environmental outfits had come to learn that few victories are permanent, and sometimes challenges emerged from issues that seemed settled. The creation of a national bird sanctuary in 1929 saved an important tract of Northwest Florida from development, but in the late 1970s some members of the Sierra Club's Big Bend chapter noticed that a 30-acre wooded tract in the St. Marks National Wildlife Refuge near the town of Panacea had been subjected to clearcutting. The chapter investigated and learned that refuge officials had leveled timber on only one-seventh of the land destined for clearing, a practice they intended to continue for years. Declining the Sierra chapter's request for evidence that the timbering would actually benefit wildlife, refuge managers continued cutting. The chapter—joined by the local divisions of Florida Audubon and the Izaak Walton League—responded with a letter-writing campaign to assistant secretary of Interior Robert Herbst, who pressured refuge officials to muzzle their chainsaws until they could produce an environmental assessment plan. The revised management plan St. Marks officials finally released in 1979 allowed no clearcutting and expanded the parcels that would be spared the saw altogether.

The 1970s opened amid a surge of optimism for environmentalists, who had gained unprecedented influence among policymakers and who soon celebrated the historic decisions on the barge canal and the Big Cypress jetport as well as the gains of the 1970-72 legislative sessions. The inevitable backlash by business groups and their supporters in Tallahassee coincided with the OPEC oil embargo, and the ensuing gasoline shortages abetted those who portrayed environmental protection as an impediment to economic health. By 1974, conservation ranked low among the priorities of most lawmakers, and Florida Audubon President Hal Scott wrote a column condemning the legislature for eviscerating much of Gov. Askew's green initiatives. The historical dynamic of environmental indifference returned to Tallahassee just as Florida Audubon and the Sierra Club were installing full-time lobbyists. Those lobbyists quickly learned to play defense, devoting much of their attention to warding off the most noxious anti-environmental bills in each session. In 1978, for example, Florida Audubon's Charles Lee successfully worked against a measure that would have given some state agencies the power to conduct dredge-and-fill operations without permits from the Department of Environmental Regulation.

Even as the legislature returned to its traditional pro-development posture following the halcyon period of 1970-1972, it recognized the continuing popularity of land-acquisition programs. The resounding voter support for the 1972 bond measure still echoed through the state, and environmental groups led by Johnny Jones and the Florida Wildlife Federation began searching for a more permanent funding source — even though political tug-of-wars had resulted in a glacial approach that left much of the money from the original bond issue unspent (and thus important lands vulnerable). Despite the great success of the 1972 Land Conservation Act, Jones — who after all represented a group composed mainly of hunters — had heard complaints that the land-acquisition program focused solely on environmental concerns and not on the need to preserve "recreational" land, i.e., hunting and fishing areas. During the 1978 legislative session, Jones drew up a bill that would generate money for land purchases of both types. Jones found sponsors, but the bill stalled over concerns about the funding mechanism — a half-cent sales tax, which would be a departure from a longstanding tradition of using the state sales tax only for general government spending. Officials in the Department of Natural Resources came up with the idea of funding land purchases through severance taxes on mineral extraction (mainly phosphate mining), and in 1979 Jones wrote a bill that drew 50 percent of the tax up to a ceiling of $40 million annually — a provision that would allow future increases without requiring a new law. The Conservation and Recreation Lands Act sailed through the legislature, setting up the mechanism that would remain in place even as new funding sources emerged in later years. Florida had entered the 1970s with a skimpy record on preserving land from development, but through the efforts of Jones, a few other lobbyists and the major environmental groups, by decade's end the state had become a model for devoting public money to the buying of natural areas.

8

GUARDING WETLANDS AND WATERWAYS

Florida's history is replete with sad tales of lakes and rivers degraded through indifference and misuse. While the polluted Lake Apopka serves as an example of such direct harm, a nearby waterway in Central Florida reflects the danger of a more circumstantial form of exploitation. The Wekiva River, rising forth from a second magnitude spring northwest of Orlando, meanders for 14 miles, growing from narrow to substantial as it accepts five tributaries on its way to a confluence with the St. Johns River. Along the way, the Wekiva offers canoeists the sight of verdant shorelines where reclusive limpkins spend their days hunting for apple snails and otters slither amid the water hyacinths. In addition to the Wekiva's aesthetic charm, its watershed contained one of the state's largest populations of the endangered Florida black bear. The river and its source had long been popular as recreation settings, and around the time that Walt Disney World began its transformation of Central Florida, developers realized the appeal that riverfront land held for potential home buyers. The state bought the area around the springhead from a local sportsmen's group in the late 1960s, opening Wekiwa Springs State Park in 1970 (the name variations reflect words in the native Creek language denoting "bubbling water" and "moving water"), but subdivisions sprouted just outside the park. And developers holding sizable tracts along the river began submitting proposals — including one for a community of 50,000 people — that promised to change the pristine Wekiva watershed into something else entirely.

The proposed city known as Three Rivers served as a catalyst in changing general concern about the Wekiva among Central Floridians into a coherent drive to save it from excessive development. In the early 1970s, local homeowners groups and Florida Audubon chapters began pushing state lawmakers to include the Wekiva in the Outstanding Florida Waters program, a designation that would create political momentum toward specific protection measures. When a lack of staffing delayed state agencies from conducting the required tests of water quality and quantity, Bill Partington of the Florida Conservation Foundation organized conservation and homeowner groups to help gather data for the process. The Wekiva and its tributaries were designated Outstanding Florida Waters in 1983 (the main river would receive National Wild and Scenic River status in 2000). In pushing for protection of the river and its watershed, environmentalists faced the complicating factor of geography—the Wekiva arose in Seminole County, flowing north to become a boundary between Orange and Seminole counties and then between Lake and Seminole counties, meaning the relatively short river was subject to three jurisdictions just at the county level. Though homeowners in 1972 convinced the Seminole County Commission to prohibit development within 200 feet of the river (an inadequate buffer in itself), it helped little when no such regulations existed on the opposite shore. In this context, Friends of the Wekiva River sprang to life in the late 1970s, formed by a group of neighbors living near the river in Seminole County.

Friends of the Wekiva River emerged as a classic single-issue conservation group following the model of Florida Defenders of the Environment, but on a smaller scale. The coalition had its genesis in a canoe trip made by two of its founders, Russell and Eleanor Fisher, who had bought five acres of land along the Little Wekiva River outside of Longwood in 1971 and built a small house there. They canoed regularly on the tributary of the main river and one day decided to put in at Sanlando Springs, several miles away, and paddle downstream to their house. A year later, they returned to the springs with some friends to repeat the trip, but exotic plants had overgrown the river, making it impassable. In the process of seeking help from local authorities to have the weeds removed, the Fishers and their friends, including Nancy Prine and Fred and Pat Harden, discovered that developers were buying up substantial tracts around the Wekiva River. Loosely organized at first, Friends of the Wekiva began fighting against more than just an incursion of noxious plants. The group decided to work toward long-term protection of the river from intensive development, and in 1981 Friends of the Wekiva River incorporated as a nonprofit.

The drive for protection of the Wekiva no doubt benefited from the fact that the Florida Audubon Society, founded in Maitland, remained headquartered about 20 miles from the river source. In lobbying state agencies toward land acquisition, Florida Audubon placed a high priority on the Wekiva River watershed, and the state responded in 1976 with the purchase of two tracts on opposite sides of the river—2,726 acres in Lake County and 1,907 in Seminole County—using money from the bond issue approved by voters four years earlier. The purchase saved important habitat and sent a signal that the state considered the Wekiva River worth protecting, but it was only a first step. After successfully lobbying the state's Environmental Regulatory Commission to have the river declared an Outstanding Florida Waterway, Friends of the Wekiva began a drive for state acquisition of a tract of land along the river's eastern edge. (Land acquisition along the Wekiva was slowed by the presence of squatters living on the river's banks and even on some small islands. The squatters claimed legal possession of the land they occupied, forcing the matter into court, and their degradation of the landscape allowed developers to question the pristine status of the Wekiva basin.) Along with Florida Audubon, the group persuaded Gov. Bob Graham and his cabinet to spend $7.3 million in Conservation and Recreation Land funds for the 8,559-acre property in Lake County that became Rock Springs Run State Preserve, an area containing a spring-fed tributary to the river and providing important habitat for black bears.

Some local developers hoped the purchase might mark the end of their irritation, and when conservation groups continued to insist on a development-free zone around the river, one developer told a reporter, "I think these people get upset over nothing. You can take everybody in

India and lose them in these preserves for a week and not find them."

In the midst of the successful push for land acquisition, the environmental groups worried about the continuing approval of development near the Wekiva, particularly in the rapidly growing Seminole County. Knowing they could not hope for the state to buy all the land needed to save the river from erosion and runoff, Friends of the Wekiva and their allies focused on a protective buffer and looked to the state level for help. The Wekiva coalition replicated two successful strategies of Florida Defenders of the Environment and other modern, single-issue alliances: gathering scientific information to bolster its arguments and adroitly courting the local media. FOWR produced a technical position paper in 1985, offering 18 recommendations to state and local governments and agencies for protection of the river. The group also met with the editorial board of the *Orlando Sentinel* to explain the nuances of the technical paper, and the newspaper embraced the issue, running a series of pro-environmental editorials under the heading "Florida's Shame" that yielded a Pulitzer Prize. The publicity and advocacy led to a turning point in 1987, when Gov. Bob Martinez accepted an invitation from Friends of the Wekiva River to attend an awareness event. After paddling a canoe down the river, Martinez returned to Tallahassee and appointed a Wekiva River Task Force, which included representatives from the Friends coalition.

FOWR and Florida Audubon had been lobbying the St. Johns River Water Management District to adopt a much wider buffer than the 200-foot Seminole County rule, and the district considered the idea before rejecting it under pressure from developers. The environmentalists, led by Charles Lee of Florida Audubon, turned first to the East Central Florida Regional Planning Council, a growth-management panel that offered support for the buffer plan, and then to Gov. Martinez, who endorsed the concept in January of 1988. The water district responded by reversing its position again and enacting a development ban. The combination of media attention and public support created momentum in Tallahassee, with even normally pro-development lawmakers wanting to join the Wekiva bandwagon. During the 1988 session, the state legislature unanimously passed the Wekiva River Protection Act, a measure that ordered the state to buy and preserve 23,000 acres near the river—a mandate that elevated the properties toward the top of the priority list, leading to the purchase of Seminole Springs State Forest and two other large tracts. The act also directed the water district to restrict construction within 550 feet of the Wekiva and its five tributaries to only one house per half mile, tightened state regulation of building near the river and ordered local governments to maintain a rural residential density in the area. Audubon's Lee suggested that the legislature use the Wekiva Act as a template for the protection of other vulnerable rivers, a recommendation the state has heeded elsewhere in limited ways.

Even with such protections finally in place, thousands of acres along the river remained in private hands, and state acquisition continued into the 1990s. At the same time, local officials approved intensive development to the edge of the buffer zone, particularly in Seminole County, where commissioners routinely made exemptions to their own comprehensive growth plans and occasionally sought to revise the plans. In response, Friends of the Wekiva led the campaign for a $20 million bond issue in Seminole County to fund the purchase of environmentally sensitive lands, and voters approved the measure in 1990. Despite the continuing threats to the waterway, Friends of the Wekiva River, a group of modest size and means, had (with help from more established allies) ensured a lasting natural zone around the river, an accomplishment that appeared highly unlikely when the group formed.

While the threat to the small but pristine Wekiva River involved the consequences of creeping development, one of the state's major bodies of water faced the possibility of a more direct transformation. Since the 1940s, when Congress passed the Rivers and Harbors Act, the Army Corps of Engineers had been making alterations to the Apalachicola-Chattahootchee-Flint river system, which flows through Florida, Georgia and Alabama. Most of the work had been restricted to areas outside Florida, but in the early 1970s some North Florida lawmakers began urging the Corps to draw up plans for correcting supposed navigational problems in the Apalachicola, an alluvial waterway that forms near the Florida-Georgia state line and runs south for 110 miles to the Gulf of Mexico, draining 17,200 square miles. The Corps happily obliged, presenting blueprints for a $200 million system of dams, canals and dikes on the river. Hal Scott, president of Florida Audubon Society, said, "I'm absolutely amazed the Corps would be so utterly stupid in this day and age to come out with that kind of proposal, even for study." When Florida Gov. Reubin Askew and his cabinet joined environmental groups in lambasting the proposal, the Corps retreated, eventually returning with two more modest options — the building of a single dam near Blountstown or a series of modifications to the river without a dam. Environmental groups criticized both options, pointing out that the river in its natural state met navigation depth requirements 85 percent of the year. In an indication of public sentiment, a 1973 hearing drew not only representatives of the Florida Wildlife Federation and other environmental groups but a phalanx of local housewives and farmers opposed to the damming of the river. As was its custom, the Corps produced studies showing positive benefit-cost ratios for either the dam or the "open river regulation," but Florida officials challenged the figures and the project stalled until the Corps finally admitted in 1980 that the proposed dam had a negative benefit-cost ratio. Though the dam was dead, environmentalists couldn't quite celebrate. The state entered an agreement with Georgia and Alabama that allowed the dredging of a barge channel in the river — a program that in the early 21st century cost taxpayers approximately $30,000 for each barge that used the river. As part of the deal, Florida received the funding to operate the 192,000-acre Apalachicola National Estuarine Research Reserve near the mouth of the river, partly to determine how best to manage delicate coastal areas.

The saga of the Ocklawaha River entered its third decade with the opposing forces engaged in a standoff. Even after the state cabinet's vote in 1976 to abandon work on the barge canal, the project remained theoretically alive through the Congressional sanction from 1962. Senator Lawton Chiles, a Democrat from North Florida, sponsored a bill in 1978 to kill the project once and for all, but canal backers shot it down. Congress finally dropped its authorization for the project in 1985, but that action left in place the existing segment of the canal, along with the dams and other structures that cost taxpayers about half a million dollars a year to maintain. With the federal government out of the picture,

Florida Defenders of the Environment and other groups could concentrate on the state legislature in their efforts to have Rodman Dam removed and allow the Ocklawaha to flow freely again. The opposition now came not from business leaders salivating at the imagined commercial benefits of a canal but mainly from fishermen who had grown attached to Rodman Reservoir. Influential legislators, most notably Sen. George Kirkpatrick of Gainesville, sided with the anglers, making audacious claims for the reservoir's economic importance to North Florida. Each annual legislative session included skirmishes over the defunct canal, with lawmakers sympathetic to the environmental cause proposing removal of the dam and lawmakers aligned with fishermen seeking to make the dam a permanent fixture. A decade after Richard Nixon stopped the canal, neither side could claim victory—though each year that passed with the dam still in place presented a nettlesome disappointment for Marjorie Carr and her allies.

Though the Ocklawaha River remained the group's chief focus, Florida Defenders of the Environment expanded its purview after a decade in existence. In 1980, FDE spawned the Environmental Service Center, a Tallahassee-based office that used the parent group's academic resources to study statewide issues. The two organizations jointly hosted conferences on growth management, water supplies and the Florida panther and held workshops to train independent environmental groups before the Tallahassee office closed in 1988.

During his first term as governor, Bob Graham decided that the state needed new land-acquisition mechanisms to complement the existing CARL program. Graham, who displayed a fondness for statements of salvation, wanted to create a program called Save Our Rivers that would provide money for the land acquisition needed not only for preservation but also for such repair projects as the one planned for the Kissimmee River. Knowing that any such bill with his name attached faced certain death in the legislature at the hands of powerful Sen. Dempsey Barron, a conservative Democrat, Graham had a clandestine chat with Johnny Jones, the experienced lobbyist from the Florida Wildlife Federation, and Jones welcomed the chance to write the bill and seek supporters in the legislature. (Because the deadline for filing bills had passed, Jones knew the measure would have to be tucked into something already under consideration.) While pondering possible funding for a new land-buying program, Jones learned that some counties raised funds through increased rates for documentary stamps, used as a tax on real-estate transactions. Consulting with officials in the Department of Natural Resources, Jones calculated that a statewide tax of five cents per $100 on the transactions would yield an annual total of at least $20 million. A heart attack during the 1981 session hampered Jones' efforts to lobby for the bill, but he managed to get the measure added as an amendment to an existing bill that passed the Senate. House Speaker Steve Pacjic, whom Jones considered a friend, balked at any tax increase the year before an election, but another influential representative, Sam Bell of Daytona Beach, intervened and convinced Pacjic to support the bill that included the "doc stamp" provision. Only after the bill had passed the Senate did Jones reveal that he had been working on Graham's behalf. Save Our Rivers began yielding between $30 million and $40 million a year for a fund administered by the state's five water-management districts, leading to purchases around the Kissimmee River and in other important riparian areas.

Water-related issues dominated the political landscape for much of the 1980s. Environmental groups had pressed the state for years to take a uniform approach to the management of rivers and lakes, and the legislature in 1987 passed the Surface Water Improvement and Management Act. Known by its acronym, SWIM required each of the five water districts to develop plans for protecting and restoring rivers, lakes, estuaries and bays affected by the actions of state agencies. The districts began drawing up their strategies, including one by the South Florida Water Management District involving water flow in the Everglades. The district, facing longstanding complaints about both the quality and quantity of water entering the Glades from its canals and pumping stations, spent two years on its plan, facing the pressure of a suit filed by the federal government (on behalf of Everglades National Park and Loxahatchee National Wildlife Refuge) over phosphorus from agricultural runoff. When the district unveiled its plan, it drew criticism from both environmentalists and agricultural interests. With the overall cost estimated at $500 million, the sugar industry—which had been polluting Lake Okeechobee for decades—agreed to pay only $40 million during the first, 10-year phase of the plan. Environmental groups noted that the $4 million annual contribution amounted to less than taxpayers in the SFWMD jurisdiction paid each year to subsidize big sugar's costs of drainage and irrigation. The federal suit was largely settled in 1991, but disputes over the Everglades—and especially the division of costs for the repair of the ecosystem—continued unabated.

Like most major waterways in Central Florida, the Wekiva River flows into the St. Johns River, which supports one of the state's largest consistent populations of West Indian manatees. The herbivorous mammal, with its benign manner and homely anatomy, has long been popular with the public (it gained legal protection in Florida as early as 1893), but its lack of agility in the water makes it vulnerable to collisions with motorboats. Florida's inland and coastline waters host a year-round population of manatees that swells during the winter, when the constant temperatures of natural springs (and the artificial warmth of discharges from power plants) provide a haven against dangerously cold waters. The manatee gained inclusion on the federal endangered species list in 1973, and five years later the Florida Legislature passed the Florida Manatee Sanctuary Act, making the entire state a refuge for the animals, a change that allowed increased enforcement of boat speed rules in areas designated as manatee zones. In 1981, Gov. Bob Graham issued an executive order creating the Save the Manatee Committee, a diverse panel including representatives of several state agencies, as well as Florida Audubon and the Outboard Marine Corporation and—in a shrewd recognition of the power of celebrity—singer/songwriter Jimmy Buffett, a sometime Key West resident then at the height of his popularity. The government committee spun off an independent group, the Save the Manatee Club, dedicated to bringing the public into the battle against extinction. Working for its first several years under the aegis of the Florida Audubon Society—and sharing its headquarters in Maitland—the nonprofit organization expanded from an initial 800 members to 10,000 in two years. Its "Adopt-A-Manatee" program, unveiled in 1984, tapped a rich vein of public sympathy, matching donors with a particular, named animal and providing them with photos and biographical details about "their" manatee. The club focused on public awareness and education, but as the membership grew it branched into other areas — scientific research, rescue and rehabilitation, and legal challenges — not just in Florida but throughout the Caribbean segment of the manatee's range. Having established credibility through its work with the U.S. Fish and Wildlife Service on a species recovery plan, the club earned an advisory role with state and local planning agencies on coastal development, boat speed rules and permit applications for water activities. The group successfully pushed for a manatee license plate, which proved popular and brought more funds into protection programs. By the end of the century, the Save the Manatee Club had swelled to 40,000 members and gained the enmity of boater groups angered by state-mandated slow zones and manatee sanctuaries.

Manatees were not the only marine animals threatened by the activities of humans. Florida's offshore waters provide a home for six species of sea turtles, all of which are on endangered lists. Marine biologists — including Peter C.H. Pritchard of Florida Audubon — brought attention during the 1980s to the disastrous effect that commercial shrimping had on the turtles. The vast nets dragged by shrimp trawlers routinely caught turtles, many of which drowned when unable to escape (the Environmental Defense Fund estimated the turtle deaths at 12,000 a year). A conservation group called the Wider Caribbean Sea Turtle Team worked with government agencies to develop Turtle Excluder Devices (TEDs) — essentially escape hatches for turtles trapped in nets — and Florida Audubon's Pritchard played a role in testing them. In 1987, the federal government required all commercial fishermen working a 60-mile stretch of the Atlantic Ocean between New Smyrna Beach and Cape Canaveral to have TEDs installed in their nets. Gov. Bob Martinez and his cabinet later voted for a permanent requirement on the use of the escape devices by shrimp trawlers in state waters. In another effort on behalf of sea turtles, Florida Audubon later persuaded the Department of Natural Resources to ban "renourishment" during the summer on beaches where turtles regularly nested.

In the same year that birthed the Save the Manatee Club, a graduate of Florida State University's law school returned to Tallahassee after working in Washington with Ralph Nader's consumer advocacy group, known as "Nader's Raiders." Neil Friedman, a former student government president at FSU, had the idea of creating an organization for environmental activism and consumer protection that would be directed by students and run by a professional staff. Under Friedman's leadership, students at FSU and the University of Florida organized petition campaigns for a ballot item that would let students individually decide to tack a small fee onto their tuition rates, with the money going to the newly formed Florida Public Interest Research Group. (The group would supplement its funding through door-to-door canvassing.) UF's president vetoed the idea, but the FSU effort succeeded and soon students were making optional contributions to Florida PIRG, as it was known. Chapters soon followed at four other state schools, with places on the board of directors corresponding to each school's level of contribution. Though the coalition had a diverse agenda, it concentrated from its inception on opposition to oil drilling in the waters around Florida. PIRG launched a "Save Our Shores" campaign in 1983, leading a successful call for a one-year moratorium on oil leases within 30 miles of the state's coastline and a postponement of drilling in areas already leased off the eastern coast. Throughout the 1980s, the group led annual drives that succeeded in extending the moratorium, and in 1990 Florida PIRG organized citizen appearances at public hearings that persuaded President George Bush to announce a 10-year ban on drilling in federal waters near the Florida Keys. Florida PIRG, working with other environmental groups, successfully lobbied that same year in the state legislature for a permanent ban on drilling in state waters (although a few companies were "grandfathered" in.) "When we started working on this, everyone told us the issue was lost," Ann Whitfield, Florida PIRG's director, told reporters. "We haven't won yet, but we're doing pretty well."

Two other organizations appeared on the Florida scene during the 1980s, bringing with them reputations that separated them from the established environmental groups. Earth First!, an organization that formed in 1980 and gained national attention for sometimes using vandalism to thwart logging and construction in western states, added a Florida chapter in 1987. Although continuing to embrace "deep ecology" and to eschew the *realpolitik* approach of the Audubon societies, the small coalition of Earth Firsters in Florida pledged to work within the bounds of the law, concentrating on direct actions such as a protest at Sea World of the theme park's practice of whale captures. Around the same time that Earth First! arrived, the Florida Greens held their first state conference at a camping area near Apopka. Spawned from a European environmental and social movement, the Greens followed a philosophy of pursuing comprehensive political changes rather than battling over individual development projects. Neither group managed to make much of an impact or to attract a substantial membership.

The Florida chapter of The Nature Conservancy, meanwhile, had continued to grow since its inception in 1961. The organization, which long had relied on scientific sources to determine its priority list, hired its first full-time staff members in 1979, and in the early 1980s it took on the task of saving no less than the Garden of Eden itself. A resident of the Panhandle area near Bristol had so anointed the high bluffs of the Apalachicola River, a vista he considered Biblical, and the name stuck for a habitat that sheltered two of the world's rarest evergreens. The steepness of the river's slopes had saved it from timbering for decades, but in 1982 word spread that a power company planned to build a 1,200-megawatt plant on 500 acres along the river. The Conservancy first persuaded the company to shift its plans to another site, and then it found a single donor who enabled the group to buy 1,158 acres and stave off the threat of a developed Eden. The tract eventually grew to 6,200 acres and became the Apalachicola Bluffs and Ravines Preserve. Around the same time, the Conservancy took part in a campaign to stop houses and a marina from being built in King's Bay at the mouth of Crystal River, a conspicuous wintering site for manatees north of Tampa. The successful drive to buy the islands brought new, statewide attention to the Conservancy, resulting in a doubling of its membership during the 1980s. The Florida chapter opened an office in the Florida Keys, beginning a continuing campaign to acquire habitats of such imperiled native animals as the Key deer and eventually helping to create the Florida Keys National

Marine Sanctuary. The Conservancy also adopted new strategies to save lands that could not be purchased outright, including a program of buying development or mineral rights from ranchers who retained ownership of their properties—a tactic of fiscal conservation that responded to the rapid disappearance of farmlands and citrus groves across the state. The group increasingly forged partnerships with state agencies, serving as a scout for properties of particular ecological importance, and in 1981 the Conservancy collaborated with the Florida Department of Environmental Protection to create the Florida Natural Areas Inventory. The inventory, a detailed and ever-changing catalog of the state's undeveloped areas, became a tool used by the state in setting its priorities for land conservation as well as for managing habitats already in public ownership. The Nature Conservancy later handed off the maintenance of the inventory to the Institute for Science and Public Affairs at Florida State University.

The Florida Conservation Foundation ran through its original grant from the Ford Foundation within a couple of years, but the entity survived into a second decade on private donations and newsletter subscriptions and continued to have influence far beyond its modest budget and circulation. The *ENFO* bulletin devoted an entire 10-page issue to conservation corridors, a concept being promoted by the issue's author, Larry D. Harris, a wildlife ecology professor at the University of Florida. Harris emphasized the danger of habitat fragmentation, especially for large mammals such as bobcats, panthers and black bears, and argued that even large wilderness preserves were no substitute for a statewide system of connected green space. Shortly after the newsletter's publication, Florida Conservation Foundation director Bill Partington received calls from several state agencies interested in the concept. Partington organized a workshop on conservation corridors and in 1986 began a drive for legislation that would include consideration of the "wildlife highways" in the growth management process. Not surprisingly, lobbyists for development interests wasted little time in scuttling any talk of such a bill, yet Partington persisted, keeping the concept alive until the tepid support of the Game and Fresh Water Fish Commission doomed any possible legislation. Though the concept of wildlife corridors never earned legal recognition, it became widely accepted among both activists and government regulators as a goal for land preservation.

Another issue of the *ENFO* newsletter focused on a matter first brought to public attention in 1982 by the *Miami Herald*'s investigative team (including a young reporter named Carl Hiaasen). The *Herald* published a series of articles uncovering plans for a colossal development on North Key Largo—a new city destined to be more populous than Key West, complete with condominiums, hotels, luxury homes, yacht clubs, marinas and subdivisions, including the 2,800-unit Port Bougainville. The project would have destroyed 12,000 acres of hardwood hammock and mangrove wetlands on the largest remaining undeveloped portion of the Keys and threatened two offshore sanctuaries, including John Pennekamp Coral Reef State Park. Local environmental groups—including the Florida Keys Citizens Coalition, Friends of the Everglades, Florida Audubon and the Sierra Club—objected to the project even before the *Herald* exposed all the details of faulty government regulation that led to its approval. The Keys Coalition, led by Captain Ed Davidson, then also the president of the Keys Audubon Society, produced its own report in 1981, pointing out conflicts of interest in the regulatory process and accusing the local water authority of using misleading information to justify a water pipeline for the development. The Coalition charged that local authorities had completely disregarded the Keys' designation in 1975 as an Area of Critical State Concern, a status intended to raise the threshold of acceptable development projects. The *Herald* concurred, saying the history of Port Bougainville "displays a total breakdown in the way government monitors growth."

Even after the *Herald*'s series appeared, the Department of Community Affairs, a state agency, approved the project, prompting Friends of the Everglades to file a complaint in circuit court. Other environmental groups joined in, petitioning for a hearing before the governor and cabinet on the issue, and the director of the Florida Department of Natural Resources came out publicly against the project. Meanwhile the charges of improprieties in the approval process led to an investigation of Port Bougainville by a Monroe County Grand Jury. Though not finding any evidence of criminal misconduct, the grand jury in its report declared,

"(T)he performance of governmental agencies involved will stand as a landmark in ineptitude." The publicity surrounding Port Bougainville gave Florida Audubon the ammunition to file a lawsuit against the developers and the Florida Keys Aqueduct Authority on the basis of potential threats to endangered animals on the island and in the adjacent John Pennekamp Coral Reef State Park. After gaining a favorable ruling that effectively ended the project, Florida Audubon began pushing the state to purchase the available land on North Key Largo and prevent the threat of future development. Gov. Bob Graham issued an executive order in 1984 creating the North Key Largo Habitat Conservation Plan Study Committee, with Florida Audubon represented. The panel's ultimate plan reduced potential development on the key from the original 17,000 original units to a maximum of 3,500 units. The legislature approved a bond issue to raise $100 million and hasten land purchases, and the Florida Department of Environmental Protection shifted the area toward the top of its acquisition list, beginning a series of purchases that eventually totaled 3,600 acres, using approximately $60 million in CARL funds. The state completed its buying in 1992 and combined the acquisitions with other state-owned land to form the North Key Largo Hammocks State Botanical Site, the largest stand of West Indian tropical forest in the United States.

In the case of Port Bougainville, demonstrably irresponsible government oversight helped environmentalists make their case against the proposed development. Conservation groups made a similar argument in opposing a bridge planned as part of an eastern bypass around fast-growing Jacksonville during the same period. The Dames Point bridge, first conceived in the early 1970s, would cross the St. Johns River northwest of downtown Jacksonville, completing the loop of Interstate 295 by blazing a course through miles of undeveloped land. Environmental groups and other critics charged that the impetus behind the bridge was a wish to accommodate Offshore Power Systems, a company that had purchased land from the Jacksonville Port Authority with the intention of building a facility just off Dames Point in which it would manufacture floating nuclear power plants. Local alliances, including the Sawmill Slough Conservation Club, urged the state Department of Transportation to use an existing highway for the southern connection to the bridge rather than build a new road, which would cost more and destroy nearly 20 times as much wetlands. The matter eventually went to Gov. Graham and his cabinet, who approved the project, leading to the bridge's completion in 1988. The activists, however, did convince planners to use the existing Southside Boulevard rather than the more environmentally damaging route to the east.

The publishing list of G.P. Putnam's Sons in 1986 included a first solo novel by a *Miami Herald* reporter in which a columnist for a fictional Miami newspaper organizes a revolutionary band called *Las Noches de Diciembre*, who suffocate the head of the Chamber of Commerce by stuffing a rubber alligator down his throat and feed an elderly woman to a crocodile, among other acts. In the fictional person of Skip Wiley, Carl Hiaasen let loose his grimmest fantasies of guerrilla action to stem the tourism-fed development that had so degraded the region in which he grew up. The novel ends with the admittedly demented Wiley on a place called Osprey Island, an imaginary slip of land in Key Biscayne, trying to chase off a bald eagle as he awaits the explosions that will launch construction of a 16-story condominium. With its combination of scathing satire and bitter humor, the wickedly titled *Tourist Season* gained renown far outside South Florida, establishing Hiaasen (then 33 years old) as one of the nation's most promising young writers. A steady stream of novels followed, and before long Hiaasen was on the bestseller lists and one of his books became a movie starring Demi Moore. A former investigative reporter who worked on the *Herald's* expose of the Port Bougainville project, Hiaasen injected each novel with his outrage over the greed of developers and the venality of public officials who have allowed so much of South Florida to become, as one of his characters puts it, "a suburban tundra purged of all primeval wonder save for the sacred solar orb." Through the use of fiction to combat the very real assaults on natural Florida, Hiaasen played a groundbreaking role in the state's environmental movement. And even as he published his novels with dizzying frequency, Hiaasen continued to write a regular column for the *Herald* in which he served as a goad to the commercial and political forces that ruled South Florida.

The state of Florida drew its name from the colorful foliage that greeted the Spanish explorers who traversed the peninsula in the 16th century. From the rainbow hues of the fragile orchids to the gaudy orange of the geiger tree, from the stunning gold of the Florida aster to the delicate purple of the spiderwort, the state abounds in both wildflowers and trees that produce annual flowers. From the earliest European occupation, however, emigrants to the region have sought to improve upon Florida's horticultural bounty. The Spanish brought citrus and papaya, so well established now that they are commonly assumed to be native. While those plants served the colonizers by producing fruit, many other plants arrived in the state purely for ornamental purposes. With its mild, subtropical climate, Florida served as an outdoor greenhouse for plants imported from points across the globe, particularly South America, China and Australia.

The federal government in 1898 established an Office of Foreign Seed and Plant Introduction at Coconut Grove, with the famed horticulturist David Fairchild appointed as its first director. One of Fairchild's experiments involved the use of melaluca, or "punk tree," an Australian tree with papery bark. Fairchild suspected the tree had the capacity to absorb water from its surroundings, and he oversaw the planting of melaluca in wet areas around South Florida. The tree proved well adapted to Florida's climate and soon began spreading on its own — eventually covering 359,000 acres of South Florida and overwhelming the native flora. While Fairchild had government sanction for his plant introductions, exotic flora also reached the state through less formal avenues. In one of the most famous examples, Mrs. W.F. Fuller, a winter resident of San Mateo, near Palatka, reportedly attended the New Orleans Cotton Exposition in 1884 and came home with a flowering aquatic plant from Venezuela. She added the plant to her fish pond, and it soon took over the water surface. In cleaning out the pond, Mrs. Fuller tossed some of the plants into the nearby St. Johns River, and thus water hyacinth was introduced to Florida's waters. Within a few years, the floating plant had covered millions of acres of rivers and lakes, and by the early 20th century the government was using boats equipped with circular saws to clear the state's inland navigational waters.

Another import from Australia arrived on ships at Key West around 1860. Casuarina, a towering tree with dark, needle-like leaves, carried the name Australian pine, though it is not actually a pine. As residents in the exposed Keys learned, a line of casuarinas would produce a substantial windbreak, and the trees became popular, reaching the mainland when Henry Flagler had them planted along the streets of Palm Beach and Miami in the 1890s. Like melaleuca, the Australian pine proved able to dominate native vegetation, and it wasn't long before the trees had overtaken entire plant communities in South Florida. A similar story resulted from the introduction in the 1890s of Brazilian pepper, a leafy tree that came to be called "Florida holly" for its winter blossoms of red berries. Probably the most invasive of all Florida's exotic plants, Brazilian pepper spread voraciously, crowding out native mangroves along coastlines and creeping steadily throughout the Everglades. The Brazilian tree proved impervious to anything but cold weather, a trait that limited its northward growth to around St. Augustine, and individual trees resisted any attempts to kill them short of removal of their roots.

Environmental groups caught on to the dangers of exotic plants before the government did, but for a long time the issue lost out to more urgent matters. Florida Conservation Foundation director Bill Partington, after years of unsuccessfully trying to persuade Florida Audubon or the state garden clubs to take on the project, helped found the Florida Native Plant Society in the late 1970s—one of many side endeavors run out of his small office. He began holding monthly meetings and producing a regular newsletter (separate from *ENFO*), and his first conference on the subject drew interest from around the state. Partington, envisioning the new group as something of a small-scale version of The Nature Conservancy, wanted the society to take an aggressive approach toward the preservation of existing plant communities that were rapidly disappearing under bulldozers. The group, however, included plant sellers who demurred from the prospect of offending developers—i.e., potential customers—with a strident message. After a few years as an informal offshoot of the Florida Conservation Foundation, the Florida Native Plant Society incorporated in 1981 and eventually grew to 27 chapters across the state. Though it never became the bulldozer-stopping activist group that Partington had in mind, the society has raised awareness of the benefits of indigenous trees and plants—including one advantage that resonates even with Florida newcomers who wouldn't know a goldenrod from a Chinese tallow: native plants require less water than imports.

The election of Bob Graham as governor in 1978 gave environmentalists hopes for a reprise of the golden era of 1970-1972, when Reubin Askew oversaw the passage of several monumental conservation laws. Graham, scion of a wealthy South Florida family (and brother of former *Washington Post* publisher Philip Graham), had gained solid environmental credentials during his 12 years in the state legislature, and his obvious ambition made him receptive to sweeping proposals—such as the "Marshall Plan," Arthur Marshall's call for restoration of the Everglades. Marshall, living in the North Florida town of Interlachen after his stint at the University of Miami, had become a cohort of Marjory Stoneman Douglas in Friends of the Everglades. The organization in 1981 published a pamphlet in which Marshall summarized his plan under the title, "For the Future of Florida, Repair the Everglades." Presenting his blueprint as a sort of open letter to all government officials and state agencies with a part to play in fixing the Everglades, Marshall urged the state to speed up its restoration of the Kissimmee River, noting the ongoing sale and development of land in its floodplain. He also listed specific steps for reinstating the natural "sheet flow" of water through the Glades and combating the pollution that continued to pour in. Reprinted quarterly for the next two years, the petition attracted endorsements from what Marshall called the largest coalition ever assembled in Florida—not only every noteworthy statewide environmental group but also local Audubon chapters, garden clubs, women's groups, churches, political organizations, homeowners associations and even the Palm Beach County Archaeological Society. As a manifesto from Florida's most influential environmentalist, the pamphlet served as a basis for Gov. Graham's agenda on the River of Grass. In 1983, Graham launched a program he called "Save Our Everglades," with the goal of returning the ecosystem by 2000 to its general condition of 1900, before human manipulations had done their damage. With the backing of the state's environmental groups, Graham issued an executive order calling for the restoration of the Everglades, the Kissimmee River and Lake Okeechobee. The $150 million Kissimmee River project, a compromise that accommodated both the Corps of Engineers and cattle ranchers in the river valley, began in 1984 with the installation of weirs to divert water from the canal and into some of the river's original meanders in an attempt to restore wetlands along its banks. Though woefully incomplete as a repair to the river, the plan marked the first attempt to undo a major Corps of Engineers waterworks project. Graham's attention to the Everglades also led to congressional approval for expansion of Big Cypress National Preserve in 1988 and Everglades National Park in 1989.

In the midst of the renewed public attention Graham had brought to the Everglades, the environmental movement lost perhaps the most effective and respected member of its ranks. Marshall, whose encyclopedic knowledge of issues ranging from the Everglades to the barge canal made him, in the words of Johnny Jones, the Einstein of Florida's environmental movement, died of cancer on February 18, 1985, only 65 years old.

For several years, Florida Audubon and the Sierra Club had been trying to focus attention on flaws in the state's protection of wetlands and the absence of a coordinated system to monitor growth. The state's wetlands had been vanishing steadily for decades—down 60 percent from an original 20 million acres by the 1960s—as construction technology improved and developers became adept at building in naturally swampy areas, and environmental groups called for an end to the routine approval of wetlands development. In the 1984 legislative session, lobbyists for the two preeminent conservation groups welcomed a proposal to address the wetlands issue. The Warren S. Henderson Wetlands Protection Act would expand the jurisdiction of the Department of Environmental Regulation, giving it the authority to deny dredge-and-fill permits solely on the basis of potential harm to wildlife habitat. The act also would bolster the power of the state's five water-management districts to control agricultural practices that would affect wetlands. As is often the case in Tallahassee, though, the original bill changed shape on its way to passage, and its ultimate form worried environmentalists as much as it pleased them. The Henderson Act established in law a practice—known as mitigation—that the Department of Environmental Regulation had informally adopted a few years earlier. Under mitigation, developers who destroyed wetlands faced the penalty of either engineering new wetlands or paying the state to buy existing wetlands elsewhere. Although presumably a deterrent, mitigation in fact offered developers an "instant solution," as Florida Audubon described it, and as such threatened to stimulate further development in wetlands. Government planners—under pressure from business lobbyists—weakened the bill further, over the complaints of environmental groups, applying the stated goal of "no net loss" only to environmentally sensitive areas and not to wetlands as a whole. Within a few years of the act's passage, environmentalists criticized its effects on several grounds. They complained about long delays between the destruction of natural wetlands and the creation of their replacements and about mitigation rules that often allowed the substitute wetlands to be far from the original development site. In addition, activists charged that many of the artificial wetlands simply failed—an assertion confirmed by a Department of Environmental Regulation report in 1991 on mitigation. Florida Audubon reported on the study, which showed that only one-tenth as much functioning wetlands had been constructed as destroyed since the law went into effect. The report also detailed an almost complete lack of both compliance with regulations by developers and enforcement by state officials.

After taking on wetlands, the legislature next addressed the state's haphazard approach to growth management. Florida had first tackled the contentious issue a decade earlier, when the Local Government Comprehensive Planning Act directed cities and counties to spell out future growth patterns for their areas. A decade later, it was clear to all that the law was not working, with most local "comp plans" so vague and malleable that state oversight was impossible. Nat Reed, the former governmental and presidential advisor, had returned to Jupiter Island in 1978, and in the early 1980s Graham appointed him to the Environmental Land Management Study Committee, which was charged with assessing the results of the previous growth-management laws. Reed urged the governor to strengthen the authority of the state's 11 regional planning councils, and he suggested changes in state law that would direct development toward existing urban areas. Graham raised the issue as a priority before the 1985 legislative session, pushing for a new package of laws that would require local, regional and state authorities to draw up more detailed plans for future development and land use, with the state having veto power over problematic local planning. The environmental lobbyists—led by Johnny Jones of the Florida Wildlife Federation, Charles Lee of Florida Audubon and Casey Gluckman of the Sierra Club—threw their weight behind the proposal, which passed under the rubric of the Growth Management Act. As part of the check on local planners, the law gave citizens the right to challenge governments over compliance with comprehensive plans. In an attempt to ensure more citizen involvement, Florida Audubon published a layman's guide to the new law, written by the husband-and-wife lobbying team of David and Casey Gluckman.

With the bold new law in place, Graham organized a Growth Management Advisory Committee, a 22-person panel that included Florida Audubon president Bernard Yokel. The committee issued a final report in 1986, including an assertion that environmentalists had made for years—that growth was not paying for itself with regard to the roads and services it forced local governments to provide, meaning the state faced an "infrastructure deficit" of $72 billion over the next 10 years. With a state mandate in place for smarter growth, conservation groups dared to hope for a retreat from the routine approval of sprawling development in Florida.

Reed, however, knew better than to trust a host of anonymous local planners to adhere to the new guidelines. Deciding that the state needed an outside "watchdog" for growth management, he headed the founding in 1986 of a nonprofit organization called 1000 Friends of Florida. Loaded with well-connected officials who knew how to secure grant money for projects, the group hired an experienced staff to monitor growth-management decisions throughout the state, reporting to the board of directors on major problems and advising other environmental groups. Reed's group eventually branched into other areas, including the pursuit of affordable housing, but growth management remained its *raison d'etre*.

Florida's political dynamics ensure that the passage of any significant environmental legislation spawns a backlash, usually in the next legislative session. Not surprisingly, business and development interests entered Tallahassee in 1986 hoping to strip away as much as possible from the Growth Management Act. The business lobbyists described it as "fine-tuning." As Florida Audubon's Lee put it to a reporter at the time, "Their fine-tuning has extended beyond the fine and into the gross." Lee and his cohorts managed to fend off most of the revisions, leaving the growth-control measure to face an uncertain fate at the hands of city and county commissions throughout the state.

Though the 1980s produced several significant laws in Florida, nationally it was a period of regression on the environment—largely through the influence of James Watt, whom Ronald Reagan appointed as Secretary of the Interior. Watt's indifference to conservation soon led to calls for his ouster, and the Florida Sierra Club did its part by organizing a "Not Watt Rally" in Tallahassee and collecting 34,000 signatures (out of 1 million gathered nationwide) on a petition demanding Watt's removal. Watt, a lightning rod for environmental groups, resigned in 1983 over a dispute involving a coal-leasing program.

Following on the momentum of Graham's Save Our Everglades program, Florida Audubon's Lee spearheaded the formation of the Everglades Coalition, which joined several state and national groups and replaced an alliance that had fallen apart during the 1970s. The Coalition, which began holding annual conferences in the mid-1980s, advocated expansion of Big Cypress National Preserve and called for changes in the planned construction of Interstate 75 from Naples to Fort Lauderdale that would allow more water flow. The most promising means of adding to Big Cypress involved a land swap among the Department of the Interior and two Florida corporations—a deal that met resistance from some environmental groups. Lee played the decisive role in convincing national partners to support the plan, and in 1988 Congress approved the idea. Under the unusual arrangement, Collier Enterprises and Barron Collier Companies transferred the land in Big Cypress— along with tracts in Fakahatchee Strand and the Ten Thousand Islands— to the federal government in exchange for an abandoned Indian school property in Phoenix, Arizona.

As the 1980s neared a close, the CARL land-acquisition program also approached the end of its mandated 10-year existence. Environmental groups called attention to the need for another statewide commitment to land acquisition, and Gov. Bob Martinez—recognizing the continued public popularity of the programs—created the Commission on the Future of Florida's Environment in 1989. The panel, chaired by Nat Reed, comprised developers, farmers and environmentalists, including Lee, who vigorously advocated a new, long-term funding source for land purchases. The majority of the commission agreed, setting the stage for lawmakers in the next session to take up the issue. Florida Audubon and the state's other major environmental groups called for two expanded elements of the earlier programs—eminent domain authority and emergency acquisition. The power of eminent domain, enabling the state to purchase land from unwilling sellers, had previously been limited to specific properties designated by the legislature, unless the state cabinet produced a unanimous vote. Under the version pushed by environmental groups, a mere majority vote of the cabinet would suffice. The proposed change in emergency acquisition would allow a five-vote majority of the cabinet to approve immediate purchases of land threatened by imminent development. Florida Audubon suggested the futuristic name Preservation 2000 for the program.

Environmental lobbyists had long recognized the limits of their influence in Tallahassee, but they knew that certain issues—such as land acquisition—were difficult for many lawmakers to oppose. When the legislature met in the spring of 1990, it considered the largest layout for land purchases in state history—$3 billion over a decade, based on the annual approval of $300 million. The Preservation 2000 bill moved through both houses with the two new provisions intact, and Martinez eagerly signed it into law. In addition to funding the CARL and Save Our Rivers programs, P-2000 (as it came to be called) directed 10 percent of the money to the Florida Communities Trust Program, which offered matching funds for local governments in land-buying campaigns. The government didn't wait long to make use of the increased power of eminent domain. A few months after the P-2000 law passed, the governor and his cabinet gave approval for condemnation proceedings on properties around the Wekiva River.

In all, 1990 turned out to be one of those rare years when environmentalists had as much to celebrate as to lament. On top of the P-2000 passage, voters in five counties approved tax increases dedicated to funding land purchases. The legislature, meanwhile, strengthened protection for manatees with a measure allowing the Department of Natural Resources to adopt more effective rules on boat use in areas populated by the slow-moving creatures. Conservation groups also welcomed the rulings of state hearing officers denying permits for two proposed marinas that threatened delicate ecosystems, one in the Florida Keys and the other adjacent to Rookery Bay National Estuarine Sanctuary on the western coast. It was enough to prompt Audubon's Lee to declare, "Last year (1990) proved to be the most significant yet for the advancement of environmental protection in Florida."

Bob Graham created the Save Our Rivers program during his first term as Governor of Florida in 1981. State Library and Archives of Florida.

9

Struggling to Preserve Past Successes

Despite more than two decades of studies and attempts at restoration, Lake Apopka remained the state's most polluted lake, with a dwindling population of alligators so damaged by pesticide exposure they were unable to reproduce. In 1985, the legislature created the Lake Apopka Restoration Council, a group with local representation (including one designated environmentalist) that worked with state agencies to come up with plans for repairing the lake. A year later, a citizens group called People for Lake Apopka Now (PLAN) formed as a watchdog over the lake's repair, and it immediately challenged the council's suggestion of cultivating water hyacinths over much of the lake in an attempt to draw nutrients out of the water. The council soon abandoned the idea. PLAN, working with the Florida Wildlife Association, later challenged an agreement between the council and muck farmers intended to reduce phosphorus runoff into the lake, arguing that a proposed filtering ditch was insufficient and that loopholes weakened the council's consent order. The case eventually went to the governor and cabinet, and the Apopka activists settled for a partial victory as the farmers' water withdrawals were eventually reduced by two-thirds, meaning less runoff would enter the lake. The passage of the Surface Water Improvement and Management (SWIM) Act in 1987 added momentum by listing Lake Apopka as one of seven first-priority bodies of water in the state

The citizens group received a jolt in 1991 when the board of the St. Johns Water Management District voted to give the muck farmers permanent permits to continue discharging water into the lake. PLAN found an ally in the West Orange Chamber of Commerce, which formed a committee to organize local opposition to the continuing pollution of the lake. The committee recognized the need for a separate advocacy group, and PLAN gave way to Friends of Lake Apopka, headed by Jim Thomas, an environmental biologist and former president of Friends of the Wekiva River and Orange Audubon Society. Friends of Lake Apopka worked with elected officials and larger environmental organizations, setting its sights on Tallahassee. The legislature in 1996 passed the Lake Apopka Restoration Act, which contributed $20 million toward the state's buyout of the muck farms around the lake and also directed the St. Johns Water Management District to begin immediate negotiations for the purchases. Though the measure marked a final decisive step toward a wide-scale salvaging of the lake, some environmental groups complained about provisions in the act they considered overly generous to the farmers in assessing the value of their properties. The federal Department of Agriculture added $26 million to the pot, and the water district gradually bought up about 20,000 acres of land and began a complicated repair project that yielded a major setback in the winter of 1998-1999, when more than 700 birds, mostly white pelicans, died in the former farmland that had been flooded. An investigation found staggeringly high concentrations of various pesticides in the birds, leading to a lengthy delay in the agency's plans to flush the chemicals from the soil. Friends of Lake Apopka, though chagrined by the bird deaths, continued to advocate an aggressive strategy for the restoration. Meanwhile, the Zellwood Drainage and Water Control District officially dissolved in 2000, nearly 60 years after the legislature created it for local farmers as an entity with the powers of an autonomous government.

The saga of the Ocklawaha River entered its third decade amid a tense political standstill. Florida Defenders of the Environment, continuing its quest for the breaching of Rodman Dam, gained increasing support from state leaders. Heeding a 20-volume report by the Florida Department of Environmental Protection and the St. Johns Water Management District, Gov. Lawton Chiles in 1995 ordered the DEP to begin securing the permits needed to remove the dam, and his successor, Jeb

Bush, also publicly supported restoration of the river. In the legislature, however, the maneuvering of a few powerful lawmakers blocked funding for the necessary projects. The legislators—most notably longtime Sen. George Kirkpatrick, for whom the dam was renamed in the late 1990s—insisted that the value of the 9,000-acre Rodman Reservoir as a bass fishing haven outweighed all other factors. Kirkpatrick and, after he left office, Sen. Jim King of Jacksonville regularly pushed bills intended to establish the permanence of Rodman Reservoir, whether by having it declared a state recreation area or directing money toward boat ramps at the reservoir. Marjorie Carr, president emeritus of FDE and the leader of the fight against the Cross Florida Barge Canal from the beginning, died in 1997 without seeing the river flow freely to its natural confluence with the St. Johns.

Despite the legislative delays, by the early part of the new century the removal of Rodman Dam seemed increasingly inevitable. With the reservoir covering federal land in the Ocala National Forest, the U.S. Forest Service exerted pressure on state officials to drain Rodman Reservoir, finally setting a deadline of 2006. An alliance of fishermen emerged under the name Save Rodman Reservoir, filing an appeal against the Forest Service's official plan and arguing that the removal of the dam would cause environmental harm. Four decades after Carr and David Anthony began questioning the Corps of Engineers over the canal project, the situation had reached a complete reversal: FDE used its cadre of academics not to refute the claims of a federal agency but to defend them when the fishermen attacked the Forest Service's impact statement. Despite the glacial pace of change, the FDE's executive director, Nick Williams, could say, "This is an exciting time in the effort to restore the Ocklawaha River."

Still, four years after the supposed deadline, the dam remained in place, as key legislators continued to promote the importance of Rodman Reservoir as a recreation area.

Though environmental groups tend to maintain unified fronts, they are subject to the same tensions and divisions as other nonprofits and businesses. A rare example of a public dispute broke forth in the early 1990s involving the Save the Manatee Club (SMC). Since its inception in

1981, SMC had operated essentially as a committee of Florida Audubon Society. After a decade, some officials with the club became displeased with the arrangement and argued that the group needed autonomy. When the leaders of Florida Audubon voted to keep the club under its dominion, Judith Vallee, the group's executive director, issued what Florida Audubon called an unauthorized press release announcing plans to separate. Singer Jimmy Buffett, who had launched the club with Gov. Bob Graham, got involved in the dispute, publicly advocating independent status for SMC. Florida Audubon first suspended Vallee and then, when she refused to return to work under the same circumstances, fired her. Save the Manatee Club officials took the case to court, and Florida Audubon agreed in 1993 to sever its ties with the club, which remained in Central Florida and incorporated with Vallee as its leader.

Despite that diversion, the Save the Manatee Club and other environmental groups remained engaged in efforts to increase protection for the animals. The club persuaded legislators to approve a specialty license plate — the state's first with an environmental theme — that became popular with drivers and yielded money for manatee protection. As the club became increasingly aggressive, however, it faced rising hostility from boaters unhappy about state-imposed speed restrictions. Shortly after incorporating, the Save the Manatee Club began filing challenges to state permits for marinas and other projects that it said would harm the animals. In 2000, SMC led an alliance of 18 state and national organizations that sued the U.S. Fish and Wildlife Service and two other federal agencies, charging that their plans for manatee protection failed to meet the requirements of the Endangered Species Act. State and federal officials eventually worked out a settlement of the suit that involved new protected havens for manatees in several key waterways (beginning in Brevard County) as well as new rules to curb the building of marinas in areas known to host the slow-moving mammals. While SMC officials said the plan didn't go far enough, enraged boaters' groups filed legal challenges. A judge dismissed the boaters' arguments in 2002, clearing the way for the Florida Fish and Wildlife Conservation Commission to move forward with protective plans for 16 "hot spots" in 10 counties.

Environmental activists also have clashed with state agencies over proposed changes in the status of certain animals. The trend began in 1995, when the Florida state wildlife commission voted to classify the white ibis as a threatened species. Cattle ranchers, fearing restrictions on the use of their property, raised such a protest that the state legislature threatened to decrease the wildlife agency's budget. In response, the commission began taking steps to revise the way it determined species listings and eventually adopted draconian requirements—an 80-percent decline in 10 years for endangered status and a 50-percent decline in 10 years for threatened status. Activists suggested that no animal in the state would meet those guidelines, yet the commission went forward with plans to consider revising the status of the red-cockaded wood-pecker from "threatened" to "species of special concern," even though the bird's population had dropped by an estimated 20 percent in the pre-vious 20 years and despite overwhelming recommendations from envi-ronmentalists and biologists against any change in status. The state commission also raised the prospect of lifting a ban on the hunting of the Florida black bear, a threatened species whose historic range has been narrowed mostly to state and national forests in six areas of the state, before tabling the notion, to the relief of environmentalists and the dis-appointment of hunting groups. Despite the success of environmental groups in a legal challenge to force wider protection for manatees, activ-ists nervously awaited the results of studies by both state and federal agencies to determine whether the animal's population has risen to the point it no longer warrants endangered status. Meanwhile, as the federal government removed the bald eagle from the endangered species list in 2007, activists charged wildlife agencies in Florida with relaxing their protections of the national symbol by allowing development to encroach inside nesting buffers.

Laurie Macdonald, Florida program director for Defenders of Wild-life, led a chorus of opposition from environmental groups against the wildlife commission's changes.

"I think many people involved in these evaluations are trying to look at the facts and trying to fit the facts to today's rules and regulations," Macdonald said. "Like with the red-cockaded woodpecker, if you look at the criteria in certain ways, yeah, it qualifies for down-listing. But we don't think the criteria are appropriate to be used. … I didn't see huge political pressure on them to adopt these rules, but there's that general wave of pressure from consumptive interests, those who use the land in extractive ways, there is just huge pressure on our resource agencies to minimize the amount of protection that is given to wildlife or to water resources or to native habitat. And so I think certainly there's that wave that pushed them toward it.

"I think, I hope, that we'll find the (Fish and) Wildlife Conservation Commission will voluntarily do a review of this rule that's been adopted and that they'll see the criteria just are not appropriate for many, many species."

In 2003, the FWC changed its official status for red-cockaded woodpeckers from threatened to species of special concern. In subsequent years, the FWC also removed bald eagles and peregrine falcons from its endangered-species list.

Manatees, with their anthropomorphic traits and their obvious vulnerability, have always drawn a certain measure of human sympathy. Other animals have remained fairly invisible to the general public as they faced similar declines. One of them, the Florida scrub jay, serves as an indicator of the effects of more than a century of development in the state. The Florida scrub jay, a species of special concern, lives a highly circumscribed existence — dependent on a specific type of habitat known as scrub that exists only in the dry uplands of the peninsula. Because that same land is the most convenient for building, development has gobbled up much of Florida's scrub habitat and reduced populations of scrub jays by more than 90 percent, with an estimated population of between 7,000 and 11,000 in continuous decline. In some cases, landowners intentionally destroyed scrub habitat to prevent any future hindrances should the birds become federally endangered. (Disruption of natural fire cycles also has affected scrub areas, and state and federal agencies now conduct prescribed burns on some public land for the benefit of the birds.) In the early 20th century scrub jays occupied nearly every county of the peninsula, but by its end the bird had been concentrated into a few segments of the state — primarily the Cape Canaveral/

Merritt Island area, Ocala National Forest and the Lake Wales Ridge, including Archbold Biological Station, a preserve near Lake Placid that has hosted studies of the birds for more than three decades. With the scrub in the state's central highlands reduced by 85 percent—largely for citrus crops—The Nature Conservancy formed a partnership in the 1990s with the state and the U.S. Fish and Wildlife Service to purchase much of the remaining land for protection as the Lake Wales Ridge Ecosystem Preserve. In addition to scrub jays, Eastern indigo snakes, gopher tortoises and dozens of other threatened or endangered animals and plants depend on Florida scrub.

Brevard County—because of federal ownership of Kennedy Space Center and Cape Canaveral Air Force Station—holds one of the state's largest concentrations of the birds, but scrub habitat on private lands decreased markedly there with the growth around Melbourne in the 1980s and 1990s. In response, the local Audubon chapter began advocating for the scrub jay as official state bird. (The northern mockingbird had informally held that status in Florida since 1927, though it is not endemic to the state, as the scrub jay is.) A group of students from Melbourne took up the issue in 1999, alarmed over the continued bulldozing of scrub land in the area. Unable to stop the development, the children pursued the honoring of the species and found a sympathetic legislator in Howard Futch, who said the scrub jay's communal rearing of young exemplified "family values." Business groups inaccurately suggested that an official designation for the birds would prevent development of scrub land, and a lobbyist for the National Rifle Association energetically took up the issue. Marian Hammer, disparaging the scrub jay's "welfare mentality," ensured that the bill never made it to a vote. In the following year's session, some high school students revived the issue, gathering 10,000 signatures in a petition drive as Futch again sponsored a bill to have the scrub jay named official state bird. The NRA lobbyist struck back, confusing the issue by suggesting that a vote for the bird could lead to endangered species status, after which "... you can kiss your property rights goodbye." In the end, lawmakers voted to give official status to the mockingbird, already the designated bird in four other states.

Though Florida Audubon had vastly broadened its goals during its first century, the organization still devoted much of its attention to birds. In the late 1990s, the chapter unveiled a new program it called Important Bird Areas, part of an initiative by the National Audubon Society in conjunction with BirdLife International, a global coalition of environmental groups. Modeled after similar efforts in Europe and in other states, the program involved a cataloging of patches of habitat both large and small with significant value for birds in Florida. Florida Audubon tapped Bill Pranty, a veteran of the respected scrub jay studies at Archbold Biological Station and the author of the comprehensive summary *A Birder's Guide To Florida*, to head up the program. Pranty collected recommendations from local Audubon chapters and other sources, weighing four factors for each suggested area—the presence of threatened or endangered birds, the dependence of birds on the site's particular habitat, the proportion of birds from a particular species and the total population of birds regularly found at the site. A committee whittled the list of recommendations down to some 90 accepted sites, and in late 2002 Florida Audubon published *The Important Bird Areas of Florida: 2000-2002*. Though the inventory carried no legal weight for any government entities, Florida Audubon officials hoped it would guide the state in decisions on both habitat management and land preservation—just as The Nature Conservancy's Florida Natural Areas Inventory has aided state planners in setting their priority lists. The project has the ultimate goal of, in Pranty's words, "keeping common birds common."

Since the 1960s, the Sierra Club had emerged as probably the state's second most prominent environmental group behind Florida Audubon. Despite their similar objectives, the two groups differed in significant ways. Unlike Audubon, Sierra existed strictly as a national organization, with its state and local chapters not independent entities. And in Florida as elsewhere, Sierra often took a more aggressive approach than Audubon, especially when it came to court challenges. Following on the successes of the Environmental Defense Fund and other new groups, Sierra in 1971 spun off an independent organization, the Sierra Club Legal Defense Fund. Like the EDF, the Sierra Fund offered its advice and assistance to clients ranging from established national organizations to such community activist groups as Concerned Citizens of Putnam County and the Conservancy of Southwest Florida, which led the fight against the development of Marco Island. (To avoid the impression that it only served the Sierra Club, the legal group eventually renamed itself Earthjustice.) In 1990, the fund opened a regional office in Tallahassee, and the branch achieved a significant victory in 1994 when it sued to block a permit for a phosphate mine in South Florida that would have gobbled up nearly 18,000 acres and required 11 million gallons of water a day. Three years later, Earthjustice filed a challenge over Fisheating Creek in South Florida, asserting that public use of the waterway dating back to colonial times trumped the rights of Lykes Brothers, a huge agribusiness that owned land around the creek and blocked public access. A jury—citing a law from 1845 that denied private ownership of navigable waterways—ruled in Earthjustice's favor, opening the 50-mile tributary near Lake Okeechobee to the public. In the wake of the verdict, Lykes Brothers decided to sell the 18,000-acre property to the state, which turned the land into a wildlife management area.

While environmental activism usually involves outside coalitions seeking to influence government decisions, a new group emerged during the 1990s that consisted entirely of government insiders. Public Employees for Environmental Responsibility (PEER), a national organization founded in 1992, opened a Florida chapter five years later, serving as both a collective voice for conservation and a protector of state workers. Headed by two former attorneys for the Department of Environmental Protection (DEP), Florida PEER offered a discreet haven for whistleblowers in state agencies. The group called attention to a trend in which developers sued individual employees rather than state regulatory agencies—a tactic the group claimed intimidated other workers into relaxed enforcement and review of permit applications. (Individual activists for years had been subject to retaliatory legal actions known as SLAPP suits—Strategic Lawsuits Against Public Participation.) PEER extracted a public pledge from then-DEP Secretary David Struhs to seek a law protecting employees from such suits, but nothing happened and the group criticized Struhs for the failure.

Florida PEER quickly established itself as a potent factor in environmental politics. The chapter issued petitions, press releases and white papers and conducted surveys of employees, including one in which Marine Patrol and Park Patrol officers lambasted the DEP for its failure to support the enforcement of environmental laws. The group directed most of its attention toward the DEP, which it accused of ignoring laws on growth management and wetlands protection, but it also pursued charges of misconduct by local governments and officials. As a conduit for frustrated state employees to air criticisms of their own agencies, Florida PEER added a significant voice to the conservation movement.

Florida Public Interest Research Group (PIRG), founded in 1981 as a collective of students, continued to grow in the following decade, expanding from its initial chapter at Florida State University to four other campuses. The only large group in the state with an environmental focus and a predominantly young membership, Florida PIRG used a professional staff guided by a board of directors that included representatives from each of the colleges. Though the organization's fundraising relied entirely on fees voluntarily paid by students, it nonetheless drew resentment from some people—on the campuses and off—who objected to its political aims. An attorney from the Keys decided to challenge Florida PIRG's status, and he found four students at Florida State to serve as plaintiffs in a lawsuit against the Board of Regents, the agency in charge of the State University System. The first judge upheld the rule that gave students at the five schools the option of designating student fees for PIRG, but that judgment was overturned on appeal in 1995. Florida PIRG, which had also sustained itself since its inception through door-to-door canvassing, absorbed the financial blow and continued as an aggressive force with 10,000 members. The group led a successful drive for a ban on garbage incinerators in the state and fought to kill a bill it dubbed the "Polluter Secrecy and Immunity Act," which would have given industries the power to regulate their own emissions. But opposition to oil drilling in Florida and its offshore waters remained the organization's highest priority. In 1995, the same year it lost its student funding, Florida PIRG celebrated the federal government's cancellation of all oil leases around the Florida Keys. And then in 2002, its 20-year fight against oil drilling in the "Destin Dome" area of the Gulf of Mexico, just 25 miles from the Florida coast, culminated in the decision by President George W. Bush to buy out the drilling rights of three oil companies. Bush also announced plans to buy oil and gas rights in the Everglades area—including Big Cypress National Preserve and the Ten Thousand Islands National Wildlife Refuge—from a South Florida company. It may have been a transparently political gesture intended to boost the re-election campaign of the president's brother, Florida Gov. Jeb Bush, but Florida PIRG and other environmental groups nonetheless welcomed the news.

"It's a huge victory, sort of a watershed moment in the 20-year battle to keep our beaches rig-free," said Mark Ferrulo, former executive director of Florida PIRG. "We're the first group that tackled this issue in 1983 when the first leases were sold, and we decided to fight it every step of the way. We've certainly had lots of help and allies along the road, but we've been sort of the lead organization spearheading the effort against drilling."

Ferrulo left Florida PIRG in 2008 to head the newly created Progress Florida, a non-profit whose concerns included not just environmental protection but also social and economic issues.

Florida PIRG wasn't alone in contesting oil drilling in and around Florida. During the 1997 legislative session, Florida Audubon led the way in lobbying for a bill that would give the state cabinet the power to demand bonds adequate to cover the cost of cleaning up oil spills before issuing permits. (Though the state had banned drilling along its coasts in 1990, some companies—including Coastal Petroleum—held "grandfather" permission.) The bill passed, offering at least a measure of assurance that taxpayers would not be stuck with the tab for any potential oil spills. The two groups also combined in 1998 to bolster a grassroots fight against Florida Power and Light over its use of Orimulsion, a controversial tar-based fuel linked to acid rain, at its Port Manatee power plant near Tampa Bay. After an initial state cabinet vote against the proposal, FP&L mounted a lengthy and expensive lobbying campaign, while environmental groups led by the Izaak Walton League unsuccessfully pushed for a bill that would have prohibited power plants from using Orimulsion. The issue came down to another vote of Gov. Lawton

Chiles and his cabinet, and they rejected use of the fuel by a 6-1 margin.

During his laudatory career as a zoology professor at the University of Florida, Archie Carr refrained from public involvement in environmental activism—including the effort led by his wife, Marjorie Harris Carr, to stop the Cross Florida Barge Canal, although he assisted Florida Defenders of Environment in unseen ways. Carr's dissemination of facts about the natural resources of the state—both in his many books and through his academic work—contributed indirectly to the cause of preservation, and after Carr's death in 1987 a coalition headed by the Caribbean Conservation Corporation (which he had served as technical director for 28 years) launched a campaign in his name. The alliance pushed the federal government to purchase coastal land in Brevard and Indian River counties that served as crucial nesting grounds for the sea turtles Carr had spent his career studying, with the land designated as a wildlife refuge. With one quarter of the area already in public possession through purchases of either the state or The Nature Conservancy, the coalition sought a $15 million appropriation from Congress for the remainder. Envisioned as a 900-acre sanctuary covering 20 miles of coastline from Melbourne Beach to Wabasso Beach, the Archie Carr National Wildlife Refuge came into being in 1991, though lagging appropriations kept it considerably below its intended size through the end of the century. The Nature Conservancy continued its race to raise funds ahead of the inevitable development of a beach that hosts 25 percent of all loggerhead turtle nesting in the United States and 35 percent of all green turtle nesting.

Ballot initiatives, seen as a way to bypass the state legislature and allow citizens to enact laws, gained popularity in the early 1990s. (In reality, constitutional amendments merely create a broad mandate for lawmakers to draft laws on a particular issue.) In the early 1990s, concerns about the effects of commercial fishing spawned a group called Save Our Sealife, which drew up a ballot measure that would ban the use of gill nets in Florida waters and limit the size of all nets in coastal and inland waters. The newly formed alliance, led by Karl Wickstrom, publisher of *Florida Sportsman* magazine, blamed the nets for declines in fish populations—the gill nets trapped young fish and disrupted reproduction patterns, and the large nets simply captured too many fish. Florida Audubon—wary of using the constitution for wildlife management—remained neutral on the issue, but other groups wholeheartedly supported it. The Florida Conservation Association (later renamed Coastal Conservation Association Florida) led a petition campaign that eschewed the use of professional canvassers and still collected enough signatures to put the measure on the ballot in November of 1994. Voters approved the "net ban" amendment by a 44-point margin, setting up a marathon of legal challenges by the fishing industry. The Florida Conservation Association worked to help the state defend the amendment in court—Florida's Supreme Court upheld the amendment in 1997—and to fend off attempts by lawmakers to undercut enforcement of the law. Within a few years, marine biologists reported that fish stocks had rebounded dramatically, while state and federal agencies made more than 1,000 arrests for violations of the ban in the first two years.

It is generally accepted fact in Florida that the state's programs for acquisition of environmentally important lands have no match in the nation. It came as no surprise to environmental groups when certain elements began to complain about the effects of those land-buying initiatives. The phrases "property rights" and "wise use" came into favor among conservative politicians, and the words had obvious appeal for many people in Florida. As used by real-estate and business interests, as well as some private citizens, "property rights" challenged the authority of any government or agency to acquire land that the owner doesn't want to part with, no matter what public benefit might result from the transaction. Some also complained about government regulations—mandated by the Growth Management Act of 1985—that affected the freedom of citizens to do as they liked with their properties. The strengthening of the state's power of eminent domain in the Preservation 2000 Act further exacerbated long-standing resentments, and some conservative lawmakers responded with attempts to curtail the government's ability to control land use. Heading into the 1994 legislative session, some lawmakers began promoting a bill that would deny enforcement of any environmental regulation if its effect were to decrease the value of any property by 40 percent or more. The lobbyists from Florida Audubon and the Sierra Club mobilized against the bill, which fell to defeat in the next session.

That hardly marked the end of the issue. Bert J. Harris Jr., a legislator from rural Lake Placid who had pushed property-rights measures for years, was rewarded in 1995 with a bill named for him. The act promoted legal recourse for landowners who had been "inordinately burdened by governmental action" — an attempt to obviate future comprehensive plans that has not been entirely resolved in the courts. Nathaniel Reed's 1000 Friends of Florida, noting the national trend of property-rights measures, called it "the most draconian law of any in the nation" and said that it has had "a chilling effect at the local level." (Legislators in 1998 unsuccessfully tried to make the Harris Act retroactive to 1990.)

Advocates of development also launched a petition drive for a constitutional amendment defining property rights to their liking, and Florida Audubon responded with a suit challenging the wording of the proposal. A judge struck down the provision, keeping it off the ballot, but further offensives followed. In 1996, environmental groups fended off bills that would have changed the character of conservation lands by either turning them into utilities infrastructure or requiring that they bring in revenue to the state. The following year, property rights proponents tried a different strategy, beginning a campaign for ballot initiatives on three constitutional amendments that taken together would weaken the authority of state and local governments and agencies to manage growth. The sugar industry set up an ersatz grassroots organization called the Tax Cap Committee to lead the drive and then fed millions of dollars into it. Florida Audubon Society president Clay Henderson led the opposition to the proposed ballot measures, and environmentalists celebrated when the state Supreme Court struck down all three as untenably broad.

The irony of the legislative obsession with property rights stems from the feeble enforcement of the state's growth-management laws. Florida Audubon's Charles Lee said that when the legislature passed the measures of the mid-1980s, environmentalists predicted that it would take a staff of several hundred people at the Department of Community Affairs to conduct all the needed reviews of comprehensive plans and zoning changes. In reality, the agency's enforcement staff has never been more than about 30 people. Even so, Lee said that Gov. Bob Martinez, whose administration first began coping with the regulations, was committed to growth management and fully supported then-DCA secretary Tom Pelham's plans to beef up the agency. But Lawton Chiles unseated Martinez in 1990, and Lee said the Chiles administration was "openly hostile" to the intent of the 1985 and 1986 laws. Lee cites the events of 1993 as the "death" of growth management. In that year, the DCA challenged St. Lucie County over its comprehensive plan, and a judge ruled in the agency's favor, sending the issue to Chiles and his cabinet. The cabinet approved the St. Lucie plan, and Chiles used the occasion to publicly lambaste DCA Secretary Linda Loomis Shelley for questioning the local government's actions.

"At that point it just demoralized everybody in that agency," Lee said. "It was clearly a turning point from which that agency has never recovered."

Recognizing the inability or unwillingness of state agencies to enforce their own regulations, Florida Audubon tried to inject itself into the process during the 1990s. It applied to the Elizabeth Ordway Dunn Foundation (established from the estate of a Palm Beach resident active in conservation causes), and received a grant to establish the position of environmental permit coordinator who would review the issuing of permits by the Army Corps of Engineers, the Florida Department of Environmental Protection and the state's water-management districts, with a focus on wetlands. Florida Audubon hired a biologist who worked with other staff members to comment on 200 permits during the first year of the program. FAS set up a network of alerts, through which it warned local chapters and other environmental groups about objectionable projects in their areas until the money for the position ran out a few years later.

Clay Henderson, an attorney from New Smyrna Beach, succeeded Bernard Yokel as president of Florida Audubon in 1995. Henderson, a sixth-generation Floridian, had first gained renown in environmental circles in 1986 when he led the successful drive for a Volusia County bond issue dedicated to land acquisition—the first such measure passed at the local level in the state. When Florida held hearings to review its constitution in 1998—a process mandated at the time of the state's founding—Henderson used his position to push for a land-acquisition program that wouldn't be subject to the whims of lawmakers. With the Preservation 2000 program approved by the legislature in 1990 nearing its "sunset," Henderson proposed a four-part plan for land acquisition to the Constitutional Revision Commission then touring the state. Henderson suggested a permanent fund from the sale of documentary stamps, the elimination of limits on bonding, strict guidelines on the use of land acquired for conservation and exemptions from property taxes for some lands held for conservation purposes. He also came up with a name for the new land program: Florida Forever. The issue proved popular with citizens who attended the commission's 14 public meetings, and the panel approved a ballot measure for the 1998 election that would extend the state's constitutional authority to issue bonds for land acquisition. The measure included restrictions on the use of conservation lands—but not the other provisions Florida Audubon wanted—and it also proposed the combining of the Game and Fresh Water Fish Commission with the Marine Fisheries Commission into a single entity. Amendment 5, the Conservation of Natural Resources Act, sparked opposition from the National Rifle Association, but the measure gained the approval of 72.3 percent of voters—drawing half a million more votes than Jeb Bush, who handily defeated Buddy MacKay in the gubernatorial election.

Heading into the next legislative session, the state's major environmental groups formed the Florida Forever Coalition, dedicated to making sure lawmakers followed the spirit of the voter mandate. Amendment 5 had not mentioned specific funding figures, and the coalition pushed for a program that would yield at least $300 million a year for at least 10 years. Lawmakers followed those suggestions, passing the Florida Forever Act on the final day of the 1999 session, and they also created the Fish and Wildlife Conservation Commission to replace the two separate agencies.

Though pleased with the new land-acquisition program, environmentalists worried that about the provision that required approval of funding each year from the legislature and governor. With the passage of the Everglades Investment Act the following year—committing the state to paying $100 million annually from unspecified sources for Florida's share of the massive restoration plan—those groups also feared that lawmakers would be tempted to use Florida Forever money to meet the Everglades obligation. Those fears came to fruition in the 2001 session when the legislature diverted $75 million from the land-conservation pot into the Everglades fund. Environmental groups—the Conservancy of Southwest Florida prominent among them—cried foul, but Gov. Bush approved the maneuver. In subsequent sessions, conservation groups could only try to dissuade lawmakers from repeating the move—or from leaving Florida Forever short of its annual funding. Amendment 5, with its overwhelming voter approval for land acquisition, served as a blueprint rather than a guarantee.

The legislature in 2008 voted unanimously to extend Florida Forever another 10 years at $300 million in bonds annually. Yet in the following session, facing historic revenue shortfalls, the legislature raided the fund and appropriated no money for the land-acquisition program. That move prompted four former Florida governors—Reuben Askew, Bob Graham, Bob Martinez and Jeb Bush—to lobby for restoration of the money. In the 2010 session, the legislature set aside $15 million for Florida Forever.

While environmentalists lamented the failure of the growth-management and wetlands laws to control urban sprawl, developers and business interests complained about the web of regulations that they said unnecessarily delayed their projects. Such was the situation when Florida voters in 1998 elected Bush, a Texas native who had moved to Florida in 1980 and done extremely well for himself in the real-estate business. Shortly after taking office, Bush raised the issue of revamping the state's growth-management apparatus. Because of the governor's background and ties to commerce, environmentalists worried that he might weaken rather than strengthen regulations intended to curb unwise development, and an internal position paper favoring less state involvement in planning decisions seemed to confirm those fears. Environmentalists spoke out against any decrease in state authority, reminding Bush that "local control" had yielded chaotic and unchecked growth in the first place. Nathaniel Reed of 1000 Friends of Florida told a reporter, "As long as there are county commissioners who are more interested in helping developers than they are in protecting the environment, we're not going to get anywhere."

In preparation for the 2000 legislative session, 1000 Friends formed an alliance with 13 other organizations to closely monitor any proposed bills and to advocate a careful approach on revisions to growth-management laws. In the end, the expected battle fizzled before it started. The legislature, preoccupied with other issues, never devoted much attention to growth management. By the next session, environmental groups had allied themselves with Bush in seeking legislation that would tie the approval of development to the existence of classroom space — directing growth toward urban areas and discouraging sprawl. The legislature, under heavy lobbying from builders' groups, never allowed the measure to reach a vote, and by 2002 — with the governor gearing up for a reelection campaign — growth-management reform had slipped from the radar in Tallahassee, leaving the state with an ineffective system but with important safeguards still in place. At the practical level, though, growth-management efforts in the state declined as the Bush administration cut funding for the Department of Community Affairs. The rejection rate for revisions to comprehensive plans changed from an average of 15 percent during most of the 1990s to a mere 2.3 percent after Bush took office in 1999.

The major hurricane strike that Southeast Florida had somehow avoided for decades arrived in August of 1992. Hurricane Andrew, with sustained winds of 112 mph, made landfall near the Homestead Air Force Base south of Miami, leaving 250,000 people homeless and causing $30 billion in damage. The Clinton administration at first pledged to rebuild the flattened air base located between Everglades National Park and Biscayne National Park, but business leaders in South Florida eventually proposed an alternate plan — construction of a commercial airport with as many as 600 flights a day. Environmental groups, led by the

Sierra Club, mobilized against the proposal, charging that an airport would threaten both parks, but the Air Force approved the project in 1994. In an echo of the Big Cypress jetport battle more than two decades earlier, the activists faced a unified and politically connected group of developers. But favorable rulings in court and by state and federal agencies bolstered the environmentalists, whose campaign drew unexpected financial support from wealthy homeowners in Key Largo. The conservation groups persuaded the military in 1997 to hold a second review of the airport proposal, and another three years passed before the Air Force issued its report, declaring that the airport did not necessarily threaten the parks but that an alternate proposal for an office park would be a better use of the land. In the meantime, the airport had become a major political issue, with the Sierra Club picketing outside the office of Sen. Bob Graham—then considered a possible running mate for Democratic presidential candidate Al Gore—over Graham's support for the airport. Gore himself disappointed environmental groups by failing to take a position against the airport.

In the waning days of the Clinton administration—after Gore had lost his election bid—the Air Force announced that it wouldn't allow an airport to be built and instead transferred about half the land to Miami-Dade County. Airport backers challenged the decision in court and drew hope from the new Bush administration's promise to reconsider the airport proposal, but in December of 2001 the Air Force confirmed its opposition to a commercial airport on the site. After seven years, environmentalists could finally celebrate.

"I think we succeeded when people were presented with an alternative that could provide jobs and protect the environment, instead it being presented as airport or nothing," said Jonathan Ullman, Everglades Senior Representative for the Sierra Club's Florida chapter. "When people were able to visualize in their heads what would happen to their national parks (if the airport were built), they got activated."

Almost as soon as the U.S. Army Corps of Engineers finished its transformation of the winding Kissimmee River into Canal 38 in 1971, environmental groups began talking about the need to undo the nine-year undertaking. The state legislature approved restoration of the river in 1976, but C-38 remained largely unaltered for a decade and a half, as state and federal agencies conducted studies, trying to decide how best to repair the river without doing greater harm. Finally, in 1992, Congress authorized the Corps of Engineers to move forward with the Kissimmee River Restoration Project, though the plan faced further delays and turned out to offer much less than the reconstructive surgery environmental groups had called for. The Corps of Engineers pledged to fill only 22 miles of the 56-mile canal, using sand and shell along the banks left from the original dredging. It is more difficult to undo a canal than to create one, and the complicated project also involved the removal of some water-control structures and the raising of water levels in the feeder lakes to the north. The Corps of Engineers set a start date of 1999 and expected the project to last 11 years. The Corps estimated the cost of this incomplete repair at $414 million, to be split evenly between the state and the federal government, with Florida's share devoted mostly to land acquisition around the river. As with any long-term endeavor involving federal money, the Kissimmee River project depended on annual votes of Congress to provide the dollars it had already pledged. Before the first load of dirt could be dropped into the canal, Congress cast doubt on the project by dramatically undercutting funding in its budget. The first phase of the project commenced in June of 1999, and a decade later the Corps of Engineers had filled seven miles of canal and removed a water-control structure, changes that returned water to 24 miles of the river channel.

Meanwhile, the legal wrangling over the SWIM plan—the adjustment of water flow into the eastern Everglades that prompted the federal government to sue the state in the late 1980s—continued to drag on as the National Park Service and the Corps of Engineers argued over the details and farmers and other private landowners challenged the need for more land acquisition. In 1992, the state essentially gave in to the Departments of Justice and Interior and settled the suit, agreeing to more stringent regulation of water discharges from the Everglades Agricultural Area. But the plan remained stalled throughout the decade by legal challenges from the sugar industry, which held 700,000 acres of sugarcane fields in and around the agricultural zone. Also in the early

1990s, the Florida Legislature debated the Marjory Stoneman Douglas Everglades Protection Act, which proposed to set up a way of assessing fees on agriculture to help pay for cleanup efforts. When the act was later amended to delay the onset of financial penalties for polluters, Douglas angrily demanded that legislators remove her name from the law.

Like the pursuit of peace in the Middle East, the quest to repair the manmade damage to the Everglades had yielded periodic agreements that were hailed as decisive at the time but failed to produce significant change. By the early 1990s, the Everglades Coalition—an alliance of state and national environmental groups—had reached a condition of heightened urgency over the plight of the Everglades, calling for a comprehensive repair of the teetering ecosystem. Their pleas brought long overdue attention to the role the sugar industry had played for decades in the degradation of the South Florida ecosystem.

The Spanish first brought sugarcane to the peninsula in the 16th century, and the first attempt at commercial production occurred in 1767 near New Smyrna Beach. For the next century, growers periodically tried to cultivate sugarcane with limited success until a subsidiary of land magnate Hamilton Disston started a productive plantation at St. Cloud, just south of Orlando. Financial problems doomed the operation, and concerns about weather and soil composition caused a southward migration of the fledgling industry. The U.S. Department of Agriculture began studying the potential for sugarcane cultivation on the drained lands of South Florida, and in 1891 a government chemist declared that the southern shore of Lake Okeechobee offered "the promise of development ... beyond the limits of prophecy." Large companies acquired vast tracts of land around the lake in the early 1900s, and the tall cane stalks soon dominated the landscape, leading to the creation of the town of Clewiston. United States Sugar Corporation, which owned land stretching for 50 miles, was producing 92,000 tons of raw sugar a year by 1940. Sugar production depended on careful control of water levels, and the Corps of Engineers accommodated the industry with a network of levees, canals and pumping stations that drained thousands of acres in what came to be called the Everglades Agricultural Area. Sugar companies supplemented the exertions of the Corps by digging their own grids of canals and dikes. By the 1990s, Florida companies — benefiting from a complex system of federal price supports – accounted for half of the nation's sugar output. The growth of the sugar industry corresponded to the decline of Lake Okeechobee and the surrounding Everglades. To irrigate their crops, sugar companies pumped huge quantities of water out of the lake and then pumped the runoff back in — heavily loaded with fertilizers and pesticides. The natural southward flow of stormwater from the massive Everglades Agricultural Area carried nutrients that spawned unnatural plant growth in the Everglades, transforming sections of the River of Grass into lakes of cattails. Meanwhile the draining of traditional wet areas for sugarcane farming led to oxidation, which caused soil to disappear at a rate of about an inch a year.

For years, environmental groups had tried to force sugar companies to pay for the rescue of Lake Okeechobee and the Everglades from their polluting practices, but the industry carried great political power and had repelled the efforts. The rising awareness of the dire condition of the Everglades, however, led to a shift in the political dynamic, and in 1994 the legislature passed the Everglades Forever Act in response to the settlement of the federal suit over water quality. The measure empowered the South Florida Water Management District to impose taxes on sugar farmers to pay for the cleanup efforts, including the building of artificial marshes to filter runoff. Under the plan, sugar farmers also had to reduce the level of pollutants flowing northward into Lake Okeechobee and southward into the Everglades.

Despite its name, the Everglades Forever Act represented a modest step that stopped far short of holding the sugar industry financially responsible for decades of harm to the Everglades and Lake Okeechobee. And it was not enough to dissuade activists from seeking a greater contribution from the industry blamed for more than half of the pollution that entered Everglades National Park. Beginning in the 1980s, the leader of the drive had been George M. Barley Jr., a seventh-generation Floridian and — like Nathaniel Reed — an affluent real-estate developer. Barley founded a group called Save Our Everglades and settled on a specific plan — pursuing ballot initiatives that would allow Florida's voters to bypass the legislature and force the sugar companies to pay their share of an Everglades repair. The group's first attempt stalled when a judge in 1994 struck its measure from the ballot, ruling that it involved more than a single issue. Save Our Everglades regrouped, breaking the original proposal into three separate amendments and launching a new petition drive. The effort was gaining momentum when Barley's charter plane plunged into the Everglades in June of 1995, leaving doubts about the fate of the ballot initiatives. Barley's widow, Mary, and his friend and fellow philanthropist, Paul Tudor Jones, took up the cause, leading an effort that gathered far more than the number of signatures needed to place the initiatives on the ballot for the 1996 election. The centerpiece measure would enact a penny per pound tax on sugar before it went to market, a step that was expected to raise $875 million over 25 years.

Predictably, the sugar industry campaigned feverishly against Amendment 4—and it also sponsored a competing measure that would require two-thirds voter approval of any amendment that created new taxes. The sugar industry formed an organization it dubbed Citizens to Save Jobs and Stop Unfair Taxes, which paid for a pervasive advertising campaign, running television spots that drew condemnation from environmental groups and from the editorial pages of many of the state's newspapers for an array of distortions. The sugar industry ads implied that consumers would pay for the tax, going so far as to suggest the tax would cause food prices in Florida to rise, and raised the specter of a new, bloated bureaucracy squandering millions of dollars. When not calling the proposal a "food tax," the sugar ads called it a "property tax increase" that would be applied to homeowners. At one point, the industry charged that Paul Tudor Jones wanted to manipulate the worldwide price of sugar for financial gain. It became by far the most expensive ballot contest in state history, with the sugar industry investing $35 million. Environmental groups spent about $15 million in response—two-thirds of that total coming from Paul Tudor Jones' personal account—but it wasn't enough to counter Big Sugar's relentless advertising, and Amendment 4 went down to defeat, 54.4 percent to 45.6 percent. Voters did, however, approve the two other measures advocated by Save Our Everglades: the "polluter pays" amendment, which held agriculture primarily responsible for the cost of cleanup projects, and another that created the Everglades Trust Fund, a repository for private and public funds to be used by the South Florida Water Management District for conservation and combating water pollution in the Everglades. And voters also rejected the sugar-sponsored amendment that would have required two-thirds approval for new taxes.

The defeat of the sugar tax did not derail the quest of environmental groups for a true rescue of the River of Grass. The Everglades coalition worked to gain support for a plan that would split the costs between the state and federal governments, and it found allies in the Clinton administration, particularly Secretary of the Interior Bruce Babbitt. Mary Barley, Nathaniel Reed, Jimmy Buffett and Florida Audubon president Clay Henderson met with Bill Clinton, who announced his support for federal legislation to impose the sugar tax, but congressional leaders would not allow even a hearing on the issue. Congress did, however, set up a task force of federal and state agencies in 1996 and put the Corps of Engineers in charge of devising a long-term solution to the water-flow problems of South Florida — an assignment that made environmentalists nervous, given the Corps' history of catering to the wishes of industry. At the state level, a consortium created by Gov. Lawton Chiles in 1994, the Commission for a Sustainable South Florida, had been drawing up its own plans. The alliance of business leaders, sugar industry executives and environmentalists issued a report in 1996 that listed a series of steps needed for a true repair of the South Florida ecosystem. Following that general blueprint, the Corps in 1999 unveiled the Comprehensive Everglades Restoration Plan, a 3,500-page compromise of the conflicting goals of restoring natural water flow to the Everglades and ensuring adequate water supplies for agriculture and the 4.3 million residents along Florida's southeast coast. The plan, tying together 68 separate engineering projects covering almost 18,000 square miles, had an initial price tag of $7.8 billion and an expected duration of 38 years. It would eliminate 240 miles of canals and levees, restoring an estimated 70 percent of historic water flow through the Everglades, and create a system of marshes to filter pollutants out of the runoff from farms and sugarcane fields.

The Corps of Engineers' plan to capture about three-fifths of the water diverted to sea through canals depended in large part on speculative technology, an aspect of the project that particularly worried some environmentalists. One unproven aspect of the project involved "aquifer storage and recovery," a plan for pumping partially treated surface water 1,000 feet below ground to prevent evaporation. The blueprint called for the eventual construction of about 300 wells across Central and South Florida to receive up to 1.7 billion gallons of water a day. Environmental groups, particularly the Sierra Club, criticized the Aquifer Storage and Recovery project as unworkable and warned that it could contaminate the Floridan Aquifer, the massive underground reservoir that supplies drinking water for much of the state. On a more general level, many environmentalists complained that the Corps had geared its efforts more toward supplying water to agriculture and residential areas than healing the Everglades. Two earlier versions of Everglades bills that made it through the state legislature were so flawed that Chiles had vetoed them, with the approval of environmental groups. By 2000, though, most of the major conservation players—realizing the opportunity of securing a long-term commitment from the federal and state governments might not return soon—supported the latest Everglades bill in Tallahassee. Friends of the Everglades, the organization founded by Marjory Stoneman Douglas, loudly dissented from the other groups. Friends blasted the Corps of Engineers' Everglades plan as "a formula for failure," saying that it depended entirely on artificial processes and that it continued the fragmentation of the Everglades begun by the Corps half a century earlier. "A large percentage of the massive expenditures for the proposed system is dedicated to preserving the very industries that have been systematically poisoning and drying out the Everglades for the last 50 years, particularly agriculture in the Everglades Agricultural Area," Friends of the Everglades complained in early 2000.

While national environmental groups worked to gain a Congressional commitment to fund the plan, state alliances faced the equally challenging task of convincing the legislature to pledge $200 million annually for the first 10 years of the project. With Gov. Jeb Bush publicly endorsing the plan, lawmakers passed the Everglades Investment Act in May of 2000. Seven months later, lame-duck president Bill Clinton signed into law the Water Resources Development Act, completing the deal, with the funding dependent on the Congressional budget each year.

Even as they applauded the federal and state commitments to restoration of the Everglades, environmental groups remained unsatisfied with many of the details in the Comprehensive Everglades Restoration Plan.

"We support *an* Everglades restoration plan, but we believe this plan as written needs to be revised to allow for more natural restoration," the Sierra Club's Ullman said. "The key to restoring the Everglades is eliminating barriers, providing enough water for the Everglades, restoring the natural sheet flow and buying more land. That can be done as long as the agencies and politicians respond to the will of the vast majority of Floridians and not to special-interest groups who might have other goals."

In 2002, Florida Gov. Bush signed a law that solidified funding for the Everglades restoration by create a program of bonds to yield $100 million a year, with the money to be matched by federal contributions to the project. That positive step, however, was partly offset by a controversial provision attributed to Sen. Jim King that limited the rights of citizens to file lawsuits over proposed developments. Some environmental groups, particularly the Sierra Club, vehemently opposed the bill as written and urged the governor to veto it and force a rewrite without the offending provision, but Bush cited the support of Audubon of Florida, The Nature Conservancy and others in signing it.

When the details about Aquifer Storage and Recovery began to emerge in the following months, citizens and grassroots environmentalists grew alarmed at the prospect of injecting water into the Floridan Aquifer. The state's Department of Environmental Protection insisted that the water pumped underground would not taint the aquifer, despite the presence of bacteria and fecal coliform in the stored water. A pair of bills proposed in the 2001 legislative session to loosen the standards on underground water storage passed both houses but generated such grassroots opposition that the Senate sponsor withdrew his bill, and the state promised to conduct experiments before proceeding with the full plan. The dispute, which delayed the start of one aspect of the Everglades project and potentially added to its cost, showed how tenuous the entire plan could be.

10

"COULD WE HAVE DONE MORE?"

A century after Louis and Clara Dommerich hosted 13 neighbors in their Maitland home to establish the Florida Audubon Society, the state's environmental community includes dozens of entities, large and small. Audubon of Florida—which adopted a new name and moved its headquarters from Central Florida to downtown Miami in 1999—has an annual budget of about $5.5 million, a full-time, statewide staff of 50 people and a network of 44 chapters totaling 40,000 members and representing every corner of the state. The Florida chapter of the Sierra Club comprises 16 independent local groups with a collective 31,000 members. The entities operating under the general heading of environmentalism range from those and other professionally run statewide organizations pursuing broad agendas to others dedicated to particular issues—a diverse collection in itself that includes major, incorporated outfits like the Save the Manatee Club as well as the many "Friends of" coalitions that exist at the truly grassroots level. Despite the proliferation of forces in the campaign to save Florida's land, water and animals, however, it's debatable whether environmental groups collectively have much more clout than the lonely Florida Audubon Society held in the early years of the 20th century.

Even after more than a century of plunder, the mania for growth rules Florida.

"I'm concerned about a conservation ethic among the people in Florida," said Bob Bendick, former state director of The Nature Conservancy

169

of Florida. "You know, 80 percent of the people who live here were born somewhere else, and there's not yet the kind of attachment to the land in a specific way that there needs to be to protect it in the future. ... Ultimately we're not going to win the legislative battle unless there's a deeper commitment on the part of the voters to conservation in Florida. I don't think we in the environmental community have done as good a job at this as we could. People get very concerned after a disaster — well, all these potential environmental disasters are not repairable, so unless you get the commitment ahead of time and avert the disaster you're out of luck."

In trying to draw more people to their side, environmental groups face the challenge of making citizens aware of the urgent ecological threats facing Florida without coming across as so alarmist that they alienate their intended audience. Darden Rice, a longtime official with the Florida chapter of the Sierra Club, suggests that activists can best reach those with what she calls "absentee hearts" by making them more aware of the state's natural assets.

"We have to be (positive) because in order to have a blueprint for the future that inspires people it can't be all doom and gloom and cynicism," said Rice, who joined the Gulf Restoration Network in 2010. "I think as we continue to help people connect the dots that Florida is our home, that Florida is a beautiful place and we have a role to protect its beauty not just for our present use but for future generations' use, as people get more and more inspired by that sense of their role — and I see that happen more and more every day — I think that's the key to winning these victories and bringing more people on board and indeed having a Florida that 20 years from now is a nice place to live."

Nathaniel Reed, founder of 1000 Friends of Florida and a former government official in Tallahassee and Washington, concedes that Florida's conservation network — despite its important successes — has failed to tap its full potential. He said that environmental groups need to raise a collective $3 million to $5 million more each year in order to bolster their scientific staffs and revive their membership recruitment, and he considers the figure attainable through existing grants from foundations.

"Properly funded, I think we could be far more active in electing members of the legislature who are far more environmentally oriented," Reed said. "I see a great future in Florida as it occurred in California of waking the sleeping giant of the retirees to become far more environmentally oriented. … We're not going to win the Florida environmental battle without having a much more concerted effort by environmental groups pinpointing various decisions that local and state government makes that are in violation of good ecological principles. We've got to become more effective politically."

The environmental movement remains at its historical disadvantage in contending against the influence of those who profit from the never-ending deluge of neighborhoods, golf courses and shopping malls. At the state level, even the titans of conservation, Audubon of Florida and the Sierra Club, can afford to retain only a combined three or four full-time lobbyists in Tallahassee — compared to the armies representing business groups, home builders, real-estate interests, the agricultural industries and others whose goals generally conflict with those of environmentalists. At the local level, where campaign spending is an even greater determiner of success than in state and national races, county commissions tend to be dominated by businesspeople. (In Lake County, for example, a real-estate agent chaired the commission in 2002, making decisions on land use that would affect the value of properties under her control.)

David Gluckman, a longtime lobbyist who has worked for the Sierra Club, Save the Manatee Club and Florida Wildlife Federation, said, "There is no question we're playing more defense over the last 10 years as a result of two factors: the more conservative, business-oriented philosophy of elected officials and the large number of rapid successes of the '70s and '80s without a lot of hard science backup."

Charles Lee, who has lobbied in Tallahassee for Audubon of Florida since the early 1970s, agrees that victories have become harder to achieve for environmental groups. He cites as the overriding cause a change in the electoral dynamics of state politics. Campaigns have become vastly more expensive, while changes in campaign laws have limited the amount each contributor can give.

"People didn't run million-dollar campaigns for the Florida Senate (in the early 1970s), and now that's probably a minimum figure you need," Lee said. "Right now what happens is everybody's got to get that brief-case full of $500 checks. There's no choice. From the day you're elected until your next election, the thing that's on the front burner of your mind is getting those $500 checks. And you have to get them from everybody because they're cut up into little $500 increments, so you've got to basi-cally hang out the red light and solicit from everybody. ... So until some-thing dramatic is done about campaign financing, not just for the environment but for every public-interest issue, things are just going to get worse and worse because it has become just a complete money game and (politicians) have to grub money from everybody. And of course, the environmental groups don't have any money; we can't compete in that arena."

The situation makes Lee nostalgic for the days of less regulated cam-paigns. He cites the example of the late Warren Henderson, whom Lee calls the most reliable environmental advocate to hold office in the state legislature during the past 30 years. Henderson, he said, took large con-tributions from two industries to cover his campaign costs.

"He was absolutely beholden to the liquor guys and the pari-mutuel guys, but he was beholden to nobody else in the world," Lee said. "For every other issue he was a free agent, he could vote his conscience. ... It's impossible to find a Warren Henderson now."

But that doesn't mean environmental groups can't possibly contend against the well-financed lobbyists of business, agriculture and home builders. With their bulletins that go out to members, especially during the legislative session, the organizations have the potential to turn thou-sands of ordinary citizens into lobbyists. And the Sierra Club, which holds a different non-profit designation than Audubon of Florida and other organizations, faces no restrictions on endorsing candidates in elections.

"Politicians listen to two things — they listen to votes and they listen to money," Rice said. "And we're never going to have as much money as industry will, but we do have incredible sway and influence with the voters and we achieve that influence by getting out there and network-ing and educating and following up and getting people organized on these issues and voting. That's all that grassroots action and power is all about, and that's what our strength is. … Sierra Club is one of the few environmental groups in Florida that can actually turn out warm bodies to meetings across the state every single month, every week."

Despite the power imbalance between nonprofit environmental groups and billion-dollar industries, some lawmakers remain sympathetic to the common complaint from developers and builders that environmental groups have too much influence. That argument produced a provision included in the measure the state legislature passed during the second year of funding for the state's share of the Comprehensive Everglades Restoration Plan. Tacked onto the Everglades bill at the last moment, the provision amended the rules of the 1971 act that gave individual citizens the right to challenge proposed development on ecological grounds. The amendment, the handiwork of Sen. Jim King of Jacksonville, set other restrictions that precluded small, ad-hoc organizations from filing lawsuits. With its narrow definition of legal standing that required challengers to be incorporated in Florida, the bill took a direct swipe at the Sierra Club, a national organization with state and local chapters. Audubon of Florida, stressing the need to secure consistent funding for the Everglades repair, offered a public endorsement that made it easier for Gov. Jeb Bush to sign the bill—and that created a nasty rift between Audubon and other members of the Everglades Coalition, most conspicuously the Sierra Club. Whether or not the incident caused lasting dissension among traditional allies, it illustrated the lack of monolithic unity in the environmental movement, a spectrum that includes the pragmatism of Audubon of Florida and the less compromising approach of the Sierra Club and others.

Despite such disagreements, Reed said that Florida's environmental community has reached an unprecedented level of cooperation over the Everglades issue. The Everglades Coalition, an alliance of some 40 state and national organizations, holds weekly conference calls, and Reed said he has never before seen such a willingness of individual groups to cede their own turf for a collective pursuit. In a state with a myriad of environmental entities pursuing separate agendas, the Everglades Coalition could yield a more cohesive approach for other issues as well.

Rice hopes the tumult caused by the "anti-citizen" provision will actually lead to deeper collaboration among conservation groups. She suggests that the major environmental groups will put more emphasis on the summit meetings they hold before each legislative session in order to coordinate strategies — an echo of the unified lobbying efforts of the short-lived Conservation 70s alliance of three decades earlier.

"I think that everyone's going to take a big step back and look at what happened in the legislature and start to think forwardly and pull together as a coalition," Rice said, "because at the end of the day we realize environmentalists have to work together and not allow ourselves to get split by intelligent politicians, tricky politicians like Jim King. ... We're all nonprofit groups. We're all incredibly besieged sometimes, and there has to be a time when we don't just live in the present but we have to look to the future."

Mark Ferrulo, executive director of Progress Florida and previously the leader of Florida PIRG, agrees on the need for improved teamwork among the entities trying to save Florida's environment.

"I think speaking overall there's been a traditional schism between those groups who focus on pollution and human health-related environmental issues and those who focus on conservation and preservation of natural resources and lands," Ferrulo said. "I think we need to come together and both improve our communication and coordination with each other, but also we need to look for opportunities where both of those overlap. Currently we're being divided and conquered by our opposition more often than should be the case.

"I think over the next couple of years there's going to be a concerted effort by the groups to improve the working relationship and be more strategic in how we as leaders in the environmental community tackle various issues. It needs to happen. We can't continue down this path of each having blinders on when it comes to the other groups' priorities and issues. The biggest examples of victories are usually when we come together. It was all the groups that worked together to get Preservation 2000 up and running. It was all the groups presenting a united front against offshore drilling that helped us win. Unlike some other environmental issues, there weren't any groups that were split off by the opposition on those two huge environmental success stories."

Like Ferrulo's organization, the Legal Environmental Assistance Foundation (LEAF) concerns itself with public-health issues outside the purview of the state's largest conservation groups. LEAF founder Suzi Ruhl, now a legal advisor for the Environmental Protection Agency, said she hoped that in the future the mainstream environmental entities will broaden their concerns.

"What we're doing is documenting the need to address public health as part of environmental protection and recognize that you can't just focus on natural resources and critters," Ruhl said. "In Florida, the chips have fallen on the side of land protection at the expense of environmental protection, and that gives politicians the chance to hide behind what's seen as a green vote when in fact they're supporting policies that pull the plug on ecosystems. We shouldn't have to choose between land preservation and environmental protection, and I hope people will come to the point they won't accept that choice. I don't think we should have to trade off environmental protection or citizens' rights for land preservation."

Ruhl notes that in the case of opposition to the underground injection of surface water as part of the Everglades restoration plan, it was "the health card"—the specter of fecal coliform bacteria seeping into the aquifer—that stalled the legislature's attempts to weaken protections on drinking water. That example, she said, demonstrates that attention to the seemingly peripheral issues of public health and environmental justice can bolster the influence of conservation groups rather than dilute it.

It should be noted that disagreements—even public ones—among environmental groups are nothing new. The late Richard Coleman, a longtime activist and former state chairman of the Sierra Club, recalled the uncomfortable experience of attending legislative committee meetings in the early 1970s and seeing Johnny Jones of the Florida Wildlife Federation and Hal Scott of Florida Audubon argue about the merits of a bill. Such displays, pointing up the divisive issue of hunting among conservation groups, prompted Coleman to propose the first pre-legislative summit meetings.

"Most of the time I was organizing groups, the most common question was, 'Why don't you all get together and just have one giant group?' " Coleman said in 2002. "The same question is still asked today. ... There is actually a reason for this, though, that's really pretty good. In front of the legislators, having half a dozen voices for conservation representing various points of view most often is very valuable. If you go to a county meeting and there's one organization that is represented by one individual it's far less effective than if there are 15 organizations represented by 15 people."

The first conservation entity in Florida arose with a specific quest — to stave off the decimation of the state's wading birds. The Florida Audubon Society and its later allies largely succeeded in that mission. The passage of state and federal laws — as well as the transformation of public attitudes toward the wanton killing of wildlife — allowed most species to recover, if rarely to their original population levels. The snowy egret, for example, hunted to the verge of extinction by the early 20th century, rebounded in subsequent decades and now has a stable population in Florida, though it remains listed by the state as a "species of special concern." Despite the gains, however, more species in Florida are imperiled now than when the Florida Audubon Society sprang into existence. In the early years of the 21st century, it is not unchecked slaughter for commercial gain that threatens the state's animals but a combination of other forces, most prominent among them the dramatic decline in natural habitat — an indirect assault fueled just as surely by commercial factors. The state lists 40 species as endangered, with another 76 classified as either threatened or "of special concern." (The federal Fish and Wildlife Service's mostly overlapping catalog of endangered and threatened species in Florida comprises 54 types of animals.) The state and federal listings of species status — which also include more than 400 varieties of plants and trees — protect animals just as crucially as the Audubon wardens in their wooden boats did during the early 1900s, swaying decisions on everything from the timing of construction projects to the management of water levels in lakes and rivers.

Considering the impact of state and federal rulings on the imperiled status of animals, it's no surprise that the agencies involved have begun to feel the heavy hand of political pressure — most notably in the legislative backlash against Florida's conservation commission after it considered protections for the white ibis in the mid-1990s. Debates over the ecological status of certain Florida species seem likely to intensify in the coming years. The prospect of government agencies "delisting" animals — moving them off lists of endangered or threatened species — raises hackles among environmentalists. The plight of the West Indian manatee in particular fuels an ongoing and rancorous argument between environmentalists and boaters groups, with the latter insisting that the species' population has increased to the point that aggressive protections are no longer needed. In the absence of scientifically sound population estimates, the debate shows no signs of diminishing. Activists paid close attention in the early 2000s as federal and state agencies revised the status of some species. In 2003, the Florida Fish and Wildlife Conservation Commission changed the red-cockaded woodpecker from "threatened" to "species of special concern," and in 2008 the state commission — following the example of the Fish and Wildlife Service a year earlier — declared the bald eagle no longer imperiled in Florida.

"For the future it will be important not only to see what that listing category turns out to be (for each species) but what the management plan is and also how other entities besides the commission itself view this down-listing," said Laurie Macdonald, Florida program director of Defenders of Wildlife. "Let's say it's the Forest Service or a local government making a land-use decision; if they see the state wildlife commission is down-listing a species, well, doesn't that indicate it must be doing very well and they don't have to be as careful about the protections they would afford it? Doesn't it mean perhaps that not as many resources would go toward its protection? [Listings affect] funding allocations and where resources are put toward research. For the red-cockaded woodpecker, the strides that have been made in recovering the population are due to intensive management efforts, and so if those efforts were diminished the progress might not continue."

Macdonald also worries that the modest recoveries of some species in certain parts of the state might create a dangerous complacency among the public about other animals. And as human populations continue to encroach into the historic range of imperiled species, the sympathy of people for animals will be tested. Macdonald notes that in some areas black bears acquire nuisance status—and become subject to possible euthanasia—because of the actions of people who feed them. She also cites the case of an experiment in which Texas cougars were released in North Florida and tracked in order to test the feasibility of returning the Florida panther to its former habitat. In biological terms, the experiment succeeded—it proved that the area could sustain Florida panthers. But many local residents complained about the prospect of having the big cats around, fearing they might kill livestock or even attack children. The program was delayed, although Macdonald hopes the U.S. Fish and Wildlife Service will eventually proceed with it.

"It's going to take a huge amount of work in educating the public and creating public support or at least acceptance," Macdonald said. "The acceptance and tolerance of some people for these animals is very low. They're afraid of them or they feel their property is threatened by them. It has already become an important matter for biologists and conservationists to realize that public outreach is a major, major part of species recovery, and a growing part of it."

On the day the Dommerichs welcomed their fellow bird lovers into their home (a home that disappeared 50 years ago to make way for a subdivision), Florida contained only 528,000 residents. A century later, twice that number lived in Palm Beach County alone, and the state's population had swelled to 18.5 million—increasing by 23.5 percent during the 1990s before the collapse of the housing market ended the trend, at least temporarily. The relentless demand for new houses, combined with the decline of citrus growing and other forms of agriculture, fuels the rapid disappearance of green space in even traditionally rural counties. At the growth rate that preceded the housing crash—a net gain of about 900 people per day—Florida's population will swell to 32 million (plus 1 million winter residents) by the year 2050. In the early 1990s, the Southwest Florida Regional Planning Council conducted an analysis of municipal comprehensive plans from all over the state and determined that under existing growth guidelines, the state's population could reach 100 million people. Around the same time, Defenders of Wildlife predicted that at the current rate of natural habitat loss in Florida—about

860 acres a day — development would cover the entire state within 70 years.

Macdonald, noting that environmental groups sometimes produce maps illustrating how Florida will look in the future if state leaders commit to conservation goals, wonders why the forces of development don't offer Floridians a glimpse of the inevitable outcome of continuing unchecked growth.

"Why don't we see what their vision is?" Macdonald asks. "If it's appropriate for the economic and ecological health of Florida, why aren't they willing to show it? … One of the biggest problems is that in our planning and in our regulatory schemes we don't look at cumulative impact. I truly believe that if people would really think about what is best for the community as a whole, we could have ecological and economic prosperity, but instead we're in this third-world mode — come in and exploit the resources, take away what you can."

The growth patterns add urgency to the state's land-acquisition programs, but those programs have been squeezed in recent years by another trend: the tendency of lawmakers to draw upon land funds for unrelated uses. In consecutive sessions in the early 21st century, the legislature diverted money from the Florida Forever account to cover other budget expenses — despite cries of protest from environmental groups, who successfully pressed Gov. Jeb Bush to veto a transfer of $100 million from a land-acquisition fund to the general budget in 2002.

"What worries me is that there does not seem to be the genuine regard [in the legislature] for conservation that's required to save Florida's environment," said Bendick, now TNC's director of government relations. "I'm fearful to see what [lawmakers] are going to do next year and the year after because there doesn't seem to be a kind of commitment that's necessary. The history of Florida Forever and Preservation 2000 are very proud ones. The past legislators and governors should be proud of what they've done, but [2001 and 2002] have really cast a shadow over that and over the future."

Reed takes a more optimistic view. He hopes the legislative raids on money earmarked by voters for land conservation will create a backlash.

"I think you'll see really a concerted effort by environmental organizations to pass a constitutional amendment forbidding the legislature to put their hands on that money," Reed said.

Though environmentalists hoped that the growth-management laws of the 1980s would slow the incursion of development into rural areas, a lack of enforcement has largely undermined the regulations. At the same time, local governments and state agencies continue to approve new roads that open up previously remote areas to development, such as the Suncoast Parkway through Pasco and Hernando counties, the source of bitter contention by the Sierra Club and others. The state's environmental groups unsuccessfully opposed legislation in 2002 that gave the Florida Turnpike Enterprise and the Orlando Expressway Authority greater freedom to pursue road-building projects with questionable economic prospects. The changes mean that conservation groups are likely to spend more time fighting road extensions—dubbed "sprawlways"—that threaten to create corridors of development in the state's remaining pastoral sections.

The combination of lenient growth-management policies and increasingly powerful transportation entities does not bode well for wooded areas in the state's interior. For that reason, Audubon's Lee said the only reliable buffer against growth in coming decades will be land acquisition—whether public, private or a combination.

"I think a lot of environmental advocates pull the wool over their own eyes by relying too much on regulation, which only gives you the right to fight another day," Lee said. "The only way to really win is to build a constituency of support to save a particular place. That can either be completely buying it to make it a state park or something like that, or it could be buying it in the sense of buying a conservation easement or development rights."

Reed, who formed 1000 Friends of Florida in 1986 as a "watchdog" organization after the passage of growth-management laws, refuses to dismiss regulation as a useless tool in slowing development.

"You can say you're very disappointed the [legislation] has not been more forcefully augmented and overseen by Tallahassee," Reed said. "But turn the coin around and look at it without the Comprehensive Planning Act. You could have at 11 o'clock at night given a planning change anywhere in your city or county without public notice, which is what went on in Florida for 75 years. The chaos would be complete rather than semi-complete. ... At least we know where the urban boundaries are. At least we can fight over the boundaries, we can talk about infill, we can talk about cohesive development. God help us if we hadn't had the act."

Still, Reed agrees that the best way to protect land is to buy it, and that, of course, is the mission of The Nature Conservancy, which has played a role in the preservation of approximately 1 million acres in Florida since 1961. Bendick said his organization will continue to work toward saving crucial green areas from development—whether through outright purchase, through the buying of development or mining rights or through working as a scout for purchases by the state. As more large landowners continue to abandon ranching and agriculture, The Nature Conservancy faces both an opportunity and a challenge from developers eager to buy up the properties. The organization has forged a strategy for the early 21st century that involves preserving green corridors in certain parts of the state: the area from Big Cypress National Preserve through the Kissimmee Valley, a region that includes the scrub land of the Lake Wales Ridge; the swath running north from Orlando through the Ocala National Forest all the way to the Okefenokee Swamp in Georgia; and two major areas in the Panhandle, the Apalachicola River drainage basin and the forests surrounding Eglin Air Force Base north into Alabama. The Nature Conservancy has expanded its scope in recent years, working to protect marine habitats in the Keys and the Indian River Lagoon, but it regards land conservation in the state's interior as its most urgent priority, and in 2002 the group unveiled ambitious plans to protect the Kissimmee River valley by restoring 337,000 acres of wetlands and by leading the purchase of conservation easements on another 300,000 acres of farmland.

"We're looking at trying to create large, connected systems of open space that can withstand the test of time," Bendick said. "All this land to create this green framework does not have to be publicly owned, and having some of it in agriculture and forestry is a really good idea for a lot of reasons. Having more of a partnership between conservation and agriculture as opposed to an adversarial relationship could do a lot for Florida's future. ... We're viewing the area from Orlando to the Everglades as kind of a Central Park for the Florida peninsula; development would be around the edges but there would be a core of open land and agricultural protected areas — parks, restored wetlands — in the center of the state that would serve lots of functions, not least of which is to store water and provide water."

Water is the subject that seems likely to occupy Florida environmentalists more than any other during the 21st century. As early as the 1920s, St. Petersburg began losing the use of its well fields because of saltwater intrusion, and the city eventually had to begin importing water from rural sections of Hillsborough and Pasco counties — leading to legal disputes as populations in those counties grew. As the 21st century began, the Tampa Bay area offered an indication of Florida's future, with the much-delayed completion of a $150-million desalination plant.

Though the Tampa area for decades has had the most severe problems, water shortages — both immediate and potential — loom throughout the state. Water managers estimated that the water table in Central Florida dropped 10 to 15 feet from 1950 to 2000 and predicted a similar decline by 2020 if consumption trends continue. Lakes and private wells in some parts of the state went dry during the late 1990s, and some residents became accustomed to anemic water pressure in their faucets. Though there was disagreement about how much of the problem traces to a prolonged drought that began in 1998, water managers and environmentalists agree that the continued rise in water consumption will create more frequent shortages in the future. The St. Johns River Water Management District issued an alarming prediction that by 2006 some parts of its jurisdiction would begin running out of water — a claim environmentalists seized as evidence that water districts should cut back on their approval of permits for golf courses and subdivisions that use vast supplies of water. In a reprise of the "water wars" between Pinellas and Pasco counties in the 1950s, regional conflicts over water supplies have begun to take shape, with local residents challenging water district permits to large-scale developments and agricultural giants.

David Guest, lead attorney for Tallahassee-based Earthjustice, expects to see a sad replication in Florida of the regional conflicts over water supplies that have long plagued California. He predicts that large cities will follow the lead of St. Petersburg—longtime owner of Silver Springs—and attempt to purchase far-flung natural springs, eventually creating networks of water pipelines. And as the cost of desalination plants continue to decrease, Guest expects the facilities to become common along the state's coastline.

Of course, Guest notes that such drastic measures could be avoided. He points out that the average Floridian uses about three times as much water per day as the average Californian.

"By far the cheapest source of new water you can get is conservation, and in Florida we just do not do that," Guest said. "The cost here is about half of California's, and our rate structure encourages wastage. You could triple the population without requiring any additional water if we got down to California's consumption rates."

During the persistent drought of recent years, many areas of the state have faced notable declines in the water table that prompted water districts to impose restrictions on water use—generally in the form of schedules for watering lawns. Despite the ease of checking usage levels simply by reading meters, Guest said water districts remain hesitant to punish violators. And meanwhile many of the state's largest consumers of water—farms, industry and golf courses—proceed essentially on the honor system, with water districts trusting them not to exceed their permitted monthly withdrawals.

"There was a major water shortage in South Florida [in 2001], and conservation played very little role in [addressing] it," Guest said. "There were lawn-sprinkling reduction rules, and there was no enforcement. There was a study that found only 10 percent were complying with the rules. … In the water-supply world, there's a culture that complying with water rules is unnecessary—the water districts know it and the consumers know it. Water conservation here is just a publicity ploy. The water districts see the report that there's only 10-percent compliance and they say, 'Well, we did what we could.' That's the problem—we don't have leadership."

The one thing that gets the attention of state agencies, Guest said, is the threat of a lawsuit. And he promises that in the future when water-management districts fail to enforce their own conservation rules, "We're going to be suing all over every which way from Sunday."

The threat of water shortages is likely to reach a level of urgency that even politicians can't ignore as the public becomes more informed about the need to preserve water-recharge areas, which have been paved over at alarming rates. While environmentalists have had little success in seeking policies that would tie development to existing classroom space or other factors, declining water supplies might finally spur more vigorous enforcement of the state's growth-management laws—or at least focus renewed attention on the costs of relentless development.

"There's, what, 500 people coming to Florida every day and nobody's bringing water with them," Rice said. "Taxpayers are paying for the desalination plants, and we pay for the cleanup and the environmental degradation that happens ... but the developers need to be funding part of this, too, because the more desalination plants we build the more we're enabling developers to build homes to bring more people to Florida. Developers are making all the money and pushing off the infrastructure costs on taxpayers, and it's not a sustainable plan whatsoever."

The looming water crisis calls new attention to the network of canals and water-control structures built by the U.S. Army Corps of Engineers in Central and South Florida from 1948 to 1971, a system that squanders billions of gallons of fresh water every day by diverting it to the ocean and the Gulf of Mexico. Despite the seemingly obvious intent of its name, the Comprehensive Everglades Restoration Plan above all represents an attempt to guarantee adequate water supplies for the competing needs of South Florida—agriculture, residential use and the ecosystem—by retaining about three-fifths of the water now funneled to sea. If the concept of aquifer storage and recovery (ASR) proves feasible, the state will save much of that water by storing billions of gallons in 330 wells scattered across South and Central Florida. If the unproven technique fails—and if the Corps cannot come up with an adequate alternative—the repair of the Everglades could crumble under the weight of competition for South Florida's finite water supply.

Audubon of Florida's Lee said his organization has been skeptical all along about the underground water storage plan, which arose from concerns about the amount of public land needed for surface storage. Lee notes that the Everglades repair measure passed by Congress includes a commitment to "adaptive management changes," meaning that if the ASR concept doesn't work out, the Corps of Engineers must come up with another way to store the water.

"ASR has a lot of challenges—very high cost of operation, very problematic on its ability to work on a large-scale basis, " Lee said. "What we think is likely to happen is that the pilot projects will show that its potential is less than the Corps thought it was. If that's the case we need to have a backup plan in place, and that's what we've been hammering at the water district and the Corps lately, to develop a backup plan."

The Legal Environmental Assistance Foundation, meanwhile, isn't waiting for the Corps to produce an alternative method of storing water. LEAF, a small organization with limited resources, plans to continue a three-pronged approach against the aquifer storage and recovery plan— filing challenges to selected permits, educating the public about threats to the water supply and lobbying in the legislature for tougher protections of Florida's water. Though a settlement of an earlier lawsuit involving deeper, municipal-injection wells makes it difficult for LEAF to challenge the entire system of aquifer storage and recovery, the firm doesn't rule out another suit as it accumulates evidence of ASR's dangers. The irony, though, is that if LEAF persuaded a judge to take away oversight of the program from the state agency, supervision of the wells would revert to the federal Environmental Protection Agency, which already has given its blessing to aquifer storage and recovery.

"Our belief fundamentally is that the Everglades [plan] is not about restoring the Everglades but about assuring a drinking water supply for the growth in that area—that it's actually a public-water supply plan, which is inconsistent with the whole purpose behind Everglades restoration," Ruhl said. "We've been very much concerned about the plan and have had no confidence in its objective of restoring the Everglades. The other major concern—our whole role in the Everglades process— has been in looking at the impact of all of this activity on the people in the Glades, and they've been virtually ignored in the entire process, the low-income people of color living around Lake Okeechobee, in Pahokee, Belle Glade and South Bay. That's what drew us into the whole Everglades battle. It's been borderline criminally negligent the way they've been treated."

Jonathan Ullman, Everglades Representative for the Sierra Club's Florida chapter, also expresses deep skepticism about the Comprehensive Everglades Restoration Plan. He hopes that mandated quarterly reviews of restoration efforts by an independent committee of the National Academy of Sciences will provide empirical proof that underground water storage and other elements of the Army Corps of Engineers' plan are inadequate, thus forcing alternative approaches. Ullman said the Sierra Club will continue to press the Corps of Engineers and, when necessary, Congress and the state legislature, for adjustments to the massive project. In particular, the Sierra Club wants lawmakers to approve funding for the "Everglades Skyway," an 11-mile elevated section of Tamiami Trail where it crosses the Shark River Slough in the northern section of the national park. The bridge would allow a crucial flow into the Everglades of natural water currents that became blocked when the road was completed in 1930. Sierra also urges planners to concentrate more on keeping pollutants from reaching the ecosystem in the first place, rather than relying on chemical treatment or other methods of removing them from water flowing into Everglades National Park, and to concentrate more on land acquisition, particularly in the Everglades Agricultural Area.

Perhaps Ullman's greatest concern, however, is the lack of coordination among the many governments and agencies whose decisions have an impact on the Everglades ecosystem.

"The protections need to be written into law," Ullman said. "We have to understand that the federal and state protection of the Everglades can only occur with the right decisions at the local level. If South Florida's counties are going to continue to rezone wetlands areas [for development], then we are headed down a very, very bad path. The culture of sprawl development ruling South Florida has to end. They're spending money on restoration, and meanwhile important pieces of property are being permitted away. … I would suggest that the companies that own that land [in the agricultural area] consider the national priority — which is to restore the Everglades — and not develop that land. If the headwaters of the Everglades are developed, it can't be restored."

The Everglades plan, an amalgam of 68 separate engineering projects, attempts to address the competing needs of human water demands, flood protection and ecological repair. Administered by the U.S. Army Corps of Engineers, whose management of water flows in South Florida during the past half-century created many of the problems now plaguing the Everglades, the complicated project will draw nervous attention from environmental groups.

"It will depend very much on governors of Florida to make sure the plan stays on track and the Congress funding its share," Reed said. "It will depend on the Corps of Engineers actually being in the restoration business rather than the [business of] drainage and more water for cities and more water for new development and more water for agriculture. Some of us are getting very, very alarmed at the present Corps plans because we don't see enough restoration. That will be a cause for oversight by the Congress at various times in the future, I guarantee you that."

Many activists go further than Reed, disowning the CERP as a sham intended to guarantee water for the continued growth of South Florida rather than as a true Everglades repair. With reports suggesting that the project's uncertain environmental benefits won't materialize until the later years of the 38-year plan, well after the water demands of agriculture and development have been satisfied, some activists began predicting that Congress will pull the plug partway through the project — a disastrous possibility.

"It's a bogus water-supply project," Barbara Lange, co-chair on Everglades issues for the Sierra Club, told a reporter in 2002. "It's about time we all admitted it."

"I'm getting angrier by the day," added Shannon Estenoz, then the Everglades coordinator for the World Wildlife Fund and co-chair of the Everglades Coalition. "I'm starting to think we were suckers for supporting this."

Reed and others anticipate ongoing clashes over the allocation of water in South Florida, with the sugar industry, other agricultural interests and developers continually seeking a greater share at the expense of the Everglades ecosystem itself. As water becomes an increasingly valuable commodity statewide, fights over its use seem inevitable. For years, some cities have allowed private companies to tap springs for commercial use, often at virtually no charge to the bottler. Environmental groups have begun challenging applications for new commercial water wells, charging that the practice amounts to a gift of public resources to private companies. In 2001, word arose of Azurix Corporation's offer to finance part of the Everglades restoration in exchange for the right to sell part of the state's water supply. The scheme fell apart, largely because Azurix's parent company, Enron Corporation, collapsed into bankruptcy. But the fact that state officials — including the head of the Department of Environmental Protection — seemed initially receptive to the idea caused alarm in the conservation community.

Amid the rising concerns over the quantity of water supplies in Florida, environmental groups hope to direct equal attention to the matter of water quality. Florida PIRG, freed from one of its major preoccupations when President George W. Bush contradicted his own energy policy by agreeing to buy up oil leases in and around Florida, has given heightened emphasis to its role as a "watchdog" over the protection of Florida's water bodies by state and federal agencies. The group will continue to press the state's Department of Environmental Protection to fix loopholes in its "Total Maximum Daily Load" (TMDL) program, which sets levels of allowable pollution of rivers and lakes, and to broaden the state's definition of impaired waters — those subject to protection against further pollution. Environmental groups hope the TMDL program, developed in the first years of the 21st century, will bring new scrutiny to the problem of cumulative water pollution from individually small sources — in theory a new mechanism for growth management as the state considers the effects of runoff from proposed roads, housing developments and shopping malls on already-degraded rivers and lakes.

Earthjustice also lists water quality as its primary concern. Guest believes that the TMDL program will force overdue changes in the way developers deal with the problem of runoff, which carries pollutants into surface water supplies. He said existing subdivisions will have to "retrofit" some sewers and retention ponds in order to meet TMDL guidelines, a potentially costly process that will prompt builders of new neighborhoods and shopping centers to use methods that inhibit runoff. For example, he said the conventional asphalt parking lot—which deflects water—will give way to permeable surfaces that allow water to filter through the ground on its way to the aquifer. Such an experimental parking lot at the Florida Aquarium in Tampa, Guest said, absorbs water at almost the same rate as a natural forest would.

"The cost of doing the stuff you need to do to really prevent urban pollution of waters, if you do it at the time of development, is not very high," Guest said. "The expense comes if you're retrofitting. When [builders] recognize how much trouble it's going to be to do that—and it's going to be a lot of trouble—it's quite clear that new developments will be done quite differently, not really much more expensively, but differently."

Environmental activists often engage in projections about Florida's future—whether issuing dire warnings of the state's inevitable decline if unwise policies continue or offering visions of the state they hope will exist. But what do they really expect Florida to look like in the coming decades?

Gluckman foresees dramatic population growth in the Panhandle as The St. Joe Company—the state's largest private landowner—continues its recent steps toward selling off or developing some of its timber forests. He predicts the area will replace the Carolinas as the nation's leading retirement destination.

Elsewhere, Gluckman said, "We will lose more wetlands and beaches, increase the number of trees as planted vegetation comes of age in urban areas, have dirtier water because we won't spend the money to solve urban runoff, fewer fish and wildlife. I'm not very optimistic."

Another environmentalist who cannot muster much cheer about the state's future is Bill Partington, the former executive with Florida Audubon and Florida Defenders of the Environment. Partington, who moved to Winter Park in 1967, is saddened by the incremental sprawl that has engulfed Central Florida.

"I guess we all anticipated it, but nobody could visualize it until it was here," Partington said. "The state has lost its identification; you don't know what state you're in—it could be anywhere."

As an example of the state's failed growth management, Partington cites nearby Oviedo, a town whose population increased 136 percent during the 1990s.

"I really think we've lost," Partington said of the environmental movement's efforts. "But people are still going to keep trying to save what's left or trying to restore areas."

Macdonald, citing an innate tendency toward hopefulness, is one of those who plan to continue the campaign to preserve natural Florida. Though she sees evidence of progress—the reintroduction of whooping cranes in Central Florida, for example—she can't help feeling discouraged as she tries to envision the state a few decades hence.

"In another 50 or 100 years, how will we even recognize this place?" Macdonald said. "I think that we have just got to work as hard as we can right now and try to secure as much funding and policy support as possible for protection of what's left and for restoration, where possible. I have this hope that within another generation or so, there will be enough understanding of the ecological processes because of environmental education and public education, and enough recognition of the value and the necessity of natural resources for our own lives, that there will be a change in attitude and a change in action among people.

"You know how it is—the more rare something becomes, the more we value it. And I think the beauty of so many places of Florida is being lost and the important functioning [of ecosystems] for our health is being lost, and as these things become more rare then we will motivate ourselves to devote the resources needed to protect them and save them. It's an interesting question—are we going to have just a slow decline in health that will finally bring us to our senses, or will there be a sudden crash of water resources or something that will bring us to our senses?"

Bendick said Florida is on the precipice of either an ecological turnaround or a descent into catastrophe, and he finds it difficult to guess which outcome is more likely. The head of The Nature Conservancy of Florida uses the metaphor of a building to describe the state's natural systems, with the large, connected green areas serving as the foundation and girders that support not only plants and animals but also sustainable human life. Florida's structural integrity, he said, relies on declaring certain parts of the state off limits to development.

"If you think of Florida's future ... really needing a green framework to support that future, to provide habitat and clean water and recreation and attractiveness for tourism and flood protection, that green structure is essential for providing all kinds of services to Florida's plants and animals and people," Bendick said. "In the debate over growth management, we suggested that we really needed to identify those places that ought to stay rural and then marshal the money and the other things needed to have that happen. That is not happening right now. ... If growth compromises enough of these structural elements of Florida's natural systems, then the building falls down.

"I think more than probably any state in the country, the condition of Florida's natural systems hangs in the balance, and it all revolves around whether we're going to reach a critical mass to sustain these connected natural systems ... or whether they're going to be so fragmented that it all falls apart. We're struggling to have the right thing happen right now, and the next 10 or 15 years will tell. I think about a quarter or so of Florida is protected in some way today. If we could get to about a third, and it was the right third, then I think those natural systems can survive. If not, they may not survive. The jury is still out."

Reed, who makes his home on a barrier island in Southeast Florida, notes that natural forces might have a major impact on the future of Florida's development patterns. Florida hasn't experienced a comparably damaging weather event since Hurricane Andrew in 1992. Reed predicted that a cycle of hurricanes in consecutive years—or even a single devastating hurricane—would slow the tide that at its peak brought nearly 1,000 new residents into the state each day.

"That would call into question the acceleration of growth we're going through right now," Reed said. "It did in 1928-'29. Everybody thinks [Florida's economy] crashed because of the overselling of the real-estate market—it was the great hurricane of 1928 that crashed Florida."

Even without catastrophic weather, Reed thinks the westward expansion of cities along Florida's eastern coast will slow as the effects of excessive building in flood-prone areas become apparent. He also predicts that the inevitable end of the Castro regime in Cuba will alter the global balance of sugar production, diminishing the political power of Florida's sugar industry and opening up thousands of acres of the Everglades Agricultural Area for restoration.

"It's hard to predict anything in Florida because just when things seem darkest something good can happen," said the Sierra Club's Ullman, who grew up in South Florida and remembers the dramatic reversal of the proposed Big Cypress jetport. "I prefer to be an optimist, but [success] only happens through vigilance and because people understand that in order to live in South Florida, we have to keep the Everglades alive. A lot of people don't understand that."

Audubon's Lee manages to be sanguine enough that he plans to continue working on behalf of Florida's environment during the coming years. But he has no illusions about the condition of his native state as the 21st century unfolds.

"I think [optimism] depends on what your goals are," Lee said. "I think if we keep fighting we'll achieve a lot more than if we don't keep fighting. Nothing is ever going to be perfect in terms of the outcome of legislation, but we will attain a lot of goals. We'll also see Florida continue to be paved over. The question is whether we can attain goals fast enough to save places from being paved over."

Facing the unending drive for development on one side and the perplexing apathy of many Florida residents on the other, environmentalists persevere in what can sometimes seem an almost hopeless undertaking.

"One of the good and bad things about working in conservation in Florida is if we're successful we would have saved something with incomparable natural value to the state," said Bendick of The Nature Conservancy. "I don't think there's any question that without the environmental community Florida's natural systems would not survive. On the other hand, we may still fail and then we'll face the concern of, 'Could we have done more? Could we have done something else to succeed?' So we're on the edge now; we don't know which way it's going to go. But without conservationists and environmentalists, it certainly would not get there."

The National Parks and Conservation Association presented their First Citizen Conservation Award to Marjory Stoneman Douglas in 1985. State Library and Archives of Florida.

11

Heroes of conservation

There is no possible accounting of the number of people who have contributed to the protection of Florida's environment—the defense of Eden. For every prominent activist involved in a newsworthy issue, many unheralded citizens work in their own ways on behalf of the state's land and animals—calling or writing to legislators, appearing at county commission meetings or water-district hearings, attending meetings of the local chapter of the Sierra Club or Audubon of Florida. Nearly every major ecological victory of the past century has resulted not from the persuasiveness of a single activist, or even a handful of them, but from the perceived tipping point of public sentiment that even politicians could not ignore.

Of course, it often takes the leadership of individual activists to create the momentum that can yield changes in public opinion, whether on the wearing of "aigrettes," the designation of a vast swamp as a national park or the changing of a sublime river into a sterile canal. In its relatively short history, the ecology movement in Florida has produced its share of such leaders, people with the perceptiveness and passion to realize what was at stake and to become effective advocates for saving the state's natural resources. The following listing, though by no means complete, includes those without whom Florida today would be a much different place. These are some of the most prominent defenders of Eden.

MARJORIE HARRIS CARR (1915-1997)

It is no great exaggeration to call Marjorie Harris Carr the founder of the modern environmental movement in Florida. Along with David Anthony, her co-chairman on the conservation committee of the Alachua Audubon Society, Carr led a relentless, nine-year campaign against the Cross-Florida Barge Canal that overturned the monolithic support of the state's politicians, business leaders and newspapers. In the process, Carr and her allies created a template for activists based on scientifically valid arguments, adroit appeals to the media, a willingness to use the courts and, above all, tremendous persistence.

Born in Boston, Marjorie Harris arrived in Southwest Florida with her family while in grammar school and grew up in Bonita Springs, then a thoroughly rural area. She spent her childhood in the woods and canoeing on the Imperial River, her outlook shaped both by her parents, whom she later described as naturalists, and by the devastating effects of unchecked hunting by "sportsmen" in the area. As a student at Florida State College for Women (now Florida State University), she spent two summers teaching a field course in natural history back in Lee County as part of a New Deal program. Upon getting a degree in zoology, she landed a summer job as a wildlife technician for the federal government—the first woman to hold such a position—conducting studies at Welaka, near the confluence of the St. Johns and Ocklawaha rivers. While pursuing her master's degree at the University of Florida, she met and after two dates married Archie Carr, a zoology professor at the school and an elegant writer who would go on to publish 11 books. Pregnancy prevented Marjorie from pursuing a doctorate, and she became an extremely well-educated housewife, spending several years in Central America as Archie conducted groundbreaking research on sea turtles. The Carrs returned to Florida in 1950, living on a wooded property with a pond near the town of Micanopy. Marjorie raised five children and spent several years teaching biology at Gainesville High School.

Carr's fondness for nature led to her membership in the Alachua Audubon Society and the Garden Club of Gainesville. With the latter group, she helped create Paynes Prairie Wildlife Refuge, a modest park along Highway 441 that swelled into a 21,000-acre state preserve covering an area where William Bartram camped during his famed trip through Florida. Carr also played a role in restoring the health of Lake Alice on the University of Florida campus, and she started Alachua Audubon's Junior Naturalists program, which provided environmental expertise for the local school system. She became president of Alachua Audubon and co-chair of the conservation committee at a time when Audubon chapters rarely waded into contentious issues, and when in 1962 Carr and Anthony first heard about plans for the Cross Florida Barge Canal their reaction was confusion rather than opposition. Setting out to find answers about the proposed canal's effect on the primordially beautiful Ocklawaha River, Carr came to twin realizations: The U.S. Army Corps of Engineers' design would mutilate the river, and government leaders did not want the public to understand the details of its plan. While motivated in part by anger and working diligently in a letter-writing campaign, Carr remained publicly humble toward the authorities. "We conservationists don't give a hoot about the canal, either way," Carr said in 1966. "We are just pro-Ocklawaha." She told another reporter at the time, "I dislike fights very much. I loathe controversy and much prefer to be constructive. ... Sometimes being constructive leads to controversy."

Reserved by nature, Carr at first played a supporting role in public, letting others step to the microphone at public hearings in Tallahassee. Eventually, though, she accepted the public demands of her position as a leader of the opposition to the canal. Carr's effectiveness in fighting the project—first with Alachua Audubon and later with the Florida Defenders of the Environment—traced to her combination of scientific knowledge with a direct but diplomatic manner. The late Anthony recalled that one state cabinet member was so afraid of Carr that he would find an excuse to leave the room whenever he saw her arrive for a hearing.

"She could call up senators and representatives and cabinet members and twist their arms," Anthony said. "She was not at all bashful; she didn't care if you were the governor or not. ... She was a fierce adversary. Marjorie would get up [at public meetings] and say, 'Well, I'm just a poor Micanopy housewife ...' She was a master of sort of deprecating herself and then with this blast of utter logic destroying someone."

Carr later summed up her motivation in maintaining the long and time-consuming campaign against the barge canal.

"Why fight for the Ocklawaha?" she once said. "The first time I went up the Ocklawaha, I thought it was dreamlike. It was a canopy river. It was spring-fed and swift. I was concerned about the environment worldwide. What could I do about the African plains? What could I do about India? How could I affect things in Alaska or the Grand Canyon? But here, by God, was a piece of Florida. A lovely natural area, right in my back yard, that was being threatened for no good reason."

Despite all their logic and determination, Carr and her allies faced years of disappointment before the momentum turned their way. Anthony said Carr refused to let those around her consider giving up.

"She was the one who bucked us up psychologically," Anthony said. "She'd say, 'You know, the truth will out.' She was a very good motivator. Marjorie Carr made twisting your arm to do things for the cause into an art form."

Another UF professor and FDE member, Alyson Flournoy, told a reporter, "She could inspire [volunteers] to use their potential. It was very subtle, she just had a knack of knowing where people's abilities were. It was a tremendous skill to bring to grassroots environmental action."

The combination of a judge's injunction and an executive order by President Richard Nixon in 1971 stopped construction of the canal—but not before three dams had been built, including one that transformed the river and its surrounding forest into a vast, shallow pool. The object of the struggle changed from stopping a federal project to undoing its effects, which proved to be an even greater challenge. Carr's determination ran up against the influence and intransigence of a few state lawmakers who year after year blocked legislation to remove Rodman Dam and free the lower stretch of the river. But the Florida Defenders branched into other areas under Carr's leadership. During the 1980s, it spawned a separate group in Tallahassee devoted to general environmental activism and sponsored conferences on diverse subjects. Even in her late seventies, Carr co-authored a report on ways to restore the Ocklawaha River. During nearly 30 years as FDE's leader, Carr remained confident that the group's science-based arguments would eventually win out, yet as her health began to fail in the 1990s she endured the disappointment of the dam's continuing presence.

Despite her famous victory in 1971, Carr saw much to lament in Florida. Late in her life, she summed up the challenge of being an environmentalist in the state.

"Right now, we are being overwhelmed with people coming down who have no sense of stewardship of Florida," she told a reporter. "Their sense of place, their sense of stewardship, is tied to Ohio or some other place."

In 1996, Gov. Lawton Chiles presided over Carr's induction into the Florida Women's Hall of Fame. She died the following year at the age of 82, drawing encomiums from environmentalists and government officials across the state.

"No other person influenced the development of the environmental ethic in Florida more than Marjorie Harris Carr," said Charles Lee of Florida Audubon.

"People talk about her defeating the barge canal as her greatest legacy, but I think the really lasting thing she did in Florida was she taught people all over the state how to get involved in conservation," said David Godfrey of the Caribbean Conservation Corporation. "She trained an army."

A year after Carr's death, the legislature dedicated the Marjorie Harris Carr Cross Florida Greenway, a 110-mile recreation trail covering the uncompleted path of the barge canal.

Anthony said at the time of Carr's death, "It's sad to realize that Marjorie has died without the Ocklawaha running free. It was our dream to have a celebration on [its] banks."

But as Carr told a reporter late in her life, the procedural acts of recent years had made that outcome inevitable.

"So yes," Carr said, "I have seen the Ocklawaha restored."

ERNEST F. COE (1866-1951)

Like many of the champions of Florida's environment, Ernest F. Coe discovered the state as an adult, first making his home in the Coconut Grove section of Miami at the age of 59. He quickly became as enamored of the state as any native could be, and his almost maniacal quest for protection of the Everglades contributed greatly to one of the most significant environmental victories Florida has ever known.

A native of New Haven, Connecticut, "Tom" Coe (as friends called him) stayed home to obtain a degree from the Yale University School of Fine Arts—though he preferred the woods around campus to sitting in a classroom. Coe achieved success as a landscape architect—incorporating what he had seen during travels to Europe and Japan—and at the height of the Florida land boom in 1925 he and his wife, Anna, moved to Miami, where he established a new business. Soon after arriving, Coe became fascinated by the semitropical wilderness to the west, with its unusual flora and its array of animals so exotic to a New Englander. During his frequent trips into the Everglades, Coe's excitement was tempered by alarm at the widespread plunder of orchids and the continued poaching of birds. He avidly embraced an idea that others had raised: a national park in the Everglades.

Coe—a tall, lanky man given to wearing white suits and bow ties—founded the Tropical Everglades National Park Association in 1928 and began an aggressive campaign for state and federal action. Too impatient to deal with bureaucratic underlings, Coe wrote to Stephen T. Mather, director of the National Park Service, outlining the need for the park—a proposal based on Coe's careful study of the Everglades over the course of nine months (including aerial observations). At his own expense, he traveled to Washington in 1929 for the first of numerous trips to the nation's capital in pursuit of Congressional support. Over the next few years Coe hosted delegations of senators to the Everglades, escorting them in tours by boat and by blimp.

Coe found allies in Congress, notably representative Ruth Bryan Owen of Coconut Grove, who sponsored a bill that led to a key hearing in December of 1930. Following a parade of scientists who testified to the uniqueness of South Florida's sub-tropical climate, Coe offered a slide presentation of Everglades scenes along with authoritative narration in his gentle speaking style. When Coe had finished, Don B. Colton, the chairman of the House Committee on Public Lands, declared, "I do not know when I have attended a more interesting hearing."

Despite the committee's enthusiasm, it took four more years for Congress to authorize the park—and another five years before it approved funding to buy land. State legislators showed even less interest in the project, failing to commit Florida to its share of land acquisition. The idea of an Everglades park languished through the Depression and World War II. Coe, a member of the original Florida Everglades National Park Commission, continued his crusade even after the panel folded. As Marjory Stoneman Douglas put it, "No one ever wrote more letters, paralyzed more people with his insistent talk, was considered more a fanatic, than Ernest Coe." He proved particularly irritating to South Florida hunters who feared losing access to their gigantic safari grounds and in some cases threatened to turn their guns on him. Coe described himself as "too stupid to be afraid." Continuing to send out news releases that even a sympathetic magazine writer described as "long-winded, obtuse and shrill," he alienated many of his original allies, and when Gov. Milton Caldwell revived an Everglades commission in 1946, he failed to appoint Coe (who also fell and suffered a fractured knee cap that year). Even as the state moved toward committing $2 million to buy land in the proposed boundaries, Coe remained critical. Back in 1928, he had envisioned the park covering about two million acres—north to Tamiami Trail and east to Key Largo—but the state and federal dealmakers whittled it to 1.3 million acres. When authorities began planning a dedication ceremony for the park, Coe at first declared that he wouldn't attend. But friends managed to change his mind, and he sat on the grandstand at Everglades City on December 6, 1947, an 80-year-old man in his white suit and bow tie.

Coe, who in 1948 received the nation's highest horticultural honor, died on New Year's Day of 1951. Over the years, Marjory Stoneman Douglas came to be associated with the creation of Everglades National Park—though her role in the process had actually been relatively small. Douglas often reminded people of Coe's indispensable contributions to the protection of the Everglades, and he finally received fitting recognition in 1996 when the park named its new visitor center after him. In a less official posthumous tribute — but one that Coe undoubtedly would have appreciated more — separate actions increased the size of Everglades National Park and yielded protection for part of Big Cypress Swamp as well as upper Key Largo and the nearby coral reef, largely completing Ernest Coe's original conception of the park.

ALLAN D. CRUICKSHANK (1907-1974) AND
HELEN G. CRUICKSHANK (1902-1994)

As authors, educators and advocates, the husband-and-wife team of Allan and Helen Cruickshank made a forceful impression on all who encountered them — especially the public officials whose actions displeased them.

Allan Dudley Cruickshank was born in St. Thomas, the U.S. Virgin Islands, of a Scottish father and a French mother. He grew up in lower Manhattan — not an ideal location for a budding ornithologist, but young Allan had a particularly attentive eye even as a pre-schooler. One day as he ran to greet his older brother and sister on their return from school, he noticed an unfamiliar bird on a willow tree. Moving closer, Allan carefully observed what he later determined was a screech owl — and from then on, birds occupied his imagination. He began making regular trips uptown to Central Park, scouting for birds, and his hunting grounds widened when his family moved to the Bronx, then still a largely pastoral borough. At the age of 14, he published an account of a rare bird sighting in New York that earned him a correspondence with a famous biologist, Sir Julian Huxley. More importantly to his career, Allan that same year borrowed a camera from his father and photographed a king rail nest in the Bronx's Van Cortland Park — the first of thousands of his nature pictures to be published. As a high school senior, Allan converted a summer's earnings into his first camera, a 4-by-5 Graflex.

Cruickshank studied biology and public speaking at New York University, where he threw a javelin for the track team, served as sports editor of the school paper and was elected student body president as a senior. He once interrupted a track meet to climb the stadium bleachers and identify the first swallow-tailed kite ever seen in the state of New York. After just three miserable days as a fledgling stockbroker on Wall Street, Cruickshank landed a job at the American Museum of Natural History, working with the world's largest collection of bird skins. He left that position in 1935 to join the staff of the National Audubon Society, his employer for the next 37 years. Soon afterward, he met a young woman, Helen Gere, the daughter of a botanist, as she perched in an apple tree photographing a bird. The couple married in 1937.

A skilled and patient photographer, Allan Cruickshank supplied nature shots to an estimated 175 books and countless newspapers during his career, earning distinction as the only person to have captured on film each of the more than 700 species of birds in the United States. Using his own slides, he presented some 5,900 lectures to a cumulative audience estimated by National Audubon at nearly 3 million people. Tall and robust and given to wearing gaudily colored clothes, including a tam-o'-shanter, Cruickshank filled his lectures with whistles so accurate that—when he used them in the field—even experienced bird-watchers often mistook his simulations for actual birds. He taught ornithology and conservation for 22 summers at Audubon Camp in Maine, spreading his knowledge to teachers. In all, his outreach to the public during the middle part of the century was matched only by fellow author and Audubon employee Roger Tory Peterson. And unlike some Audubon officials of the time, Cruickshank didn't shy away from decrying the disappearance of natural areas he saw in his travels.

Allan Cruickshank, individually and with Helen, also a writer and photographer, published several books. The Cruickshanks' 1949 publication, *Flight Into Sunshine,* Helen's account of their bird pursuits in Florida accompanied by 121 of Allan's photos, won the John Burroughs Medal for distinguished nature writing, and *A Paradise of Birds,* a description of avian activity in Texas, captured an Oppenheimer Prize for Allan's photography. (A fellow naturalist once said, "Allan Cruickshank is a portrait photographer whose studio is the whole world.") In addition, Allan for years edited the annual edition of *Audubon Field Notes* (later called *American Birds*) that compiled the results of the Christmas Bird Counts performed by members throughout the country.

Allan and Helen traveled widely—during his prime as an Audubon lecturer, Allan became acquainted with park rangers and wildlife officials at virtually every national park and wildlife refuge in the country. The couple developed a fondness for Florida, particularly the salt marshes of northern Merritt Island, a haven for migratory wading birds and one of Allan's favored sites for photography. In 1953, the couple moved from New York to Florida, settling in Rockledge on the banks of the Indian River. When the newly created National Aviation and Space Administration began acquiring land on Cape Canaveral and Merritt Island to build its launch center in the early 1960s, Allan Cruickshank used his connections with the U.S. Fish and Wildlife Service to lobby for a wildlife refuge on the large buffer area not involved in launch operations. Merritt Island National Wildlife Refuge opened to the public in 1963 and gained a reputation as one of the premier birdwatching locales in the country, a unique wintering range for roseate spoonbills, reddish egrets, wood storks and other waterfowl. "Had it not been for [the Cruickshanks], I'm not sure we would have this refuge," said Dorn Whitmore, a project manager at Merritt Island.

Though thousands of children at Audubon Camp knew him as a gentle lover of birds, Allan Cruickshank was prone to righteous anger over abuses of Florida's environment. During the 1960s, he became a fierce opponent of the proposed Cross Florida Barge Canal, making a memorable appearance at a famous hearing in Tallahassee as he thundered his disgust toward the politicians who had approved the project. He and Helen also earned the enmity of business interests in Brevard County for opposing projects that would harm the Indian River at a time when local politicians hoped the boom of the space program would yield unending growth. Shortly after their arrival, the couple led a successful fight against a proposed oil refinery at nearby Port Canaveral—the first significant victory for conservationists in Brevard County. They also worked to change the mentality of a rural county in which the poaching of wildlife brought at most a 10-cent fine, and the Cruickshanks joined the efforts of Save Our Waterways, a local alliance opposed to the dredge-and-fill projects rampant in Brevard County during the 1960s. The couple regularly railed against the use of Sykes Creek, a teeming rookery, as a fill source for a Merritt Island mall and other projects, and at least once they picketed at construction sites. Allan's vocal criticisms in the late 1960s also helped convince the city of Cocoa Beach not to extend its bulkhead line farther into the Banana River, a move that would have destroyed thousands of acres of river bottom and a vast system of mangrove islands. Late in his life, Allan led the local charge against the Navy's consideration of Mosquito Lagoon—adjacent to the Merritt Island refuge—as the site of a submarine port.

Allan Cruickshank died in 1974, two years after receiving the Arthur A. Allen Medal by the Cornell University Laboratory of Ornithology, which deemed him "unquestionably America's foremost bird photographer." After his death, Helen continued photographing wildlife in national refuges for the U.S. Fish and Wildlife Service and giving lectures. In her seventies, she culled Allan's copious records and prepared his *Birds of Brevard County* for publication—supplying a tender biographical sketch of her late husband—and also produced a book called *Bartram in Florida*, a distillation of the famous explorer's work supplemented by her own observations. At the time of her death at age 92, she was at work on a book about her travels with Allan while planning her annual summer trip to the Bear River area in Wyoming. She left behind a vast catalog of nature slides that supplied the bulk of the Visual Resources for Ornithology, considered the world's largest collection of bird photos and housed at the Academy of Natural Sciences in Philadelphia.

The Fish and Wildlife Service honored Allan in 1984 by naming a hiking trail after him at the Merritt Island refuge. At the ceremony, Helen said: "He loved the marshes so much, it's a wonder he didn't grow fins between his toes." After Helen's death in 1997, Brevard County dedicated a nature preserve to the couple not far from their longtime Rockledge home.

LOUIS F. DOMMERICH (1841-1912) AND
CLARA J. DOMMERICH (1857-1900)

The couple whose home gave birth to the environmental movement in Florida shared not only a fondness for nature but also a European ancestry.

Louis F. Dommerich was born in Obernkrichen, Germany, the son of a college professor. After serving an apprenticeship in a German factory, he left his home country at 18 and found a position with a textile company in New York. Within 10 years he had become a partner in the firm of Oelbermann, Dommerich and Co., and he eventually took over the company, branching into banking and insurance as the firm reached $100 million a year in business. After the death of his first wife, Dommerich married Clara J. Caesar, whose family had left Germany when she was one year old. In 1885, the couple made the first of what became regular winter trips to Florida, and two years later they spent a season at the Seminole Hotel in Winter Park, just north of Orlando. The Dommerichs enjoyed taking trips on the steamers that plied the St. Johns River, but they also found the excursions alarming. Every boat on the river seemed equipped with guns, which tourists aimed at any wildlife they happened to see during their cruises. With each winter's return to Florida, the Dommerichs saw fewer birds and other wild animals.

In 1891, Louis Dommerich bought from a Confederate Army major 400 acres overlooking Lake Minnehaha in Maitland, a town adjacent to Winter Park, and he directed the building of a three-story, 30-room wooden mansion complete with turrets and gables. He surrounded the house with palm trees and planted 72 acres of orange trees, christening the land Hiawatha Grove, after the Longfellow poem. The house came to be known simply as Hiawatha. The Dommerichs and the youngest of their five children (four from Louis' previous marriage) spent their winters at Hiawatha Grove, enjoying the migrant birds—or "beerds," in Louis Dommerich's pronunciation—that abounded in rural Central Florida. As one of their winter neighbors, Harriett Vanderpool, later recounted, the decline in bird populations along the St. Johns and other waterways "forcibly struck" the Dommerichs, who "deemed it their duty in some way to arrest the wanton destruction that sooner or later must result in serious trouble to those whose living depended on crops of fruit, grain or vegetables."

After word spread in 1896 that a Boston socialite had formed the Massachusetts Audubon Society, an action that spawned similar groups in other states, the Dommerichs decided that Florida—despite its relatively meager population—needed to join the movement. Although details are limited, Clara Dommerich appears to have played the leading role in bringing the Florida Audubon Society to life. The first meeting at Hiawatha on the afternoon of March 1, 1900, had a decidedly female cast, with twice as many women present as men. Clara Dommerich took the minutes of the historic gathering, noting the election of Rt. Rev. H.B. Whipple, the Episcopal Bishop of Minnesota and a winter resident of Maitland, as president of the nascent Audubon chapter. As evidence of Mrs. Dommerich's groundwork, she reported having received "liberal subscriptions" toward the group's operations.

Florida Audubon Society set its agenda in that first meeting, appointing a committee of five (including Mrs. Dommerich) to draft a bill for the Florida Legislature seeking legal protection for birds. The inaugural members also agreed to distribute pamphlets touting the economic value of birds for agriculture, to discourage women from adorning themselves with feathers and to push for the study of birds in public schools. In celebration of the day, the Dommerichs ordered a bronze birdbath from Tiffany Jewelers in New York and installed it in the yard at Hiawatha. Mrs. Dommerich began sending out cards to acquaintances that read, "Your name has been proposed as a Member of the Florida Audubon Society ..."

Clara Dommerich died in New York the following November, and *Bird-Lore* magazine lamented that the "cause of bird-protection has lost a staunch and efficient supporter who had chosen for her field of work a state where her services were greatly needed." Bishop Whipple also died soon after the organization's first anniversary meeting, leaving Louis Dommerich to take over as president. The chapter's annual meetings continued to take place at Hiawatha through 1912, when Louis Dommerich resigned the presidency because of declining health. He died in July after an operation in New York, and his children donated $5,000 to Florida Audubon in his honor. Dommerich's heirs held on to Hiawatha until 1954, when they sold the entire property to a developer for $420,000. The builder demolished the house but named the subdivision Dommerich Estates (a nearby elementary school also bears the family name), and the Maitland library inherited the birdbath. All that remains of Hiawatha is a small manmade pond near where the house used to stand.

The Dommerichs' daughter, Paula Siedenburg, carried on her parents' ideal, remaining in Central Florida and serving as an officer with Florida Audubon Society for much of her life.

MARJORY STONEMAN DOUGLAS (1890-1998)

During her extraordinary lifetime, the former newspaper reporter wrote hundreds of thousands of words about her adopted home of Florida. But it took just three words—"river of grass"—for Douglas to change the popular conception of the state's greatest ecological treasure, the Everglades.

Born in Minnesota, Douglas spent a somewhat chaotic childhood in the Northeast. Her father, a man given to chasing fortunes that never quite materialized, moved the family to Rhode Island when Marjory was young. After his wife suffered a nervous collapse and wound up in a sanitarium, Frank Stoneman exported Marjory to Massachusetts, where she was raised by a grandmother and an aunt. The pair encouraged Marjory's love of language, supplying her with books and giving her elocution lessons. She graduated from Wellesley College in 1912 and then briefly used her communications skills in a sales position at a department store. She lived in St. Louis for a year before moving to Newark, N.J., where she met and married Kenneth Douglas, a newspaper reporter 30 years her senior. Her husband proved to be as peripatetic as her father had been, and he finally wound up in jail for misusing bank drafts. Marjory soon sought a divorce—the conditions of which involved her living in another state for two years. She moved to Miami, where her father had founded the *News Record*—Miami's first morning daily newspaper, which later became the *Miami Herald*.

Not long after Marjory's arrival in 1915, her father asked her to fill in temporarily for the newspaper's society editor, and she began compiling news from women's clubs. The temporary duty led to full-time work at the paper, and during World War I she was assigned to report on the first woman in Florida to join the Naval Reserve. Finding no one to write about, Douglas herself enlisted and went to Europe, where she remained after leaving the Navy to do publicity work for the Red Cross. Returning to Miami in 1920, she became an assistant editor at her father's newspaper and began writing a daily column called "The Galley." Given her first public platform, Marjory Stoneman Douglas advocated for women's suffrage and wrote approvingly of a campaign by local naturalists to have the Everglades protected as a national park. Having declared her support, Douglas began a process of self-education on just what exactly she was trying to save.

She left the *Herald* in 1923 and pursued a life of free-lance writing, contributing to national magazines (most notably the *Saturday Evening Post*) and developing her skills at fiction, drama and poetry — and meanwhile she built a small house in the Coconut Grove section of Miami. She became acquainted with Hervey Allen, a novelist (his *Anthony Adverse* was a bestseller) who also edited a series of books about American rivers, and he suggested in the 1930s that Douglas write a book about the Miami River. Deciding the river didn't provide sufficient material for an entire book, she asked if she might fill it out with material about the Everglades — about which she still knew little — and Allen agreed. Douglas soon discovered that nothing close to a comprehensive study of the Everglades had ever been written, and it took her three or four years of research, making trips to Tallahassee to consult state records, before she could even begin writing — which took several more years.

John Pennekamp, who had replaced Douglas's father as editor of the Herald, referred her to a state hydrologist named Garald Parker, who was studying the ground water patterns of South Florida and offered to educate the writer on the region's ecosystem. Struggling for a metaphor that would sum up the interrelated nature of the entire Everglades system, with its dependence on a southward flow of water from Central

Florida to Florida Bay, Douglas asked Parker whether the Everglades could accurately be described as a "river of grass." The hydrologist gave his blessing to the phrase.

"Some years later my colleague Art Marshall said that with those three words I changed everybody's knowledge and educated the world as to what the Everglades meant," Douglas wrote in her autobiography.

When Douglas finally submitted the book to a publisher, the response was encouraging but came with a condition—she had to trim 20,000 words of her densely written prose. "It was one of the worst jobs I ever had," Douglas later said of the self-editing process. "I took those words out almost one-by-one, a phrase here and there." After painfully extracting 19,000 words, she wired her editor and said to take it or leave it. The publishing house agreed, and an initial printing of 7,500 copies came out in November of 1947—a month before the dedication ceremony of Everglades National Park. The book, dedicated to her father, has since sold half a million copies and ranks among the most influential nature books ever published in the United States. A dense exploration of the Everglades that travels back to the centuries before European settlement, the book benefited from Douglas' gift for the indelible phrase, most memorably in its opening words: "There are no other Everglades in the world. They are, they have always been, one of the unique regions of the Earth, remote, never wholly known."

Even before the publication of her famous book, Douglas had become an early member of the Tropical Everglades Audubon Society formed by Ernest Coe and had served on the state committee pursuing the creation of a national park. But she insisted that she didn't earn the title of environmentalist until the late 1960s, when her anger over a proposed training airport in the Big Cypress Swamp—just north of the Everglades— spurred her into unrestrained activism. In her 1987 autobiography, *Voice of the River*, Douglas told of an encounter in a grocery store with a woman involved in fighting the proposed jetport. Praising the woman for her effort, Douglas was surprised by the response: "Yeah, what are you doing?" To get out of the conversation, Douglas made a vague promise to help the cause, and the next day the jetport opponents solicited her help. In 1969, Douglas asked a friend for his opinion about an environmental club based on membership dues of $1. The man handed her a dollar bill, and Friends of the Everglades was born—an organization still in existence.

From the time of the jetport battle onward, Douglas became a fixture at public hearings on developments that would affect the Everglades. A small woman whose thick glasses and floppy straw hats gave her the look of a Flannery O'Connor character, she described herself as unattractive and said her drab appearance allowed her to "get by with a lot more." Late in her life, she took full rhetorical advantage of her status as an infirm old lady.

Yet she elicited little sympathy from those who didn't share her opinions, often drawing boos and catcalls when she rose to spoke at public meetings. At a Dade County Commission meeting in the 1970s, she told her detractors, "That's all right. Carry on. I can stay here all night." She could be just as cantankerous to her allies. Whenever someone thanked her for saving the Everglades, Douglas would snap, "It's not saved yet." When Gov. Bob Martinez honored her as the fourth Great Floridian at a ceremony in 1987, she used the occasion to scold the governor for failing to do more for ailing Lake Okeechobee. As if making up for lost time, Douglas traveled the state, excoriating the forces that had contributed to the decline of the Everglades, including the sugar industry, the developers and the U.S. Army Corps of Engineers.

Douglas became an advisor—sometimes officially—to politicians, including Gov. Bob Graham, whose Save Our Everglades program of the early 1980s followed the suggestions of Douglas and biologist Arthur Marshall. Even as she passed her 100th birthday and her eyesight faded, Douglas remained politically engaged. When the state legislature showed signs of weakening the commitments of the 1994 Marjory Stoneman Douglas Everglades Forever Act, Douglas—with little patience for compromise at the age of 104—publicly demanded that lawmakers strike her name from the measure.

She died in 1998, blind and nearly deaf, still in the Coconut Grove cottage that had been her home for seven decades. At her request, her ashes were scattered over an area of the Everglades named for her. Upon her death, President Bill Clinton—who had awarded her the nation's highest civilian honor, the Presidential Medal of Freedom—took time from an official visit to Europe to add his voice to the statements of praise pouring in from environmental leaders and politicians in Florida and elsewhere. Nathaniel Reed, himself an accomplished environmental activist, described Douglas as an appealing amalgam of contradictions— "bold, brash, loving, sweet, tough, fierce, marvelously humorous."

With one immortal phrase, Douglas had taught the world to think of the Everglades as a single, living ecosystem that could not survive being fragmented to suit the desires of sugar growers, developers and politicians.

"The Everglades is a test," she said. "If we pass, we may get to keep the planet."

CARL HIAASEN (1953-)

Tourist Season, the first solo novel of *Miami Herald* reporter Carl Hiaasen, opens with the president of the Greater Miami Chamber of Commerce being suffocated with a rubber alligator and then stuffed into a suitcase. With that demented revenge fantasy, Carl Hiaasen unveiled his anger to the world outside South Florida. Hiaasen's rage—drawn from many sources but most consistently from the destruction of Florida's environment—combined with a deft satirical touch has made him not only a best-selling novelist but also a modern successor to Marjory Stoneman Douglas as the environmental conscience of Florida.

Hiaasen was born just early enough to know what South Florida was like before it became one continuous metropolitan strip from Miami to West Palm Beach. He grew up in Plantation, still a small town separate from Fort Lauderdale in the 1950s, and he and his friends explored and camped in woods that would later give way to busy thoroughfares and shopping malls. Hiaasen, whose grandfather had migrated from North Dakota to found the area's first law firm, developed two tendencies at an early age: disgust at the conquest of nature and a yen to share his opinions with others. When he and his friends encountered the increasingly ubiquitous surveyor's stakes that signaled coming development, they would pull them up in small acts of defiance. "We were kids," Hiaasen said in the introduction to his collection *Kick Ass*. "We didn't know what else to do." He received his first typewriter at the age of six and soon began typing up reports on neighborhood sports contests and distributing them to his peers. At Plantation High School, he produced a small-scale newsletter called *More Trash* (a precursor of "zines") that featured withering caricatures of teachers and administrators.

After a stint at Emory University, Hiaasen in quick succession married his high school girlfriend, became a father and transferred to the journalism program at the University of Florida. Following his graduation he landed a job as a reporter at *Today* newspaper in Cocoa, eventually branching into feature writing. He also produced a few op-ed pieces for the paper before the managing editor decided he was too young to be a columnist. Hiaasen moved on to a regional bureau of the *Miami Herald* in 1976 and worked his way up to a spot on the paper's investigative reporting team, contributing to a series that exposed improprieties in the approval of Port Bougainville and other developments planned for North Key Largo. The negative publicity stalled the projects, and the state eventually turned much of North Key Largo into a nature preserve. Hiaasen, who had ghostwritten the memoir of a doctor while in college, had an urge to write fiction, and in the early 1980s he teamed with another writer to produce three novels. In 1985, Hiaasen was at work on a satirical novel set in South Florida when the *Herald* offered him a slot as a columnist—a vantage point from which he could shed his journalistic neutrality and lambaste the area's "greedheads." Just as he was drawing the ire of South Florida's business leaders with his columns, *Tourist Season* came out to appreciative reviews. The book's plot centered on the efforts of a disturbed Miami columnist who uses decidedly radical tactics to scare away tourists and protect an island from development.

Hiaasen was just getting started. He began producing novels at a rate of one about every two years while continuing to write a regular column for the Herald in which he aggressively exposed political corruption and bemoaned the unrestrained paving of South Florida. In his books, Hiaasen ranged over such subject matter as tournament fishing, cosmetic surgery, theme parks, hurricanes, strip clubs, legalized gambling and punk rock, but each novel contained at least an undercurrent of outrage over the rape of the environment, memorably embodied in the recurring character of Skink, a former Florida governor who roamed the state's woods, subsisted on road kill and served as a vigilante for nature. The novels offered a satisfying likeness of the justice absent from real life, when—as Hiaasen made plain in his columns—the rapists of nature are usually rewarded, not punished. With the success of his books, which have been translated into 21 languages, Hiaasen no longer needed his job at the *Herald,* yet he continued to write weekly columns, unwilling to relinquish the chance to administer some measure of rhetorical justice to the "greedheads."

"I have seen very little that has happened in Florida to give me much faith in the human race," Hiaasen once said. "Somebody's got to stand up and scream bloody murder."

Hiaasen's venting took a more specific turn with the 1998 publication of *Team Rodent: How Disney Devours the World.* In addition to exploring charges of animal abuse at Disney's Animal Kingdom, Hiaasen excoriated his fellow members of the press for their fawning treatment of a multi-billion-dollar corporation operating as "a sovereign state within a state" that permanently changed the landscape of Central Florida. As in his columns for the *Herald,* Hiaasen displayed a willingness to name names in assigning blame for Florida's decline.

During a book tour to promote his novel *Basket Case,* Hiaasen told a gathering of fans, "... Everywhere I go, whether it's Canada or London, there are readers who identify with what is happening in Florida. You don't have to live here to find that a place you cared about and wanted to show your kids isn't there anymore. They've paved over the land, cut down the trees, dug a crater. It's great that so many people understand this, but it's disheartening. ... Florida is one of the most gorgeous places in America. It's a curse as well as a blessing because you can feel such helplessness about what all is disappearing."

Though he directs his anger toward those who hold power—whether political or financial—Hiaasen also decries the public apathy that allows the continuing mutilation of the natural landscape. Though he may not engage in the traditional activism of an environmental leader like Marjorie Carr, Hiaasen through his books and newspaper columns provides fuel to the resistance effort. Even if only one percent of Hiaasen's legion of fans parlayed their admiration into concrete action, the impact—in Florida and elsewhere—would be incalculable.

"I've always seen myself as just one more voice in the battle to save a little something of Florida for future generations," Hiaasen said. "I don't think writers can change the world, but we can put a spotlight on a problem—and hope that others who care take notice."

MAY MANN JENNINGS (1872-1963)

One of the most accomplished women in Florida's history, May Mann Jennings never held public office yet had access to power from an early age and made adroit use of it. She championed women's suffrage, child labor laws, public education and many other social issues, and she contributed immeasurably to the preservation of the state's natural lands.

May Mann's childhood mixed comfort and tumult. Born in New Jersey, she spent her childhood in Crystal River near the Gulf Coast, the oldest daughter of Austin Mann, a prosperous state senator. After his wife died of tuberculosis, Mann sent 11-year-old May and a sister to St. Joseph's Academy, a convent school in St. Augustine, where May stayed for seven years before graduating as valedictorian. At 18, May met and promptly married William Sherman Jennings, a judge from Brooksville, a cousin of the noted orator and presidential candidate Williams Jennings Bryan and a political aspirant himself. Jennings was elected governor in 1900, and he eagerly embraced the popular call for draining the Everglades. Naturally his wife supported his policies, but May's later actions gave an ironic cast to the governor's agenda.

After William Jennings lost his reelection bid, the couple moved to Jacksonville (with a second home in Miami) and May Mann Jennings soon took an active role with the Jacksonville Women's Club, an organization unafraid of getting involved in political issues. By 1914, May had risen to the presidency of the Florida Federation of Women's Clubs, and she threw the weight of her authority behind an issue some South Florida members had been fruitlessly pursuing—the preservation of Paradise Key, the largest stand of royal palms in the state and an area threatened by a proposed road. The federation first secured a donation of 960 acres from the widow of railroad magnate Henry Flagler, but that left a swath of the hammock owned by the state. Making full use of her political connections, May personally lobbied Gov. Park Trammell on the matter, and she hosted a visit by the trustees of the Internal Improvement Fund—the first time she had seen the hammock herself. The state agreed to turn the land over to the federation, but the legislature offered no money to maintain a public park, leaving May Mann Jennings to lead the federation in a time-consuming fund drive. She presided over the christening of Royal Palm State Park in 1916; it took her another five years of exhaustive lobbying to win funding for the Florida's first state park. Her strivings on behalf of Royal Palm provided the impetus for legislative action that created the state park system.

When a group of South Florida naturalists began pressing the federal government for a national park in the Everglades, Jennings (whose husband had died in 1920) joined the call, offering to donate Royal Palm as part of the proposed park. She lobbied for bills passed by the Florida Legislature during the 1930s that yielded the acquisition of 325,000 acres of land in the Everglades and established the Everglades National Park Commission. The drive for a national park lost momentum during World War II, but Gov. Spessard Holland and his successor, Millard Caldwell, revived the issue, and Caldwell appointed Jennings to a recast Everglades National Park Commission. When President Harry Truman oversaw the dedication of Everglades National Park on December 6, 1947, Jennings took her place on the grandstand at the age of 74.

Amid her efforts on behalf of Royal Palm and the Everglades, Jennings remained engaged in a myriad of pursuits. As the head of the Florida Federation's conservation department for 19 years, she led campaigns for the protection of rivers and estuaries, increased enforcement of bird and wildlife laws and the declaration of February 14 as Bird Day in Florida. A longtime officer with Florida Audubon, she argued against the killing of pelicans during World War I, when popular sentiment held that the birds were filching $1 million worth of state-owned fish a day. When some newspapers advocated the systematic thinning of rookeries, Jennings lobbied in Tallahassee against any such state plans.

Jennings' experience with the preservation of Royal Palm spurred her toward a passion for conservation in general. Seeing the rapid disappearance of native woods throughout the state, she proposed the taxing of timber and the creation of a forestry department, which would use surplus tax funds for land acquisition. Jennings commissioned her son, Bryan, to draft a bill, and then she helped achieve its passage in 1927, creating the Florida Board of Forestry (now called the Division of Forestry). By the time Stetson University bestowed an honorary doctorate on her in 1931, Jennings had come to be called Florida's "mother of forestry."

May Mann Jennings, probably the best-known woman in Florida during her prime, died in Jacksonville in 1963 at the age of 90. She regretted that having spent the first year of her life in New Jersey kept her from claiming to be a native Floridian. Nonetheless, a dormitory at the University of Florida bears her name.

John C. "Johnny" Jones (1932-)

John C. Jones — known to most as "Johnny" — does not fit either of the templates from which most of the state's environmental heroes have emerged. Possessed of neither the wealth (and therefore freedom) of the early activists nor the scientific training of the later breed, Jones found a niche for himself during the "golden era" of ecology — the late 1960s through the 1970s. Making of use of sincerity, mental sharpness and a talent for persuasion, he virtually invented the role of the environmental lobbyist.

Jones has lived his entire life in West Palm Beach. As a child, he fished and hunted with his father and uncles in what remained a largely rural part of the state. As a teenager, he made his first visit to the Kissimmee River — a lovely, winding waterway that he came to cherish. He also fell in love with the daughter of the man who introduced him to the river, and a few months before his 17th birthday Johnny married Mariana Beebe. The couple raised five children, and Jones worked for 14 years as a plumbing contractor in his father's business before forming his own company in 1963. His gregarious personality made him a natural to lobby in Tallahassee on behalf of the Master Plumbers Association, which he began doing in the mid-1960s. Around that time, he also took an active role with the Florida Wildlife Federation, a group dedicated mostly to protecting the rights of hunters. The federation elected Jones vice president in 1969 and president two years later, and he served as an informal lobbyist, traveling to the capital when important bills were up for discussion. Under Jones' leadership, the Florida Wildlife Federation took on a broader agenda almost indistinguishable from those of the state's better-known conservation groups.

The federation installed Jones in 1972 as a paid lobbyist, and he took part in one of the most environmentally valuable legislative sessions the state has ever known. He lobbied on behalf of the Environmental Lands Act, an unprecedented land-acquisition measure, and then accepted Gov. Reubin Askew's appointment as vice chairman of Lands For You, a group that traveled the state urging voters to approve the $240 million bond issue the act required. The measure passed overwhelmingly.

Jones perfected his lobbying tactics during the 1970s, renting a three-bedroom apartment in Tallahassee each spring so that he could host members of the federation from the districts of lawmakers who stood in the way of bills. On particularly important issues, he sometimes arranged to bring groups of federation members to Tallahassee by bus or plane, a tactic he recalls as being highly effective. Jones also used more subtle means of persuasion, passing out pocket knives and nature photos to legislators and their staffs as he became familiar with nearly every lawmaker. Jones' lobbying technique combined relentlessness with benevolence, and the result prompted one powerful legislator to moan to him, "What Johnny wants, Johnny gets."

"I always tried to make friends with people," Jones said. "There were only one or two guys in the whole history I just could not get along with. … If a guy didn't vote for me, I didn't beat him up. If a guy votes for you 80 percent of the time, you should love him."

Lawmakers came to depend on Jones, sometimes asking him to draft legislation for them. In the act that gave him the greatest satisfaction, he crafted the Kissimmee River Restoration Act of 1976, which committed the state to undoing the conversion of Jones' beloved meandering river into a broad ditch running between Lake Kissimmee and Lake Okeechobee. Jones also helped to write the 1979 bill that created the

Conservation and Recreation Lands (CARL) Act, a program that widened the 1972 mandate to include land for parks and hunting areas. Subsequent funding updates have retained the CARL formula.

Florida Audubon Society and other groups followed the lead of the Florida Wildlife Federation, installing full-time lobbyists of their own in Tallahassee. Their goals usually corresponded, though Jones sometimes clashed with other environmentalists over the matter of hunting on protected lands.

In 1970, Jones met Arthur Marshall, the longtime biologist with the U.S. Fish and Wildlife Service who had recently started an ecology program at the University of Miami. The two men 15 years apart in age seemed an odd pair—Jones portly, diplomatic and self-educated, Marshall lean and blunt, the holder of two degrees—yet in addition to their shared concern for the Everglades they learned they had lived as children in the same section of West Palm Beach. Jones welcomed the role of student to Marshall's professor, and their association blossomed into a deep bond. Jones said that the program for restoration of the Everglades—embraced at the conceptual level by Gov. Bob Graham and incorporated nearly two decades later into the $7.8 billion federal-state program—arose from discussions on his patio among Jones, Marshall, Marjory Stoneman Douglas and representatives of other environmental groups.

Jones proudly recalls that a month before Marshall died in 1985, the great ecologist planted a kiss on him and said, "John, you're the bestest friend a man could ever have."

Within a year of his friend's death, Jones encountered a case of depression that forced him to vacate his position with the Florida Wildlife Federation and leave Tallahassee behind. He eventually got a job as a consultant with the Palm Beach County Solid Waste Authority, but in 1988 as he sat at a traffic light an eight-ton truck crashed into his car, leaving him with several ruptured vertebrae—injuries that confined him to a wheelchair. During his recovery, doctors discovered cancer, prompting the removal of one of his kidneys, and complications from a later heart bypass operation led to diminished use of his right arm and constant pain in his hand. Through it all, he remained attuned to the state's pressing environmental issues, staying in touch with longtime activist Nathaniel Reed and officials with state agencies. As he discusses the successes of his years in Tallahassee, Jones often relies on his wife of more than 50 years, Mariana—"my computer"—to supply a detail. Fittingly, the couple learned in 2002 that the state has designated a 10,294-acre tract north of West Palm Beach as the John C. and Mariana Jones/ Hungryland Wildlife and Environmental Area.

The following year, Johnny Jones was inducted into the Everglades Coalition's Hall of Fame.

CHARLES LEE (1950-)

Charles Lee's career has coincided with the modern era of environmental lobbying in Tallahassee, and he has been identified more than anyone else with the pursuit of conservation goals through the state legislature.

Whereas some of Florida's notable activists started late in their lives, Lee, director of advocacy for Audubon of Florida, stands as an environmental prodigy. He grew up in Miami during the height of the dredge-and-fill era, and throughout a childhood largely spent fishing he witnessed the relentless development of northern Biscayne Bay.

"I saw the world I was used to devoured by 'condominia,' " Lee later told a reporter. "I watched one favorite snapper hole after another get filled in."

Lee combined his anger over the environmental plunder with a gift for expression, writing so many letters to the local newspapers that an editor with the now-defunct *Miami News* put the teenager in touch with some activists in the area. By the age of 16, Lee was a board member of the local Izaak Walton League chapter and also active in Miami's Tropical Audubon Society. As a teenager, he met the famed *Miami Herald* editor John Pennekamp, who presented him with a youth conservationist of the year award from the National Wildlife Federation.

Around the time Lee earned an associate of arts degree from Dade Junior College, he met Florida Audubon Society president Hal Scott at a party hosted by Dade Thornton, the organization's board chairman. Scott offered Lee a job at "a mighty $100 a week" as his administrative assistant in the Maitland headquarters. It would be a one-year assignment, after which Lee planned to return to school and pursue a law degree.

He never made it to law school. Before long, Florida Audubon was sending Lee up to Tallahassee for at least part of each legislative session. At first Lee had an uncompromising attitude toward the business of lobbying and earned a reputation as a gruff "pit bull."

"I think everybody who goes naively into that process is at first very much misled about what they can accomplish and also very uninformed on how things do get accomplished," Lee said. "So you spend your first few years just learning the ropes."

In an early success, Lee helped convince lawmakers to commit $40 million—"in those days a huge piece of money"—to match a federal contribution toward the purchase of land in Big Cypress Swamp. By the age of 30, Lee had become a well-known figure in Tallahassee, the public face of the state's preeminent environmental group. He played a role in landmark measures including the Conservation and Recreation Lands Act (1979), the Save Our Rivers program (1981), the Warren S. Henderson Wetlands Protection Act (1984) and the Growth Management Act (1985). With the state's land-acquisition program winding down in the late 1980s, Lee took part in the Commission on the Future of Florida's Environment, a panel chaired by Nathaniel Reed.

"We were very much outnumbered by the business interests on that committee," Lee said, "and really we could get them to agree to do only one thing and that was land acquisition. They were very hostile to any regulatory advancements. We reached sort of the 'what to do' stage of deliberations, and I worked to get a consensus around land acquisition."

The result was the Preservation 2000 program, which dedicated $3 billion over a decade to land purchases, making Florida a national leader in the preservation of environmentally endangered areas. Lee also led the effort in the mid-1980s to revive the Everglades Coalition, a working alliance of some 40 state and national environmental groups. Among his other accomplishments, he helped line up congressional support for an unusual land swap that added 125,000 acres to the Big Cypress National Preserve.

Lee became senior vice president of Florida Audubon at the age of 34 and now ranks perhaps only behind Reed as the best-known environmental activist in the state and ahead of him as the one most often quoted in the media. Based in Winter Park even after his employer moved its headquarters to Miami in 1998, Lee remains a peripatetic fellow. His travels to Tallahassee include not just legislative sessions but also many state cabinet meetings, and he is a familiar face at hearings of water management districts and other agencies throughout the state. He said he routinely drives about 75,000 miles a year.

Lee has come to understand that even good laws don't necessarily have the intended effects. Because of chronic understaffing in state agencies, for example, the important growth-management measures of the mid-1980s have had little practical effect.

"Any new piece of legislation you have to look at it realistically, and what it can do and what it will do are two different things," Lee said. "Enforcement and funding are always key pieces to how well a law will succeed. I think all of our environmental laws have been reduced in their effectiveness to one degree or another due to a lack of enforcement and a lack of funding. The Growth Management Act is probably the primary example of that."

Over the years Lee evolved from his early "naïve" approach to a pragmatic strategy recognizing that environmental groups would never have the same influence in Tallahassee as developers and agricultural interests, groups with vast reserves of money to contribute to politicians. A registered Democrat, he developed a good rapport with the administration of Republican Gov. Bob Martinez in the late 1980s and with another Republican, Jeb Bush, a decade later. Lee typifies the outlook of Florida Audubon, with its emphasis on realism. Though he seeks chances to push for environmentally helpful legislation, he spends much of his time in Tallahassee working to lessen the damage of bad bills.

Lee's willingness to compromise on behalf of Florida Audubon has sometimes rankled people from other environmental groups, particularly when he publicly supported a bill in 2002 that pledged money for the Everglades restoration but included a provision limiting the rights of citizens and organizations to file legal challenges over proposed developments.

Officials with other organizations—notably the Sierra Club, which stood to suffer most from the provision—publicly criticized Lee for agreeing to the amendment. He responded by saying he had worked to soften the sting of something destined for approval.

"The only way you can make your ideals a reality is to figure out the way to work the system," Lee told a reporter. "Your ideals are a nice thing for a scrapbook, and nothing more."

David Gluckman, a lobbyist who has worked for Florida Audubon, the Sierra Club and other conservation groups since the late 1970s, said Lee faces the same tension between pragmatism and idealism that all environmentalists face when they try to achieve tangible results.

"I worked for Florida Audubon for 17 years and I've been as mad as anyone with Charles from time to time," Gluckman said. "However, there is no question that he has been a major figure in Florida's environmental movement since the early '70s, and he's still here. Because he's been a paid professional all those years, there will always be folks who will decry his actions, even if approved and supported by the Audubon board. … Professionals in this system must compromise in order to continue to fight on other issues. We don't always like it, and the 'purists' who don't need to compromise hate it, but it's what we do. Charles may leave a few more unhappy people along the way than the rest of us, but in the long run he's had some pretty good successes."

ARTHUR R. MARSHALL (1919-1985)

A government insider turned outsider, Art Marshall ranked as the undisputed expert on the Everglades and added immeasurable credibility to the environmental movement during the crucial period of the 1960s and 1970s.

Born in Charleston, South Carolina, Marshall grew up in West Palm Beach and Miami—the former still a small town bounded by woods and wetlands during his childhood, though the construction of the Hoover Dike around Lake Okeechobee in 1930 began the process of separating the populated coast from the Everglades. His boyhood memories of swimming in a pristine Biscayne Bay fueled his later anger over the state policies that allowed so many bays to be destroyed.

Marshall enlisted in the Florida National Guard at age 18 and joined the Army four years later—just in time for World War II. As a first lieutenant in the 81st Chemical Motor Battalion, he saw his first action of the war in France during the pre-dawn invasion of Omaha Beach on June 6, 1944—D-Day—and the death of his company commander during the operation brought him a battlefield promotion to the rank of captain. During 11 months in Europe, Marshall took part in the liberation of 1,000 Jews from Ohrdruf, the first German concentration camp to be captured. He also became acquainted with General George Patton, whose famously rugged demeanor apparently matched Marshall's own.

After the war, Marshall spent some time working in a fledgling construction business in Miami with his brother, John, before he arrived at the University of Florida in 1949 as a 31-year-old freshman unsure about his career course. He earned a bachelor's degree in biology and added a master's in marine biology from the University of Miami in 1956. He took a job with the U.S. Fish and Wildlife Service, working as a biologist and eventually becoming supervisor of the Vero Beach field office of the Bureau of Sport Fisheries and Wildlife. It proved to be a frustrating experience for Marshall, who detested the state's longstanding practice of routinely approving projects that used dredged material to transform shallow bays into land that could be built on. Marshall and his colleagues faced an unending stream of applications for dredge-and-fill permits.

"We knew we had to combat this," he once told a reporter. "It was clearly going to destroy the life in these bays. We sat there in that office, five or six of us with graduate degrees, and did nothing. No one would listen to us. We'd recommend permits for dredging and filling be denied, and over and over again the commissions would ignore us."

As an employee of a government agency, Marshall faced unwritten restrictions on his ability to publicly advocate for environmental issues—especially when it involved challenging government policies. But he did what he could. In the early 1960s, he led a campaign to save Pelican Island—the nation's first wildlife refuge—from development. For his efforts, Marshall received from fellow activists a plaque calling him the "fearless leader of the Loyal Order of Piling Painters," a reference to the scatological habits of pelicans. He hosted visits from congressmen and officials with federal agencies during the drive to protect what became Biscayne National Monument (now Biscayne National Park), and he assisted with a court case in 1970 that saved 11 acres of Pinellas County bay bottom from dredging and set a precedent for the protection of bays. He played a supporting role in the fight against the Cross Florida Barge Canal, and in the late 1960s he had the opportunity to combine his philosophy with his official duties when Dade County officials began planning a training airport in Big Cypress Swamp, just outside Everglades National Park. Marshall served as a primary author on a Department of the Interior report about the jetport's likely environmental effects, a report that helped sway White House officials to kill the jetport plan.

Meanwhile Marshall began seeking out chances to appear before conservation groups—particularly chapters of the Izaak Walton League—and to donate his expertise on a myriad of topics.

"I used to make speeches to as few as seven people," he recalled. He also supplied the environmental groups with scientific papers and newspaper stories, leading a friend to dub him a "biopolitician." Though he was careful to avoid outright activism, Marshall still drew the displeasure of elected officials, and at least one of them—U.S. senator Spessard Holland—tried to pressure Marshall's superiors into muzzling the biologist.

Feeling that his "hands were tied" in his government job, Marshall left the Department of the Interior in 1970 to found the Division of Applied Ecology at the University of Miami—and to continue his quest to educate the public about the Kissimmee River-Everglades system. He remained in demand by environmental groups as well as government officials, and in 1971 Gov. Reubin Askew tapped him to lead a task force on water issues. The task force's recommendations formed the core of the land and water management package that passed in the 1972 legislative session. Marshall also served for two years on the board of South Florida's water management agency, during which he tried to steer the district away from its traditional narrow focus on each proposed development and toward a more "integrated" approach that took into account the needs of the entire ecosystem.

Marshall had two particular gripes about Florida's environmental policies—the fragmentation of government agencies and the lack of a formal role for academics and citizens in the process. In a 1972 paper entitled "A Proposal To Establish the Florida Environmental Institute," he offered a corrective. Noting that some people "already see Florida as the 'New Jersey of the South,' " he wrote, "The kinds of decisions we face cannot be made by agencies of government alone, nor by educational institutions alone. They must be made by those who are affected by the results of those decisions—the people of Florida." The proposed institute would be a non-profit organization, designed to study environmental problems in an "integrated" way and then serve as an independent advisor for state government and the public, and it would also have an educational component, taking in a few college students each year as interns. Marshall estimated the annual cost at $800,000, which would come from private donations, foundation grants and possibly government grants. The concept, unrealistic in its assumption of government's willingness to be advised, went nowhere, but after Marshall's death a foundation formed in his name followed the basic structure of his proposal. Marshall also worked with Archie Carr and others to sketch out an undergraduate environmental studies program at the University of Florida.

Another of Marshall's concepts received more attention—his blueprint for fixing the Everglades, which came to be known as the Marshall Plan. (He used the word "repair" rather than speaking of restoration, saying, "To restore the Everglades, I'd have to move 300,000 houses.") Marshall emphasized the need to unleash the historic "sheet flow" of water southward into the Everglades, a natural process that had been disrupted by the Corps of Engineers' aggressive flood-control projects, most notably the replacement of the Kissimmee River with a drainage canal. "The effectiveness of all the elements [of the plan] for repairing the Everglades system and restoring its natural resources is totally dependent on filling the Kissimmee ditch," Marshall wrote. "There is no doubt of that." He crystallized his suggestions into a four-page petition that drew support from every major environmental group in the state.

"Art Marshall dared to suggest that the entirety of South Florida was a single ecological system," said Estus Whitfield, an environmental adviser to several Florida governors.

Though in private life a gentle fellow, Marshall wasn't afraid to express unpopular opinions, often in a blunt manner. He once dared to say, "Growth should be stopped rather than managed or controlled. In the same way a lake can have too much nutrients in it ... a city can have too many people in it." His continuing public statements on political matters drew warnings from his academic superiors, and the funding for his position at the University of Miami disappeared after just three years. Marshall and his wife, Kay, moved to North Florida, where the family owned a piece of land in the small town of Interlachen. Drawing on his construction experience, Art built a modest house (known to friends as "Fort Marshall"), leaving the woods around it intact and using a design that kept energy needs to a minimum—it was cooled by cross-ventilation and heated by a wood stove using dead trees found on the property. "He lived his philosophy," said Johnny Jones of the Florida Wildlife Federation, a close friend. At his rural outpost, Marshall tended to a garden and hosted various family members, including his brother John, whose career as a developer offered fodder for many debates.

In Interlachen, Marshall served as a visiting faculty member at the University of Florida, became chairman of the St. Johns River Water Management District, worked as an environmental consultant and continued his support of conservation groups, sending out a constant stream of correspondence under the masthead, "Arthur Marshall, Ecologist." In the last few years of his life, he organized the Coalition to Repair the Everglades, a group that included Douglas and Jones and greatly influenced Gov. Bob Graham's Save Our Everglades program of the early 1980s.

When the longtime pipe smoker was diagnosed with lung cancer in 1984, he knew that he would not live to see the repair of the Everglades, but he hoped he had spread his understanding of the ecosystem widely enough that others would carry on the effort armed with a scientific argument. Marshall died in February of 1985.

Trim and bespectacled, Marshall had a professorial appearance even before he became an academic. He spoke fluent Spanish, an ability that helped him study the effects of rainforest clearing in Central and South America and to translate excerpts from "Don Quixote" — a thematically fitting subject — for friends. Above all, Marshall pursued the life of an integrationist. He taught other environmentalists to see the area from Orlando south as a single ecosystem, and he sought unity between government agencies and private groups, between academics and the public and between the state and federal governments — as in the shared purchase of the Big Cypress Swamp, which set a precedent for the joint commitment to an overdue Everglades repair more than a decade after his death.

"He dragged us into the 20th century, ecologically, in this state," said former Florida Audubon Society President Bernard Yokel. "He was described as a maverick, and he was. He was tough-minded. He was tenacious."

"Art was to the environmental movement what Einstein was to mathematics," Johnny Jones said. "He was the smartest environmentalist in Florida, probably in the country."

Gov. Bob Graham likened Marshall to famed naturalist John Muir, founder of the Sierra Club.

Marshall, who avoided joining environmental groups so that he could maintain ideological independence, received countless awards, including conservationist of the decade from the Florida Wildlife Federation in 1984. After his death, Nathaniel Reed and Gov. Bob Graham led a campaign that raised $1 million to create an endowed chair in Marshall's name in ecological science at the University of Florida, and Congress added his name to the Loxahatchee National Wildlife Refuge, a chunk of the Everglades near Marshall's boyhood home of West Palm Beach.

Marjory Stoneman Douglas also paid tribute to Marshall, revising the afterword of her famous book to give more credit to the scientist and his vision for the way to fix the troubled ecosystem. "Although my phrase 'River of Grass' first awakened people to the notion of the Everglades as a river," Douglas said, "it was Art Marshall who filled in all the blanks."

KEN MORRISON (1918-) AND HELEN MORRISON (1919-)

For more than half a century, the Minnesota natives have been among Florida's most assiduous and effective citizen activists.

The Morrisons arrived in Florida with luminous credentials. Ken, who accepted a job in 1956 as director of Mountain Lake Sanctuary (now known as Bok Tower Gardens), had served for the previous seven years as editor of *Audubon Magazine*, the official publication of the National Audubon Society. Before that, he had worked as a free-lance writer in Minnesota and as publications editor for the state's conservation department.

The couple wasted little time in becoming familiar with the conservation network in their new state, and four years after their arrival Ken founded the Ridge Audubon Society, a chapter covering eastern Polk County, including the small town of Babson Park, where the Morrisons settled on eight acres of scrub land along Crooked Lake to raise their children. By the early 1960s, Ken had achieved enough statewide renown to be elected president of the Florida Audubon Society.

Around that time, concerns over the fate of the Ocklawaha River began to percolate through the environmental community. Though they lived far from the river, the Morrisons joined the earliest opposition to the U.S. Army Corps of Engineers' plan to truncate the Ocklawaha as part of the Cross Florida Barge Canal project. They traveled to the river to take part in a "boatathon," and Helen produced a turning point in the campaign when the couple drove to Ocala for a meeting of the Florida Canal Authority in 1965. The river's defenders had been fruitlessly seeking a public hearing on the barge canal project, and during the public comments that night Helen stood and addressed the chairman of the Canal Authority, L.C. Ringhaver, the head of a heavy-equipment company in Ocala. She pressed Ringhaver to set a date for a public hearing, and she remained standing until—whether charmed by her decorous manner or cowed by her persistence—he promised to do so.

"Helen was always very polite and sweet, smiling and disarmingly friendly to all," said Bill Partington, director of Florida Defenders of the Environment during the barge canal fight. "She was ladylike and seemingly harmless but devastating."

The commitment Helen secured that night in Ocala led to a notorious meeting of the governor's water resources committee in early 1966. The Morrisons were present in Tallahassee that day for the hearing that not only put canal proponents on the permanent defensive but also, in the judgment of many, marked the advent of a truly statewide conservation movement.

"That was almost the start of unifying the environmentalists in Florida to become active," Ken Morrison said. "I mean, they'd been active in their communities, but that sort of began the statewide emphasis that later resulted in organizations becoming active in these things."

"It was very interesting because I think in some instances it was such a surprise to have people go to Tallahassee from all over the state — some of them rode the bus — and they were just intent on bringing what they felt," Helen said, "even some of them who had never seen the Ocklawaha River but knew it should not be harnessed into a canal."

Later in the campaign against the canal, Ken offered an invaluable assist to the newly formed Florida Defenders of the Environment when he suggested that the group solicit signatures from scientists across the country on a petition that would be forwarded to President Richard Nixon. FDE found 162 scientists to sign the letter, one of several crucial influences that prompted Nixon to halt construction of the canal in January of 1971.

Even as they became energetically involved in issues of statewide concern, the Morrisons also led the efforts to protect habitat around the ecologically important Lake Wales Ridge in the area where they lived. Ken helped convince The Nature Conservancy to purchase the 3,000-acre Tiger Creek Preserve, a virgin tract near Lake Wales containing unique species of plants. (It has since swelled to 5,000 acres.) Under Ken's leadership, Ridge Audubon worked to protect the Green Swamp, which covers part of Polk County and provides the headwaters for four major rivers, making it, in Ken's words, a "water tower" for Central Florida. Alarmed by continued dredging projects in the swamp, Ken wrote to state attorney general Robert Shevin and suggested that the state intervene under the section of the Florida constitution that held the state responsible for conserving natural resources. To his surprise,

Shevin concurred and got an injunction, which effectively ended all dredging in the Green Swamp. Not satisfied with that victory, Ridge Audubon successfully campaigned to have the Green Swamp designated an area of critical state concern, creating a more daunting obstacle to future development.

Never content to watch from a distance, Ken and Helen have ventured to Tallahassee "many dozen" of times (in Ken's estimation) for cabinet meetings or legislative hearings, sometimes making the seven-hour drive from Babson Park three times during a legislative session. When it seemed crucial, they drove to public meetings elsewhere in the state as well. Partington sometimes hosted the couple in his Winter Park home, and he soon came to expect more than just the two guests when the Morrisons drove up from Babson Park.

"Helen and Ken came up here a few times and stayed overnight and when they did that she'd always have some kind of crippled or orphaned animal, whether it was an opossum or a baby bird or an owl, she always had something," Partington said. "She couldn't leave it home; she had to bring the thing with her."

Since moving to Florida, Ken Morrison has served on the board of directors of nearly every major environmental organization in the state at some point, as well as that of the national Defenders of Wildlife. During his 25 years at Bok Tower Gardens, visitors would find his desk piled high with papers—most of it in the form of newsletters from conservation groups. He is one of the few environmental activists willing publicly to admit involvement with the Florida League Against Progress (FLAP), a mostly underground alliance that uses humor and mischief to discourage people from moving to the state.

In addition to the many words the Morrisons have spoken on behalf of the environment at public meetings over the decades, they have had hundreds of letters published in the opinions pages of newspapers across the state. Though Ken is the writer by training, the letters usually bear Helen's name as well. In 1984, Ken published a book, *Mountain Lake Almanac*, which combined his observations along the Lake Wales Ridge with more universal ruminations on the natural world. Almost two decades later, in his eighties, he was at work on what might be considered a sequel.

At an age when even the most devoted conservationist might be less inclined to worry over the future of Florida, Ken and Helen Morrison were still paying close attention to such matters as Polk County's comprehensive plan and the fate of Rodman Dam and — Helen's abiding concern — environmental education in public schools.

The Morrisons' own four children didn't need to rely on schools for their nature lessons. The couple's son Steve works for The Nature Conservancy at its Tiger Creek Preserve office, and their daughter Sally works as a ranger for the Florida State Parks system.

"You work on different things and you're never sure to what extent your efforts are contributing toward the total success or failure of projects," Ken said. "We feel good about what we have done, and other people have said that we've been successful in accomplishing various things. So we like to think that's right."

BILL PARTINGTON (1928-)

Though little known outside the flock, Partington played an indispensable role in the campaign against the Cross Florida Barge Canal and later contributed greatly to the growth of a fact-based approach to environmental campaigns.

A Massachusetts native, Partington spent a decade running a family business, meanwhile pursuing his real interest — reptiles — working with a professor at Brown University doing research on turtles. In 1965, he learned that the Pine Jog Conservation and Education Center, a facility run by Florida Audubon Society in West Palm Beach, was searching for a director. Partington got the job, moved to Florida and immediately became enmeshed in environmental issues. When some conservation-minded locals decided it would be a good idea to form an alliance of groups, Partington organized the Federated Conservation Council, which brought together 25 entities — garden clubs, civic chapters and traditional environmental outfits — and he began producing a monthly newsletter. The council worked to combat dredge-and-fill projects in Southeast Florida and to protect islands in the Intracoastal Waterway from development. In its most notable success, the alliance stopped plans to develop part of John Prince Park, the last remaining natural marsh area of any size in West Palm Beach, and convinced county commissioners instead to set it aside as a permanent nature area.

Florida Audubon's board of directors decided in 1967 to create a new executive position dedicated to conservation issues, and Partington landed the job, relocating near the state headquarters in Maitland. As Audubon's assistant director, he monitored the activities of the state government, producing a newsletter, sending out alerts to local chapters on urgent legislative matters and organizing trips to Tallahassee for public hearings. He also became a part-time lobbyist, spending much of each legislative session in the capital, borrowing a desk from a sympathetic state senator to work on environmental bills, often in collaboration with Nathaniel Reed, an advisor to Gov. Claude Kirk. Among the ad-hoc efforts Partington oversaw with Florida Audubon was the formation of the American Alligator Council, a small group (including University of Florida biologists Archie Carr and Wayne King) that worked toward the passage of a New York law banning the sale of alligator products—a tactic that reduced gator hunting in Florida by drying up the market.

While still in West Palm Beach, Partington had joined the forces contending against the planned barge canal that would devastate the Ocklawaha River, and he continued to follow the issue as a Florida Audubon official. When several members of Audubon's Gainesville chapter decided to form a separate group in 1969 entirely dedicated to the canal fight, they hired Partington as the director of Florida Defenders of the Environment. He and David Anthony, a canal foe since 1962, traveled to New York to meet with leaders of the Environmental Defense Fund, a pioneering organization in the use of legal tactics for conservation causes. Guided by the EDF, Partington and Anthony drew up a lawsuit seeking an injunction against the Army Corps of Engineers, the builder of the canal. "It was awful from a legal point of view," Partington recalls of their draft, "but it worked." In January of 1971, with the canal approximately one-third complete, a U.S. district judge issued the injunction against the Army Corps of Engineers. Four days later, President Richard Nixon directed the Corps of Engineers to abandon the project. The legal maneuverings continued for years, but the canal was effectively dead.

While engaged with Florida Defenders of the Environment, Partington was approached by The Conservation Foundation, a Washington-based group that hoped to establish independent centers for environmental education and advocacy in every state. Partington suggested creating the Florida chapter under the auspices of Florida Audubon, but the Washington group—having gained a $100,000 grant from the Ford Foundation—wanted the center to be autonomous from any existing entity. Partington agreed to take the helm of the new group, which formed in 1971 as the Florida Conservation Foundation. Based in Winter Park, it included the Environmental Information Center, a clearinghouse that produced a not-quite-monthly newsletter called *ENFO*. The newsletter, usually a monograph, drew heavily upon the expertise of academics and quickly gained a reputation as essential reading not only for activists such as Art Marshall but also for employees of regulatory agencies. The Foundation also organized national conferences and seminars, including one on nuclear power at which Marjory Stoneman Douglas debated representatives of the industry. "We were respected even by our enemies," Partington said of the Florida Conservation Foundation.

Under the foundation's aegis, Partington set up separate entities, some of which served a short-term purpose and two of which—the Florida Native Plant Society and the League of Conservation Voters—spun off as independent groups. One of Partington's projects, the Florida Solar Coalition, worked with the Department of Energy to distribute blueprints for building a solar water heater, and the coalition produced a book written by Partington's wife, Joan. Partington also played an active role in encouraging a citizens group to contend against development around the Wekiva River, and he helped form an environmental studies program at Rollins College. His career as an environmental instigator in Florida lasted only about two and a half decades, but during that period Partington's fingerprints could be found on a multitude of initiatives. A skilled jazz pianist, he thrived as something of a conservation bandleader, bringing together activists in important collaborations.

Or, to use the metaphor of Ken Alvarez from his book *Twilight of the Panther*, "Partington is a one-man environmental army."

JOHN D. PENNEKAMP (1897-1978)

The man who helped transform the wishes of others into the reality of Everglades National Park often downplayed any suggestion that he belonged in the pantheon of Florida's great environmentalists.

"They call me a conservationist," Pennekamp told a reporter late in his life. "But I'm not. They probably would shoot me for saying this, but I could live without seeing the Everglades."

Whatever his motivations, Pennekamp's tangible contributions to the environmental movement are apparent for all to see.

Born and raised in Cincinnati, Pennekamp set a course for himself in the newspaper business from childhood. He joined the *Cincinnati Post* as a copy boy at the age of 14 and soon moved up to a reporter's position and then became city editor of the paper. During the 1920s, at the height of the Florida land boom, Pennekamp pitched a story to his superiors about the many wealthy Cincinnatians moving to Florida—notably a millionaire industrialist named William McQuillan. The paper sent Pennekamp to South Florida to writer a story, and while there he accepted an offer to become editor of the *Miami Herald*. Not until years later did Pennekamp reveal that he had been smitten with the millionaire's daughter, Irene McQuillan, while she still lived in Cincinnati. Three months after Pennekamp arrived at the *Herald*, he and Irene were married.

Pennekamp established such a reputation for integrity as an editor and columnist during the following two decades that when Gov. Spessard Holland in 1944 revived state interest in the languishing drive for a national park in the Everglades, he turned to *Herald* publisher John S. Knight and suggested that if Pennekamp publicly advocated the idea the state legislature would fall in line. Knight agreed and asked Pennekamp to work toward getting lawmakers to pay for the land needed to create the park, to which Pennekamp asked what park he was talking about.

The editor quickly educated himself on the details. Under the joint arrangements between the federal and state governments, Florida needed to buy about 400,000 acres of privately owned land inside the planned park boundaries, at an estimated total cost of $2 million. With the legislature controlled by a group of North Floridians dubbed the "Pork Choppers" for their skill at steering appropriations toward their home districts, Pennekamp didn't expect lawmakers to produce the entire amount. He decided that an appropriation of $400,000 could spark enough private donations to cover the needed $2 million. Pennekamp arranged a meeting with a group of the Pork Choppers at a fishing camp in Orange Springs, and after a lunch of chicken, greens and cornbread, the men settled into a game of poker. "Just nickel and dime stuff," Pennekamp later said, "but before long I had taken $30 from them." Growing annoyed at the editor's success, a particularly influential legislator, B.C. Pearce of Palatka, asked how much Pennekamp wanted the state to offer for the Everglades purchases. Taking another gamble, Pennekamp asked for the full $2 million. Pearce replied, "Well, why don't you go ask the legislature for it instead of trying to pick *our* pockets?" Pennekamp knew that with the Pork Choppers, an oral commitment was binding. The legislature came through, and on December 6, 1947, Pennekamp sat beside President Harry Truman on the grandstand at Everglades City for the official dedication ceremony.

Though modest about his credentials as a conservationist, Pennekamp recognized the significance of his role as the closer in a two-decade quest to protect Florida's premier ecological wonder.

"Everglades National Park is my greatest achievement because if I hadn't done it there would be no park," Pennekamp said years later. "Nobody will deny that."

In the midst of his pursuit of Everglades funding, Pennekamp was involved in another skirmish that brought him national recognition. The *Herald* in 1944 ran two articles and one cartoon lambasting local judges, and one judge responded by convicting the *Herald* — and Pennekamp, as its associate editor — of contempt. The *Herald* appealed, and the case went to the U.S. Supreme Court, which in 1946 unanimously overturned the contempt of court ruling, establishing John Pennekamp as a First Amendment hero. It was far from the only public tussle involving Pennekamp during his 52 years with the *Herald*. When Tom Watson, the state's attorney general, spoke out against the spending for an Everglades park late in the process after remaining silent for years, Pennekamp publicly blasted him. Watson, a candidate for governor in 1948, responded with a letter that the editor proudly retained the rest of his life in which Watson promised to spit in Pennekamp's face if the two ever met.

When the legislature created the Florida Board of Parks and Historical Memorials in the late 1940s, Pennekamp accepted a nomination as its inaugural chairman and held an unpaid position on the board for more than two decades. During his tenure, state parks doubled in number and annual attendance swelled from 7,500 to about 10 million. He played a crucial role in the creation of Cape Florida State Park in Key Biscayne, which opened in 1969.

Like Everglades National Park, the preserve that stands as Pennekamp's legacy arose from the ideas of others. In the late 1950s, a coalition of marine biologists led by Gilbert Voss of the University of Miami petitioned the federal government to protect the coral reef off Key Largo, an area suffering from raids by opportunists who sold chunks of coral to tourists along U.S. 1. When the National Audubon Society advocated for an underwater preserve, Pennekamp mediated in talks among officials from the federal and state governments as well as commissioners from Monroe County, which owned part of the submerged land targeted for a park. The negotiations moved forward with astonishing speed, and the combined donations created a park extending from Key Largo to the edge of the continental shelf. At the dedication ceremony in 1960, Gov. LeRoy Collins surprised Pennekamp by declaring the nation's first underwater preserve as John Pennekamp Coral Reef State Park. "His pen has struck down the despoiler," Collins intoned, "and exalted those who would preserve." The editor later induced a Key Largo landowner to donate 2,400 acres, including an island and three miles of ocean frontage, for the park's headquarters. Pennekamp often visited the park named for him—or at least its above-ground segment—and he told the story of the time a park concessionaire suggested that he provide pamphlets to answer some of the questions asked most often by visitors. When Pennekamp asked which question topped the list, he learned that guests wanted to know "how long you've been dead."

Despite his protestations on his status as a naturalist, Pennekamp often fished with friends near Cape Sable—especially after the scare of a heart attack when he was just 40. He also regularly covered environmental topics in his column, "Behind the Front Page," which ran in the *Herald* for 35 years until he retired in 1977, a few months before his death. As early as 1963, years before Art Marshall unveiled his blueprint for rescuing the Everglades, Pennekamp addressed the annual meeting of the National Audubon Society and raised the specter of a looming water crisis in South Florida. A few years later, he told the Florida Institute of Park Personnel, "Conservation is no hobby. ... (W)ithout conservation, the earth will continue on its hell-bent course to become as bleak and lifeless as those photographs we have been seeing of the moon."

Without Pennekamp, there's no telling what the Everglades might look like now.

NATHANIEL P. REED (1933-)

Nat Reed ranks as a rarity among environmentalists in Florida: someone who has been genuinely effective both as a government insider and as an activist outsider.

Reed's father, Joseph V. Reed, who later gained renown as a Broadway producer, bought the bankrupt Hobe Sound Company in 1932, a year before Nathaniel Pryor Reed was born, turning it into a profitable real estate and holding company that supplemented the family's already considerable wealth. Nat Reed grew up in an atmosphere of great privilege, living most of the year in Greenwich, Conn., and spending summers at Jupiter Island, a slender coastal barrier north of West Palm Beach. The family traveled frequently, and at the age of 15 Nat made a walking tour from Oslo, Norway, to the Arctic Circle.

Though the family business involved real estate (as well as ranching and citrus), Joseph Reed's financial security and his appreciation for nature allowed the Hobe Sound Company to develop its properties carefully, often leaving natural areas intact. His family's environmental sensitivity imprinted itself on Nat at an early age.

"My passion always was outdoors—it was fishing, which was my first great love, and then it became butterflies and moths and then trees, and just everything about my life has been fastened on the outdoors,"

Reed said. "I had a very caring mother and father. We were just a very outdoorsy family. All of my brothers had an abiding concern (for the environment). Everybody cared; I just seemed to care a little bit more."

After graduating from Trinity College in Hartford, Conn., Reed joined the United States Air Force's intelligence services and spent five years in Europe, Northern Africa and the Middle East. He rose to the rank of first lieutenant, and he said the experience of commanding other lieutenants and enlisted men prepared him for the positions he would later hold in Tallahassee and Washington. It wasn't that Reed planned to seek any government position. When his military service ended in 1959, he returned to Florida with the intent of merely working in the family business. He couldn't help being dismayed, however, by what he saw happening to South Florida: The Army Corps of Engineers was busy fragmenting the Everglades into manageable units of water, with plans in the works to transform the winding Kissimmee River into a canal.

"The underdog situation (for environmentalists) was very apparent; that kind of caught me," Reed said. "And it just seemed like the Florida I knew so well was disappearing rapidly. ... From 1960 on I began to go to the various meetings of Florida Audubon Society and The Nature Conservancy and I began to speak out around the state."

Reed's life changed in 1966, when he served as an advisor to fellow Republican Claude Kirk in his long-shot campaign for governor. Reed urged Kirk to incorporate environmental planks into his platform, particularly a promise to curtail the selling of state-owned submerged lands for dredge-and-fill projects, a practice that had been routine for years.

"That was great fun," Reed said of the Kirk campaign. "Whenever he had a question about something serious about the environment he said, 'Ask Reed.' That was a marvelous opportunity to speak to a whole range of issues that were of great importance to me."

Kirk defied predictions by winning the 1966 election, and Reed and his wife Alita were among those invited to a post-inauguration picnic luncheon at the governor's office the following January. At one point Kirk escorted Nat and Alita down a corridor and took them into what Reed calls "a tiny cubbyhole." Kirk said, "If you really believe in trying to save Florida, stay with me—here's your office. I'll get you a secretary." Reed said yes.

With that exchange, Reed—who had held positions as a Jupiter Island city councilman and as co-chairman of a state panel on marine antiquities—became at age 33 the first official environmental advisor to a Florida governor. The press made much of the fact that a multimillionaire had taken a $1-a-year job, but Reed made it clear from the outset that his was not a token position. He installed himself in the undersized office and—in keeping with his military background of using a "network" of sources—tacked up a wall map that listed contacts with every local environmental group in the state. He welcomed activists to his office and plotted legislative strategy with some of them. Reed didn't hesitate to criticize such controversial projects as the Cross Florida Barge Canal and the Big Cypress Jetport, and he once appeared at a meeting of the State Chamber of Commerce and lambasted the group for its anti-environmental positions.

Bill Partington, an official with Florida Audubon and Florida Defenders of the Environment in the late 1960s, recalls a meeting in which the cabinet considered a proposal for a development in the Keys disguised as a shrimp farming operation. In Kirk's absence, the cabinet unanimously approved the project, prompting Reed to vociferously denounce the cabinet members. (Amid negative publicity and Kirk's return for the next meeting, the cabinet reversed its decision.) The strident approach earned Reed the enmity of business groups and the nickname "Mr. Clean" from the state's newspapers. The patrician activist, with his lanky, 6-foot-5 frame and his impeccable attire—he always wore sharply pressed pants even for a stroll through Big Cypress Swamp—seemed to fascinate the media.

It wasn't just philosophical rivals who could receive Reed's scorn. Even representatives of environmental groups sometimes found him brusque in his disagreement.

"He has a seriousness to him, and I think we've all been stepped on at one time or another by him," Partington said, "but he's quick to turn around and get your help on something again. To him the issues are much, much more important than any of the personalities that might be injured."

In a 1968 speech to Florida Audubon, Reed said, "Conservationists must become a firm, hard lobby." He followed up those words the next year by helping to found Conservation 70s, a coalition of environmental groups dedicated to lobbying in Tallahassee. Though the group didn't last long, it brought conservation groups a new level of visibility and influence in state politics.

Despite early opposition from the legislature, Kirk and Reed tackled the major environmental issues of the time. Reed's influence helped Kirk transform the philosophy of the trustees of the Internal Improvement Fund—consisting of the governor and cabinet—which made decisions on dredge-and-fill projects. The approval of permits changed from routine to unlikely to virtually impossible during Reed's four and a half years in Tallahassee.

"Claude Kirk was no environmentalist himself, but he depended on Nathaniel Reed to guide him," said Ken Morrison, one of Florida's most prominent environmental activists. "When the governor was in public, Reed had to stay right close to him so that if any question came up that Kirk couldn't answer, why Reed could whisper in his ear what to say."

In 1967, the legislature approved Kirk's idea for a Department of Air and Water Pollution Control (the predecessor of the Department of Environmental Protection), and the governor appointed Reed first as a member and later as chairman. Reed directed his attention first to the woeful status of sewage treatment in Florida and, with support from Kirk, gradually pressured cities and counties into building long-overdue facilities. "Mr. Clean" then addressed the equally serious problem of industrial pollution. With Kirk's approval, Reed took an uncompromising position on the need for companies to meet the requirements of the federal Clean Water Act, sometimes presiding over "enforcement conferences" held in areas with notable pollution problems. Reed recalls a moment of triumph coming at one such conference in Escambia County, where the government officials at first faced undisguised hostility from citizens, most of whom worked for one of the companies facing state scrutiny for ongoing environmental offenses. Reed arrived one morning to find that the women of the local garden club had laid flowers on the table of the government officials, and he knew the public had been swayed. The conference led to an agreement between the state and local industries on pollution levels in Escambia Bay.

"It was one of the most magical moments in my life," Reed said. "The general public said, 'We don't want to smell it, we don't want our children to have to swim in it, we don't want to drink it, we're sick and tired of seeing dead fish.' And we knew we'd won."

The anti-pollution efforts, though, may have cost Kirk in the 1970 election, when Democrat Reubin Askew unseated him as governor. It could well have been the end of government service for Reed, who had three children and had been reluctant to leave Jupiter Island in the first place. Askew, however, crossed party lines and asked Reed to join his administration. Reed accepted, but within a year he received a call from an old friend, Rogers Morton, who had recently become Secretary of the Interior. Reed soon went to Washington as Assistant Secretary of the Interior for Fish, Wildlife and National Parks.

"Tallahassee prepared me for my five years as assistant secretary brilliantly," Reed said. "The education I got in the governor's office, learning how to write the kind of memorandums [Kirk] could read quickly and understand, satisfied [President Richard] Nixon to a T. ... By the time I got to Washington I was very comfortable with government."

Upon his arrival in Washington, Reed made it known that he would not be awed by his surroundings. During a hearing before Congress, the unknown bureaucrat stunned lawmakers with a lively denunciation of the Army Corps of Engineers' practice of routinely altering rivers throughout the nation. In another early action, Reed set a firm timetable for the nation's wildlife refuges and national parks to draw up overdue lists of wilderness designations—and then assigned a senior staff member to the issue. Reed kept his attention on Florida, playing point man in the federal government's purchase of half a million acres in the Big Cypress Swamp, but he also made a particular priority of land preservation in Alaska, first while in the Department of the Interior and later as chairman of an organization called Americans for Alaska.

Reed served in Washington through Nixon's re-election and his replacement by Gerald Ford, and he probably could have retained his post in the administration of Jimmy Carter, but he decided to leave government after an expected two years that had turned into 10. In one of his final acts, he signed a memorandum to the Army Corps of Engineers recommending the removal of dams from the Ocklawaha River. Reed's return to Florida fueled speculation about a possible run for office — he had been rumored as a candidate for governor in 1974 and for the U.S. Senate in 1976. After seriously mulling a run for governor in 1978, he instead took on the role of campaign manager for fellow Republican Jack Eckerd, who lost to Bob Graham. In the midst of the campaign, Reed accepted an appointment to the South Florida Water Management District's board of directors. He held the position intermittently for 14 sometimes-contentious years.

"What I tried to do was completely transform that agency from a flood-control, water-delivery-to-agriculture agency into a water-management agency," Reed said. "I had some successes and I've obviously had some failures."

In the mid-1980s, the state legislature gave needed attention to Florida's chaotic growth patterns, passing a series of laws that in theory gave Tallahassee much greater oversight into the growth plans of cities and counties. Reed had paid close attention to the results of similar laws in Oregon, where a group called 1000 Friends of Oregon led by the state's former governor had arisen to serve as a self-appointed monitor over growth management. In 1986, Reed got together with some of the state's leading political figures — Gov. and soon-to-be Sen. Bob Graham, U.S. Rep. Buddy MacKay and Florida Department of Community Affairs chief John DeGrove — all of whom agreed that Florida needed an organization like the one in Oregon.

"Everybody else had some kind of formal governmental job," Reed said. "And so everybody turned to me. I said, 'Listen, I'm running a family business and trying to raise three children,' and they said, 'You're it.'"

Reed became the first chairman of 1000 Friends of Florida, an entity that shadows the Department of Community Affairs, challenging zoning changes and revisions to comprehensive plans that threaten the environment. He continues to serve on the group's board of directors, a status he also has held for the National Audubon Society, The Nature Conservancy, National Resources Defense Council and the National Geographic Society.

Reed has reversed the pattern of his youth, making the longtime family home (named "Dragonsnook") on Jupiter Island his primary residence and spending summers in Maine. He takes pride in the environmental stewardship of his family and its neighbors in Southeast Florida. A group of Jupiter Island residents in the 1960s set aside a valuable tract for what became Blowing Rocks State Preserve, and the Reed family has donated hundreds of acres over the years to expand Hobe Sound National Wildlife Refuge—including three miles of ocean frontage that could have yielded a fortune from developers.

Though he has been out of government for more than 30 years, Reed often travels to Washington and finds that he remains welcome in many Congressional offices—though the reception tends to be chillier among the Western contingent, a carryover from Reed's policies at the Interior Department. Though nominally a Republican, he had better relations with officials in the Clinton Administration than those in the current Bush Administration and admits that he would have preferred to see Al Gore elected—an outcome he thinks the candidate squandered in 2000 by failing to taking a stand against a proposed commercial airport in Homestead.

"I call myself an independent Republican," Reed said. "I stay in the Republican Party so I can vote in the primaries in my county, which has become 100 percent Republican. I'm frank to say that I like to embarrass the far-right wing of our party by having more common sense than they do."

Though he remains thoroughly engaged in the environmental battles of the day, Reed acknowledges that he misses the direct influence he held during his days as a government official. He bears a particular fondness for the late 1960s, a turning point in Florida when Reed was the state's most visible crusader against the degradation of the environment.

"I came at a moment when Florida was getting restless and emerging from its environmental slumber and was beginning to get really interested," Reed told a reporter in 1970. "Nobody could be luckier than I. I hit it dead square center ... right on target."

KATHERINE BELL TIPPETTS (1865-1950)

During more than a century of existence, Florida Audubon Society has had only one female president. Katherine Tippetts, however, was by no means a token appointment.

Like many of the early leaders of Florida's conservation movement, Tippetts emerged from the leisure class. Born Emily Katherine Bell to an aristocratic family in Maryland (her mother's ancestors had arrived on the Mayflower), she spent her childhood amid private teachers and became fluent in five languages. She married a newspaperman, William H. Tippetts, a European correspondent for several papers, and the couple spent several years living in both New York and Europe. During this period, Katherine became acquainted with some of the world's major literary figures, and she cultivated a writing career of her own, first as a contributor to periodicals and later as a writer of novels, using the pseudonym Jerome Cable. In 1902, William Tippetts' failing health prompted the couple to move to St. Petersburg, where they bought a 50-room hotel and renamed it the Hotel Belmont. After her husband's death in 1909, Katherine Tippetts took over management of the hotel and other business ventures. She devoted most of her energy, however, to non-commercial matters, including a love of nature, founding the St. Petersburg Audubon Society in 1909 and serving as its president for 33 years.

Tippetts advocated the idea of bird sanctuaries, and she persuaded 11 cities in Pinellas County to declare official protection for birds within their borders. A photo from the era shows Tippetts standing beside a sign featuring a painting of a pelican and the words, "ST. PETERS-BURG — BIRD SANCTUARY — NO SHOOTING — Under Penalty of Fine + Imprisonment." She led an eight-year campaign for the designation of a state bird, and in 1922 the Senate agreed to honor the mockingbird — the winner in a vote by children. Equally concerned about the area's waterfowl, Tippetts compiled information about roseate spoonbills on an island near her home on Pinellas Point and worked with federal agencies to gain an executive order from President Warren Harding setting aside three islands as federal sanctuaries, part of what eventually became Pinellas National Wildlife Refuge.

The St. Petersburg Audubon Society hosted the annual meeting of the state organization in 1916, and four years later Florida Audubon selected Tippetts as its president. During her five years at the helm, Florida Audubon successfully lobbied the state legislature to make bird study compulsory in public schools and arranged for teacher training courses at the state colleges in Gainesville and Tallahassee. Tippetts also played an aggressive role in the legislature's creation of the Florida Fish and Game Commission. Under her leadership, Florida Audubon widened its purview beyond birds, gaining state protection for some native trees and flowering plants.

In a bid to increase her influence in Tallahassee, Tippetts unsuccessfully ran for a seat in the Florida House of Representatives — becoming only the second woman to mount a candidacy. In 1924, she resigned as president of Florida Audubon and took a position as vice president at large for the Florida Federation of Women's Clubs, at the time a virtual equal of the Audubon chapter in environmental advocacy. Tippetts eventually became national conservation chairman of the General Federation of Women's Clubs, and she also served as an officer with the American Forestry Association and the National Park Association. Equally engaged in civic activism, Tippetts helped establish a children's hospital in St. Petersburg.

By the time of her death in 1950, Tippetts was affectionately known to many in St. Petersburg as "The Bird Woman."

Conclusion

In the pursuit of conservation, victories are rarely permanent and new challenges constantly arise. Environmental advocates are perpetually on the defensive, reacting to threats and attempting to preserve what others want to pave over.

There is no reason to expect that dynamic to change in the near future.

Florida's economy has long relied on a steady influx of new residents into the state, a phenomenon that has made construction among the state's dominant industries. Around the turn of the 21st century, Florida was gaining about 1,000 new residents a day. The relentless population growth cost Florida in the loss of wetlands, scrub habitat and green space in general, with a resulting decline in animal species, from scrub jays to Eastern indigo snakes, dependent on certain ecosystems.

The collapse of the national real-estate boom yielded the unthinkable in Florida: population growth came to a standstill in 2008. The turnabout offered environmental advocates a partial respite from the constant development pressure and raised hopes that the state's leaders might begin steering the economy away from the building-intensive approach that prompted a writer for *The New Yorker* magazine to label Florida "the Ponzi state." Instead, though, local governments began suspending or reducing impact fees—county levies designed to offset the need for new roads, schools and parks caused by new subdivisions—under the guise of job creation, thereby signaling that little had really changed.

Meanwhile, the Deepwater Horizon explosion in the Gulf of Mexico raised new concerns about oil drilling near Florida's coasts. The rupture, which eventually spewed more than 200 million gallons of oil from the sea floor, occurred one year after the Florida House of Representatives hurriedly passed a bill that would have allowed oil exploration within three miles of the Florida coastline, reversing a long-standing ban on near-shore drilling. The bill stalled in the state Senate, and the Deepwater Horizon disaster scuttled any chance such a measure would be revived in the 2010 session.

Environmental advocates, however, knew it might not be so long before legislators made another push to allow drilling near Florida's coasts. How soon that comes may well depend on the facts that emerge about the long-term environmental effects of the worst oil spill in U.S. history.

Climate change is a related area of ongoing concern for conservationists in Florida. The effects of the planet's warming in recent decades had already become apparent in Alaska and other northern regions by the early 21st century, and climate scientists predicted that rising oceans in coming decades would drastically alter the coastline of Florida. Environmental advocates will continue to lobby for more rigorous conservation policies as well as the increased use of alternative forms of energy, including solar power and biofuels. Though conservation groups in Florida and elsewhere have traditionally opposed nuclear power, an energy source that contributes fewer harmful greenhouse gases to the atmosphere but creates radioactive waste, some are beginning to welcome nuclear power, however cautiously, as a lesser evil than oil—and coal-based power plants.

Water will undoubtedly figure into many conservation battles in the coming decades. Florida's incessant population growth already has strained the capacity of some cities and counties to meet the demand for water, causing conflicts between municipalities competing over finite sources. Environmental groups will continue to press for increased use of reclaimed water for irrigation and other ways to reduce consumption of the precious resource.

Beginning with the campaign to protect wading birds from slaughter at the turn of the 20th century, many conservation struggles in Florida have been connecting in one way or another to the Everglades. The "River of Grass" will continue to be a source of deep concern for environmental groups. Securing annual federal funding for the Comprehensive Everglades Restoration Plan is likely to be an ongoing challenge, and meanwhile conservation groups will watch closely to see if the plan's dozens of individual projects deliver the promised benefits for the imperiled ecosystem. In addition, environmental advocates will push for other necessary steps to help the Everglades, including the purchase of more conservation land north of Everglades National Park and the building of a skyway to barriers to water flow into the region.

Decades of ineffective growth-control policies in Florida prompted one of the most interesting and controversial environmental gambits in recent years, a proposed constitutional amendment nicknamed Florida Hometown Democracy that would require voter approval for all changes to local development plans. Proponents, led by Lesley Blackner, a Palm Beach lawyer, argued that Amendment 4 was needed because city and county governments routinely alter their comprehensive plans to allow proposed construction projects. The state's established conservation groups endorsed Amendment 4, even if some environmentalists privately wondered about its practical consequences. Early polling showed the public favoring the proposal, though perhaps not overwhelmingly enough to guarantee the 60-percent threshold required for passage of constitutional amendments.

Not surprisingly, developers and business groups fought back by raising millions of dollars to fight Amendment 4. So alarming was the prospect of local referendums on development plans that opponents admitted Florida's growth-control process was broken, though they argued that Amendment 4 was the wrong way to fix it. Though the proposal was soundly defeated, the battle demonstrated that Florida's conservationists are still capable of pushing back against the state's dominant financial and political forces.

The challenges for the environmental movement in the second decade of the 21st century will come as much from within as without. The activists of the 1960s and 1970s are dead or aged, and retirees now dominate many local Audubon and Sierra Club chapters. Without citizen activists willing to do the trench work of calling and writing to legislators to lobby them on bills, the environmental movement depends too heavily on its small cadre of paid professionals, who will always be outnumbered and outspent by corporate lobbyists. Conservation groups must find new ways to attract and retain younger members.

There is hope. High school and college students in recent years have identified themselves increasingly with "green" causes, even if that label is often vaguely applied. Whether such environmental concern proves to be a mere fad or translates into committed activism is an open question that will figure greatly into the future successes or failures of conservation groups in Florida and elsewhere.

For more than a century, Florida's environmental advocates have struggled to preserve the natural splendors that enchanted William Bartram when he first beheld them in the late 18th century. Without the ongoing commitment of conservationists, following upon the selfless efforts that began with a meeting of 15 people at Louis and Clara Dommerich's Maitland home in 1900, Florida is destined to become a place in which the artificial thoroughly displaces the natural, a place where scrub jays and gopher tortoises join Carolina parakeets and ivory-billed woodpeckers as mere historical curiosities and where nature itself becomes largely an anachronism.

BIBLIOGRAPHY

CHAPTER 1

Adams, Alexander B. *John James Audubon, A Biography.* New York: Putnam, 1966.

Audubon, John James. Audubon, Maria R., editor. *Audubon and His Journals.* New York: Chelsea House, 1983.

Belleville, Bill. 2000. *River of Lakes: A Journey on Florida's St. Johns River.* Athens, Ga.: University of Georgia Press.

Brown, Robin C. *Florida's First People.* Sarasota, Fla.: Pineapple Press, 1994.

Coker, William S. and Shofner, Jerrell H. *Florida From the Beginning to 1992.* Houston, Tex.: Pioneer Publications Inc., 1991.

Cruickshank, Helen G., editor. *Bartram in Florida 1774: The Adventures of the Great American Naturalist, Explorer, Artist.* Cocoa, Fla.: Florida Federation of Garden Clubs, Inc., 1986

Douglas, Marjory Stoneman. *Everglades: River of Grass.* Sarasota, Fla.: Pineapple Press, 1997.

Fagin, N. Bryllion. *William Bartram: Interpreter of the American Landscape.* Baltimore: The Johns Hopkins Press, 1933.

Gannon, Michael, editor. *The New History of Florida.* "Original Inhabitants" chapter by Jerald T. Milanich. Gainesville, Fla.: University Press of Florida, 1996.

Oeland, Glenn. "William Bartram: A Naturalist's Vision of Frontier America." *National Geographic,* March 2001.

Proby, Kathryn Hall. *Audubon In Florida.* Coral Gables, Fla.: University of Miami Press, 1974.

Tebeau, Charlton W. *A History of Florida*. Coral Gables, Fla.: University of Miami Press, 1971.

Wright, J. Leitch Jr. *Creeks and Seminoles: Destruction and Regeneration of the Muscogulge People*. Lincoln, Neb.: University of Nebraska Press, 1986.

CHAPTER 2

Graham, Frank Jr. *The Audubon Ark: A History of the National Audubon Society.* New York: Alfred A. Knopf; 1990.

Fuller, Walter P. "Who Was the Frenchman of Frenchman's Creek?", *Tequesta, The Journal of the Historical Association of Southern Florida*, 1969, p. 45-59

Pierce, Charles Williams. "The Cruise of the Bonton," *Tequesta*, 1962, p. 3-64

Williams, Robert W. "History of Bird Protection in Florida." Howell, Arthur H., *Florida Bird Life*, Florida Department of Game and Fresh Water Fish, Tallahassee, 1932.

-------. "The Audubon Society," *The Auk*, April 1888, p. 288.

Summerlin, J. "Slaughter in Florida." *The Audubon Magazine*, July 1887, p. 139.

----------. "Wholesale Destruction of Birds in Florida." *The Audubon Magazine*, September 1887, p. 178-180.

Scott, W.E.D. "The Present Condition of Some of the Bird Rookeries of the Gulf Coast of Florida, First Paper," *The Auk*, April 1887, p. 135-143

Scott, W.E.D. "The Present Condition of Some of the Bird Rookeries of the Gulf Coast of Florida, Second Paper," *The Auk*, July 1887, p. 213-221

Scott, W.E.D. "The Present Condition of Some of the Bird Rookeries of the Gulf Coast of Florida, Third Paper," *The Auk*, October 1887, p. 273-281

Chapman, Frank M. "A List of Birds Observed at Gainesville, Florida," *The Auk*, July 1888, p. 267-277.

------------. "The Audubon Movement." *The Nation*, Sept. 14, 1905, p. 214.

Scott, W.E.D. "A Summary of Observations on the Birds of the Gulf Coast of Florida," *The Auk*, January 1889, p. 13-21

Scott, W.E.D. "An Account of Flamingoes Observed in the Vicinity of Cape Sable, Florida," *The Auk*, July 1890, p. 221-229

Royall, J.B. "The Florida State Game Commission," *The Florida Naturalist*, October 1937, p. 1-5

-------. "State Game Department Report," *The Florida Naturalist*, October 1931, p. 18-19

Longstreet, R.J. "President's Report," *The Florida Naturalist*, October 1936, p. 47-48

Hadley, Alden H. "Reminiscences of the Florida Everglades," *The Florida Naturalist*, January 1941, p. 21-29

Marth, Del and Martha J. Marth. *The Florida Almanac 2002-2003*, Pelican Publishing Company, Gretna, Louisiana, 2002

Derr, Mark. *Some Kind of Paradise, A Chronicle of Man and the Land in Florida*, William Morrow and Co. Inc., 1989

CHAPTER 3

Blackman, Lucy Worthington. 1935. *The Florida Audubon Society 1900-1935*. Winter Park, Fla.: Florida Audubon Society.

Dommerich, Clara J. Minutes of Florida Audubon Society meeting, March 2, 1900, Maitland Historical Society.

Blackman, Lucy Worthington. 1939. *The Florida Federation of Women's Clubs 1895-1939*. Jacksonville, Fla.: Southern Historical Publishing Associates.

Buchheister, Carl W., and Graham, Frank Jr. Jan., 1973. "From the Swamps and Back." *Audubon* magazine.

Dieterich, Emily Perry. "Birds of a Feather: The Coconut Grove Audubon Society, 1915-1917," *Tequesta,* 1985, p. 5-27

-------. "Editorial," *Bird-Lore*, April 1899, p. 63

-------. "Reports of Societies," *Bird-Lore*, June 1900, p. 96-97

Vance, Linda D. "May Mann Jennings and Royal Palm State Park," *Florida Historical Quarterly*, July 1976, p. 1-17

Tebeau, Charlton W. *Man In the Everglades*, University of Miami Press, Coral Gables, 1968

Chapman, Frank M. "Pelican Island Revisited," *Bird-Lore*, January-February 1901, p. 3-8

Vanderpool, Mrs. I. "Early Days of the Florida Audubon Society," *The Florida Naturalist*, July 1932, p. 64-66

Vanderpool, Mrs. I. "Florida Society," *Bird-Lore*, September-October 1901, p. 183

Marrs, Mrs. Kingsmill. "Florida Audubon Society," *Bird-Lore*, November-December 1901, p. 220.

Blackman, William. "Economic Value of Birds to Farmers and Fruit Growers." Florida Audubon Society pamphlet, Florida Audubon Society papers, Rollins College special collections.

Some Kind of Paradise, A Chronicle of Man and the Land in Florida.

Graham, Frank Jr. 1990. *The Audubon Ark: A History of the National Audubon Society.* New York: Alfred A. Knopf.

Landfried, Tracy. "The Early History of the Florida Audubon Society, 1900-1905." Florida Audubon Society papers, Maitland Historical Society.

Orr, Oliver H., Jr. 1992. *Saving America's Birds: T. Gilbert Pearson and the Founding of the Audubon Movement.* Gainesville, Fla.: University Press of Florida.

Tritaik, Paul. "Pelican Island National Wildlife Refuge," *The Florida Naturalist,* Spring 1997, p. 8-10

Poole, Leslie Kemp. "The Florida Story Begins with Audubon Wardens," *The Florida Naturalist,* Spring, 2000, p. 6-9

Marrs, Mrs. Kingsmill. "State Reports, Florida," *Bird-Lore,* November-December 1907, p. 332-335

Persons, Todd; Harrod, Karen, editor; Scott, Hal, and Friedman, Alexander J. 1975. *The Florida Naturalist* magazine, special edition.

----------. "The Audubon Societies." *Bird-Lore,* July-August 1908, p. 186-187

--------. "The Audubon Societies," *Bird-Lore,* January-February 1909, p. 51-53

-------------. "State Audubon Reports," *Bird-Lore,* November-December 1909, p. 309-310

Marrs, Mrs. Kingsmill. "State Audubon Reports," *Bird-Lore,* November-December 1910, p. 287-288

Marrs, Mrs. Kingsmill, "State Audubon Reports," *Bird-Lore,* November-December 1911, p. 365-366

Marrs, Mrs. Kingsmill, "State Audubon Reports," *Bird-Lore,* November-December 1912, p. 429-430

---------. "The Audubon Societies," *Bird-Lore,* March-April 1912, p. 135-136

Florida Bird Life

Pearson, T. Gilbert. "Report of the Secretary," *Bird-Lore,* November-December 1912, p. 383-392

Pearson, T. Gilbert. "The Audubon Societies," *Bird-Lore,* January-February 1913, p. 67

Marrs, Mrs. Kingsmill. "Florida," *Bird-Lore,* November-December 1913, 446-448

Pearson, T. Gilbert. "Plume Hunters Arrested," *Bird-Lore,* July-August 1913, p. 276-278

CHAPTER 4

Blake, Nelson M. *Land into Water – Water into Land*, University Presses of Florida, Tallahassee, 1980

Carter, Luther J. *The Florida Experience: Land and Water Policy in a Growth State,* The Johns Hopkins University Press, Baltimore, 1974

Gifford, John C. *On Preserving Tropical Florida*, compiled by Elizabeth Ogren Rothra, University of Miami Press, Coral Gables, 1972

Levin, Ted. "Forever Glades," *Audubon*, July-August 2001, p. 38-61

McCally, David. *The Everglades: An Environmental History*, University Press of Florida, Gainesville, 1999

A History of Florida, Tebeau

Gannon, Michael, editor. *The New History of Florida*, University Press of Florida, 1996

Douglas, Marjory Stoneman. *The Everglades: River of Grass*, Pineapple Press, 1997

Some Kind of Paradise

Man In the Everglades

Douglas, Marjory Stoneman, with John Rothchild. *Voice of the River*, Pineapple Press, Englewood, Florida, 1987

Vance, Linda D. *May Mann Jennings: Florida's Genteel Activist*, University Presses of Florida, Gainesville, 1985

Pratt, Theodore. "Papa of the Everglades National Park," *Saturday Evening Post*, August 9, 1947, p. 32-50

Wright, E. Lynne. *More Than Petticoats: Remarkable Florida Women*, The Globe Pequot Press, Guilford, Conn., 2001

Baker, John H. "The President's Report to You," *Audubon*, January-February 1945, p. 45-54.

Simpson, Charles Torrey. *In Lower Florida Wilds*, G.P. Putnam's Sons, New York, 1920

Leviero, Anthony. "President Pleads For Conservation," *The New York Times*, December 7, 1947, p. 1

Blackman, Lucy Worthington. *The Florida Audubon Society 1900-1935*, Florida Audubon Society, (no date).

Royall, J.B. "The Florida State Game Commission," *The Florida Naturalist*, October 1927, p. 1-5

-------. "Report of the 31st Annual Meeting," *The Florida Naturalist*, April 1931, p. 58-65

The Florida Almanac 2002-2003

Hadley, Alden H. "Campaigning for Conservation," *The Florida Naturalist,* October 1936, p. 1-5

Hadley, Alden H. "Report on the Audubon Educational Program for Florida," *The Florida Naturalist,* April 1941, p. 69-72

-----------. "In Memoriam, Alden H. Hadley," *The Florida Naturalist,* July 1951, p. 76-77

Straub, William L. *History of Pinellas County,* The Record Company, St. Augustine, 1929

Arsenault, Raymond. *St. Petersburg and the Florida Dream, 1888-1950,* University Press of Florida, Gainesville, 1996

Sprunt, Alexander Jr. "The Work of the National Association in Florida – Past and Present," *The Florida Naturalist,* January 1938

Mason, C. Russell. "Annual Report of the President," *The Florida Naturalist,* April 1937, p. 52-54

--------------. "State Game Department Report," *The Florida Naturalist,* October 1931, p. 18-19

Drobney, Jeffrey A. *Lumbermen and Log Sawyers: Life, Labor, and Culture in the North Florida Timber Industry, 1830-1930,* Mercer University Press, Macon, Ga., 1997

Miller, James J. *An Environmental History of Northeast Florida,* University Press of Florida, Gainesville, 1998

Kimbrough, Rhonda L. (Heritage Program Manager, National Forests in Florida). Correspondence with author, March 2002.

--------. *Reference Anthology of National Association of State Foresters, 1968,* Florida Society of American Foresters papers, University of Florida collections

Harbin, Linda (title, Florida Division of Forestry). Correspondence with author, April 2002

Wells, Mildred White. "Florida Clubwomen See Dream Realized in Everglades Park," *The General Federation Clubwoman,* December 1947, p. 6-8

Willey, Day Allen., "The Naval Stores Industry," *Scientific American,* October 10, 1908, p. 245.

------------. "Florida Celebrates Pulp Boom." *Business Week,* January 22, 1938, p. 39-40.

CHAPTER 5

Barbour, Thomas. *That Vanishing Eden*. Little, Brown and Company, Boston, 1944

The Florida Almanac 2002-2003

Some Kind of Paradise, A Chronicle of Man and the Land in Florida

Chesson, M.W. "Land Reclamation In Phosphate Industries." *The Florida Naturalist*, April 1963, p. 35-37.

Storer, John. "FAS' Beginnings ... John Storer Remembers." *The Florida Naturalist*, June 1972, p. 75-77

----------. "A Century of Conservation in Florida." *The Florida Naturalist*, Spring 2000, p. 6-13.

Tanner, James T. "The Ivory-billed Woodpecker." *The Florida Naturalist*, January 1943, p. 21-22.

Christy, Bayard. "The Vanishing Ivory-Bill." *Audubon Magazine*, March-April 1943, p. 99-102.

Mills, Herbert R. "Broadcasting DDT." *The Florida Naturalist*, July 1946, p. 57-63

Mills, Herbert R. "Another Look at DDT." *The Florida Naturalist*, July 1949, p. 71-78

--------. "Want Pollution of Peace River Stopped." Tampa Tribune, July 4, 1919, p. 3.

Blakey, Arch Fredric. *The Florida Phosphate Industry: A History of the Development and Use of a Vital Mineral*. Wertheim Committee, Harvard University, Cambridge, Mass., 1973.

------------. Bulletin of the Florida Chapter Sierra Club, January 1972.

Bobroff, Bob. "Phosphate Company Closed In Peace River Slime Case." *Orlando Sentinel*, December 23, 1971, 14A.

--------. "Florida Audubon Adds Least Tern Sanctuary," *The Florida Naturalist*, January 1959, p. 2.

Whisenhunt, Matt H. "Effect on Wildlife of Highpowered Insecticides." *The Florida Naturalist*, April 1959, p. 73-74.

Peters, Harold S. "Is A Control Program for Imported Fire Ants Necessary?" *The Florida Naturalist*, April 1959, p. 69-72.

---------. "Additional Land and Money for Key Deer." *The Florida Naturalist*, July 1961, p. 127.

Belleville, Bill. "Where Tiny Deer Reign." *The Oxford American*, Fall 2001, p. 72-78.

Defenders of Wildlife [http://www.defenders.org/habitat/highways/new/target/keydeer.html]

Di Silvestro, Roger. "What's killing Key deer?" National Wildlife Federation, [http://www.nwf.org/nationalwildlife/keydeer.html]

Klimstra, W.D. "The Key Deer." *The Florida Naturalist*, Winter 1985, p. 2-5.

Greenberg, Jerry. "Exploring the World's First Undersea Park." *Audubon Magazine*, May-June 1961, p. 141-147.

Brookfield, Charles M. "America's First Undersea Park." *National Geographic*, January 1962, p. 58-88.

----------. "Florida's underwater flower garden." Florida Magazine, *Orlando Sentinel*, July 1, 1979, p. 9-13.

Tebeau, Charlton W., and Ruby Leach Carson. *Florida From Indian Trail to Space Age, A History, Volume 2.* The Southern Publishing Co., Delray Beach, Fla., 1965.

Burt, Al. "Mr. Pennekamp Visits His Park." *Miami Herald*, undated, John D. Pennekamp papers, University of Florida collections.

----------. "Sanctuary Notes." *The Florida Naturalist*, January 1960, p. 39-40.

Mason, C. Russell. "Alligators Given Complete Legal Protection." *The Florida Naturalist*, October 1961, p. 194.

----------. "These Are the Florida Audubon Sanctuaries." *The Florida Naturalist*, October 1961, p. 215-218.

----------. "Hialeah Race Course Becomes Florida Audubon Sanctuary." *The Florida Naturalist*, July 1962, inside cover.

Graham, Frank Jr. *The Audubon Ark: A History of the National Audubon Society*, Alfred A. Knopf, New York, 1990.

Land into Water – Water into Land

-------. "The Corkscrew Is Rescued, and We Thank You." *Audubon Magazine*, September-October 1968, p. 5.

Alden, Peter, and Rick Cech and Gil Nelson. *National Audubon Society Field Guide to Florida.* Alfred A. Knopf, New York, 1998.

Finn, Melvin A. "For Fahkahatchee Strand ... The Time Is Now!" *The Florida Naturalist*, July 1965, p. 85-87.

----------. "Merritt Island Wildlife Refuge Established." *The Florida Naturalist*, October 1963, inside cover.

Dickerson, David. "Nature trail dedicated to Cruickshank." *Today*, October 9, 1984, 1B

Eichhorn, Karl (Indian River Audubon Society). Interview with author, March 27, 2002.

-----------. "The Kennedy Space Center Story." [http://www-pao.ksc.nasa.gov/kscstory/ch18/ch18.htm]

Benson, Charles D., and William Barnaby Faherty. *Moonport: A History of Apollo Launch Facilities and Operations.* Published as NASA Special Publication-4204 in the NASA History Series, 1978.

Tritaik, Paul. "Pelican Island National Wildlife Refuge." *The Florida Naturalist,* Spring 1997, p. 8-10.

Gladwell, Malcolm. "The Mosquito Killer." *The New Yorker,* July 2, 2001, p. 42-51.

----------. "Audubon Societies Agree To Coordinate Programs." *The Florida Naturalist,* July 1960, p. 138.

-------------. "Florida Audubon Society Continues Campaign To Save Bald Eagle." *The Florida Naturalist,* April 1963, p. 56.

Cokinos, Christopher. *Hope Is the Thing With Feathers: A Personal Chronicle of Vanished Birds.* Jeremy P. Tarcher/Putnam, New York, 2000.

Pranty, Bill. *A Birder's Guide to Florida.* American Birding Association, Inc., Colorado Springs, Colo., 1996.

Carr, Archie. *A Naturalist in Florida: A Celebration of Eden.* Yale University Press, New Haven, Conn., 1994.

----------. " 'Boycott Alligator Product' Audubon Society Recommends." *The Florida Naturalist,* January 1967, p. 2.

Woodward, Alan R., and Clinton T. Moore. "American Alligators in Florida." U.S. Geological Survey, [http://biology.usgs.gov/s+t/noframe/d052.htm]

Philp, Kenneth R. "Turmoil at Big Cypress: Seminole Deer and the Florida Cattle Tick Controversy." *Florida Historical Quarterly,* July 1977, p. 28-44.

-----------. "Cattle-dipping vats in Florida." Florida Department of Health. [http://www9.myflorida.com/environment/water/watertox/vats.htm]

--------------. "Help Save the Key Deer." *The Florida Naturalist,* July 1951p. 73.

Levin, Ted. "Forever Glades." *Audubon,* July-August 2001, p. 38-61.

Chastain, Mrs. Robert L. "Pine Jog Nature Center." *The Florida Naturalist,* October 1962, p. 115.

CHAPTER 6

The Florida Almanac 2002-2003.

The Florida Experience: Land and Water Policy in a Growth State.

Barber, Henry Eugene. *The History of the Florida Cross-State Canal.* Doctorate dissertation to University of Georgia, Athens, Ga., 1969.

Bull, Roger. "Failed barge canal project leads to Cross Florida Greenway." *Florida Times-Union,* January 19, 2001.

Tobias, Lucy. "Cross-state canal long a dream, nightmare for Floridians." History of Marion County, *Ocala Star-Banner.*
[http://www.starbanner.com/History/full_hist_sec4_c.html]

Couse, John. Correspondence with Florida Defenders of the Environment. Florida Defenders of the Environment papers, University of Florida collections.

Hensley, Ed. "Canal Opponents Urged To Support Plan." *Orlando Sentinel,* January 26, 1966, 1C.

Carr, Marjorie Harris. Correspondence. Florida Defenders of the Environment papers. University of Florida collections.

Anthony, David. Interview with author, April 8, 2002.

Partington, Bill. Interview with author, April 17, 2002.

Beal, Dennis. "Nixon Marks 'Finis' To Barge Canal." *Orlando Sentinel,* January 20, 1971, A1.

------------. "Conservation Successes and Repurcussions." *ENFO,* March 1971, p. 1-6.

---------. "The Cross-Florida Boondoggle." *ENFO,* June 1974, p. 1-20.

Poor, Peggy. "This Was a Forest Primeval." *Orlando Sentinel,* January 10, 1971.

---------. "On Barge Canal Halt – Repercussions Develop." *The Florida Naturalist,* February-March 1971, p. 8.

----------. "President's Action Halts Florida's Favorite Folly." *Audubon Magazine,* March 1971, p. 115.

----------. "Down with the Ditch." *Time,* April 19, 1943, p. 24.

Persons, Todd, and Karen Harrod; additional material by Hal Scott and Alexander J. Friedman. "The First One Hundred Years." Special edition of *The Florida Naturalist,* 1975.

----------. "Barge Canal refuses to die." *Audubon Magazine,* July 1972, p. 100.

The Everglades: River of Grass.

Semple, Robert B. "Everglades Jetport Barred By a U.S.-Florida Accord." *The*

New York Times, January 16, 1970, p. 1A.

Marshall, Arthur R., Florida Report Coordinator. *Environmental Impact of the Big Cypress Swamp Jetport.* U.S. Department of the Interior, September, 1969.

McDavitt, Jack. "Hopes Officially End For Jetport Near Everglades." *Orlando Sentinel,* January 16, 1970, A1.

George, Jean. "Victory In The Everglades." *Reader's Digest,* August 1970, p. 73.

---------. "Saving the Big Cypress Swamp." *Time,* December 6, 1971.

Steen, John. "Reed To Lead Fight To Save Big Cypress." *Tampa Tribune-Times,* May 16, 1971, 8A.

Lee, Charles. "1988 In Review – Conservation." *The Florida Naturalist,* Spring 1989, p. 10-11.

--------. "Stepping Up the Pace on 'last oil frontier.' " *Business Week,* April 10, 1965, p. 86.

Marlowe, Dick. "Disney Highway Of Water To Create Downstream Flood." *Orlando Sentinel,* May 30, 1971, 10B.

Scott, Hal. "Decisions – Decisions." *The Florida Naturalist,* April 1974, p. 14-16.

Associated Press. "Big Cypress Oil Plans Draw Blast." *Orlando Sentinel,* March 11, 1971, 3B.

-------. "Does Florida Need Refineries?" *ENFO,* April 1974, p. 1-11.

--------. "The Ocala Oil Gamble." *ENFO,* February 1974, p. 1-6.

Pritchard, Peter C.H., and Herbert W. Kale. *Saving What's Left.* Florida Audubon Society, Casselberry, Fla., 1994.

Foglesong, Richard E. *Married To the Mouse.* Yale University Press, New Haven, Conn., and London, 2001.

Sierra Club papers, University of Florida collections.

--------. "FAS Gets New Executive Director." *The Florida Naturalist,* February-March 1971, p. 3.

Ward, Fred. "The Imperiled Everglades." *National Geographic,* January 1972, p. 1-27.

McAleenan, John. "Nat Reed Says, 'Enough.' " Florida Magazine, *Orlando Sentinel,* October 9, 1988, p. 9-14.

Reed, Nathaniel P. Interviews with author, May 2002.

Long, Jim. "Florida's 'Mr. Clean' Shifts His Attack to Community Sewage Disposal." *Florida County Government and Port Authority,* May-June 1970, p. 11-34.

Van Gieson, John. "Suspend Officials, Reed Tells Askew." *Miami Herald*, April 5, 1971, 1B.

-------. News release, Office of the Governor of Florida, July 1, 1969.

Walker, James. "State Pollution Leaders Quits To Take U.S. Post." *Tampa Tribune*, April 2, 1971, 1B.

Douglas, Marjory Stoneman. *Florida: The Long Frontier*. Harper and Row, New York, 1967.

Levin, Ted. "Champions of Conservation: Marjory Stoneman Douglas." National Audubon Society. [http://magazine.audubon.org/century/champion.html#Mdouglas]

CHAPTER 7

Associated Press. " 'Eco-Commando Force' Strikes Dade Sewage Treatment Plants." *Orlando Sentinel*, April 23, 1970, 6C.

Lawrence, D.G. "Kirk Observes Earth Day By Signing Alligator Bills." *Orlando Sentinel*, April 23, 1970, 2C.

Associated Press. "Conservation 70s Living Hand To Mouth Existence." *Orlando Sentinel*, November 22, 1970, 2B.

Dasmann, Raymond F. *No Further Retreat: The Fight To Save Florida*. MacMillan Co., 1971.

Gluckman, David. "Citizen Lawsuits – A Florida Reality." *The Florida Naturalist*, August-September 1971, p. 1-2.

-------------. Friends of Lake Apopka. [http://www.fola.org/f.hist/hist.html]

Jackson, Jerry. "Farming on Lake Apopka Land Is Still A Family Affair." Orlando Sentinel, June 16, 1996, 1D.

Poole, Leslie Kemp. "Lake Apopka: A patient on the critical list." *ENFO*, December 1988, p. 1-8.

Associated Press. "State biologists kill panther in tranquilizer dart accident." *Orlando Sentinel*, January 20, 1983, C5.

Maehr, David S. *The Florida Panther: Life and Death of a Vanishing Carnivore*. Island Press, Washington, D.C., 1997.

Alvarez, Ken. *Twilight of the Panther*. Myakka River Publishing, Sarasota, Fla., 1993.

Newell, David. "Panther!" *Saturday Evening Post*, July 13, 1935, p. 10-15.

------------. "The Environmental Information Center." *ENFO*, January 1971, p. 1-4.

Lord, Linda A. *Guide to Florida Environmental Issues and Information.* Florida Conservation Foundation, Winter Park, 1993.

------------. "Florida Panther." National Parks and Conservation Association. [http://www.eparks.org/wildlife_protection/wildlife_facts/florida_panther.asp]

Sharp, Brian. "Let's Save the Dusky Seaside Sparrow." The Florida Naturalist, April 1969, p. 68-70.

Kale, Dr. Herbert II. "Mostly Birds." *The Florida Naturalist,* Summer 1987, p. 5.

Jean, Charlie. "Uphill battle" over–last dusky dies." Orlando Sentinel, June 18, 1987, 1A.

A Birder's Guide to Florida.

Some Kind of Paradise, A Chronicle of Man and the Land in Florida.

------------. "Restoring the Kissimmee River May Be Florida's Environmental Armageddon." *ENFO,* February 1977, p. 1-8.

Hinnant, Lee. "Kissimmee's fans hail money for river." *Tampa Tribune,* December 29, 1987, 1B.

Waitley, Douglas. *The Last Paradise: The Building of Marco Island.* The Pickering Press, Coconut Grove, Fla., 1993.

-----------. "Urgent! Your Letters Are Needed To Stop Marco Island Dredge and Fill Project!" *The Florida Naturalist,* August 1975, p. 28.

Lee, Charles. "Conservation in the 80s: The Florida Audubon Program." *The Florida Naturalist,* October-December 1981, p. 5-13.

-----------. "Florida Conservation Resume." *The Florida Naturalist,* December 1973, p. 29-30.

Beacham, Frank. "Ecologists Band vs. Base Site." *Today,* January 25, 1973, 1A.

Entwistle, Bob, and Betsy David. "Oil, Bird Habitats and Conservationists." *The Florida Naturalist,* October 1973, p. 27-32.

Associated Press. "Phillips Seeks Okay To Explore For Oil In Big Cypress Area." *St. Petersburg Times,* March 11, 1971, 1B.

Associated Press. "Company can drill for gas in estuary." *Orlando Sentinel,* January 21, 1983, C3.

Toner, Jim. "Fight Vowed Over Forest Oil Decision." *Orlando Sentinel,* January 6, 1974, C3.

Associated Press. "Ecologists Watch As Forest Drilling Nears." *Orlando Sentinel,* October 27, 1974, C10.

Bucking, Larry. "U.S. Okays Amoco's Drilling in Ocala Forest." *Orlando Sentinel*, April 10, 1975, B3.

Groer, Anne. "Court Gives U.S. Control of Atlantic Offshore Oil." *Orlando Sentinel*, March 18, 75, A1.

------------. "Positive Leadership – FAS & Oil." *The Florida Naturalist*. February 1972, p. 38-39.

------------. "Those Exxon Ads." *The Florida Naturalist*, October 1976, p. 24-25.

Woodburn, Ken. "A Brief History of Florida's Environmental Movement." Sustainable Florida. [http://sustainable.state.fl.us/fdi/fscc/news/state/woodburn.htm]

----------. "Conservation News and Issues." *The Florida Naturalist*, August 1978, p. 26-27.

CHAPTER 8

Fisher, Eleanor. Interview with author, April 4, 2002.

Osinski, Bill. "Volunteers Organize To Save Wekiwa." Orlando Sentinel, February 3, 1974, C3.

Associated Press. "State Purchases 2 Wekiva Tracts." *Orlando Sentinel*, August 25, 1976, 4B.

Yokel, Bernard. "President's Line." *The Florida Naturalist*, Spring 1988, inside cover.

Lee, Charles. "Vice President's Line – The Wekiva River Protection Act: A Model For Saving Florida's Rivers." *The Florida Naturalist*, Summer 1988, p. 10.

Renner, Lisanne. Environmental group asks state to protect more river area." *Orlando Sentinel,* October 6, 1982, W4.

Moore, Ann. "Wekiva residents ask county to look at projects." *Orlando Sentinel*, November 14, 1984, C1.

Johnson, Ian. "Ecologists worry over growth's threat to Wekiva River." *Orlando Sentinel*, August 8, 1984, B3.

Moore, Ann. "Friends of Wekiva want basin checked." *Orlando Sentinel*, March 27, 1985, D1.

Renner, Lisanne. "Water board reconsiders Wekiva buffers." *Orlando Sentinel*, April 14, 1988, D1.

Renner, Lisanne. "Defenders of Wekiva draw up battle plan." *Orlando Sentinel*, May 12, 1988, D1.

White, David. "Governor receives Wekiva bill." *Orlando Sentinel*, June 4, 1988, D1.

O'Neal, Donna. "Cabinet adds teeth to Wekiva buffer." *Orlando Sentinel*, December 21, 1988, D1.

Spear, Kevin. "More than rules needed to stop Wekiva bulldozer, activist says." *Orlando Sentinel*, February 10, 1990, D1.

Spear, Kevin. "State buys 3,397 acres along Wekiva." *Orlando Sentinel*, March 30, 1990, B1.

River of Lakes.

Bacchus, James. "Ecologists Battle For Apalachicola." *Orlando Sentinel*, June 24, 1973, B3.

Leitman, Steve, and Doug Alderson. "Apalachicola River: Is the Dam Finally Dead?" *ENFO*, February 1980, p. 1-5.

Associated Press. "Tri-state pact allows dredging of Apalachicola." *Orlando Sentinel*, Sept. 6, 1980, C5.

Associated Press. "200 Protest Plan To Dam Apalachicola." *Orlando Sentinel*, June 28, 1973, B3.

----------. "Apalachicola: Our Last Clean Major River Endangered by Corps of Engineers Development Plan." *ENFO*, December 1976, p. 1-8.

----------. "Ocklawaha River Restoration." Florida Defenders of the Environment. [http://www.fladefenders.org/ocklawaha.html]

White, David J. "Feds Say Remove Dam by 2006." *The Monitor*, Florida Defenders of the Environment, Spring 2002, p. 1-6.

----------. "Marjorie Harris Carr Cross Florida Greenway." Florida Department of Environmental Protection. [http://www.dep.state.fl.us/gwt/cfg/]

Jones, John C. Interviews with author, April 2002.

----------. "Evolution of Ecosystem Restoration Efforts." National Park Service. [http://www.nps.gov/ever/eco/restore.htm]

Levin, Ted. "Reviving the River of Grass." *Audubon*, July-August 2001, p. 54-57.

Lipman, Larry. "Governor: We'll Heal Everglades." *Orlando Sentinel*, August 10, 1983, A1.

Van Meter, Victoria Brook. *The West Indian Manatee in Florida*. Florida Power & Light Company, Miami, 1989.

----------. "Manatee Info." Save the Manatee Club. [http://www.savethemanatee.org/info.htm]

Sadusky, Nancy, communications director, Save the Manatee Club. Interview with author, March 27, 2002.

Pritchard, Peter C.H. "Sea Turtles: A Cornucopia of Issues." *The Florida Naturalist,* Spring 1992, p. 8-12.

Zimmerman, Michael. "New hope for turtles off Florida coast." *Orlando Sentinel,* October 18, 1987, G3.

Associated Press. "Cabinet Oks permanent rule for turtle escape devices." *Orlando Sentinel,* January 10, 1990, D5.

Ferrulo, Mark, executive director, Florida Public Interest Research Group. Interview with author, April 3, 2002.

Associated Press. "Lawmaker, activists fight for permanent drilling ban." *Orlando Sentinel,* September 29, 1989, C3.

Renner, Lisanne. "Ecological radicals take root." *Orlando Sentinel,* August 1, 1988, A1.

---------. "Florida Chapter Makes a Difference Over Last 40 Years," *Florida Chapter News,* The Nature Conservancy, Fall 2001, p. 1-2.

Bendick, Bob, state director, Florida chapter, The Nature Conservancy. Interview with author, May 15, 2002.

Harris, Larry D. "Wildlife Corridors." *ENFO,* November 1985, p. 1-10.

Barada, William R. "The Key Largo Fiasco." *ENFO,* June 1983, p. 1-10.

---------. Izaak Walton League.
[http://www.iwla.org/history/chdv_hst.html#florida]

Knetsch, Joe. "History." Florida Department of Environmental Protection. [http://www.dep.state.fl.us/lands/history.htm]

---------. "Florida Audubon Society Annual Report 1992." *The Florida Naturalist,* Summer 1993, insert.

Crowder, Reg. "The Dame Point Bridge." *ENFO,* May 1982, p. 1-6.

---------. "Past Projects." Jacksonville Transportation Authority. [http://www.jtaonthemove.com/jtaeng.past.htm]

Hiaasen, Carl. *Tourist Season.* G.P. Putnam and Sons, New York, 1986.

McMahon, Bucky. "The Anger Artist." *GQ,* June 1996, p. 92-98.

Haehle, Robert G., and Joan Brookwell. *Native Florida Plants.* Gulf Publishing Company, Houston, 1999.

---------. "Non-native Invasive Terrestrial Plants in the United States." St. Johns River Water Management District and the University of Florida Center for Aquatic and Invasive Plants.

--------. "Biological Pollution." *ENFO*, December 1972, p. 1-8.

-----------. "U.S. Senator Bob Graham Biography." [http://graham.senate.gov/biography.html]

Marshall, Arthur R. *For the Future of Florida, Repair the Everglades.* Friends of the Everglades, 1982. Arthur R. Marshall papers, University of Florida collections.

Associated Press. "Graham lauds gains in Everglades but says barriers remain." *Orlando Sentinel*, November 6, 1983, B5.

Lee, Charles. "Vice President's Report." *The Florida Naturalist*, Summer 1987, p. 2-3.

Burt, Al. "Glades protector dies of cancer." *Miami Herald*, February 20, 1985, 1A.

Yokel, Bernard. "President's Line." *The Florida Naturalist*, Summer 1986, p. 14.

Yokel, Bernard. "President's Line." *The Florida Naturalist*, Spring 1991, inside cover.

Blemenstyk, Goldie. "State told to prepare for growth." *Orlando Sentinel*, March 18, 1983, B1.

Blanton, Donna. "Legislators agree on growth plan." *Orlando Sentinel*, May 30, 1985, B1.

Yokel, Bernard. "President's Line." *The Florida Naturalist*, Summer 1989, p. 1.

Yokel, Bernard. "President's Line." *The Florida Naturalist*, Spring 1987, p. 1.

------------. 1000 Friends of Florida. [http://www.1000friendsofflorida.org/]

Blanton, Donna. "Lobbyists try to amend growth act." *Orlando Sentinel*, March 25, 1986, D1.

Sierra Club Bulletin, various issues, Sierra Club papers, University of Florida collections.

Lee, Charles. "1988 In Review – Conservation." *The Florida Naturalist*, Spring 1989, p. 10-11.

Associated Press. "Changes in state plan worry environmentalists." *Orlando Sentinel*, Feb. 14, 1985, B1.

-----------. "History of Florida's Conservation Land Acquisitions." EDIS document FE 331, Institute of Food and Agricultural Sciences, University of Florida, January 2002.

Lee, Charles. "Conservation." *The Florida Naturalist*, Summer 1990, p. 10.

Yokel, Bernard. "President's Line." *The Florida Naturalist*, Fall 1990, p. 9.

Kleman, Kim. "The Federal Battle of Florida's Wetlands." *ENFO*, April 1986, p. 1-4

Lee, Charles. "Conservation." *The Florida Naturalist,* Summer 1991, p. 13.

Allen, Dale. "Preservation 2000: Florida's Environmental Future." *ENFO,* April 1990, p. 2-3.

CHAPTER 9

----------. "Kissimmee River Restoration." South Florida Water Management District. [http://www.sfwmd.gov/org/erd/krr/index.html]

Toth, Lou, Chief Scientist, South Florida Water Management District. Correspondence with author, May 2002.

Associated Press. "Suit to save Everglades is settled." *Orlando Sentinel,* July 12, 1991, A1.

Associated Press. "State adds 158,000 acres to wish list." *Orlando Sentinel,* November 6, 1988, 5B.

---------------. "Kissimmee River Restoration." Audubon of Florida. [http://www.audubonofflorida.org/science/kissrivrest.htm]

----------. "Kissimmee River Restoration." State of Florida Executive Office of the Governor. [http://www.state.fl.us/eog/govdocs/opbenv/saveglades/everglades/html/kissimee.htm]

Zaneski, Cyril. T. "Anatomy of a Deal." *Audubon,* July-August 2001, p. 48-53.

More Than Petticoats: Remarkable Florida Women.

Yokel, Bernard. "President's Line." *The Florida Naturalist,* Summer 1992, p. 14-15.

Sellers, Laurin. "Manatee club leaves docile image in its wake." *Orlando Sentinel,* July 15, 2001, B1.

Lelis, Ludmilla. "New rules settle manatee lawsuit." *Orlando Sentinel,* May 15, 2001, C1.

Associated Press. "Boaters fail to sink new slow-speed waterways." *Orlando Sentinel,* May 24, 2001, D3.

Lelis, Ludmilla. "Judge OKs slow zones for boats." *Orlando Sentinel,* April 18, 2002, A1.

Pittman, Craig. "Advocates: New criteria put species at greater risk." *St. Petersburg Times,* December 10, 2001, 1B.

Pittman, Craig. "Agency keeps bear hunt ban." *St. Petersburg Times,* November 24, 2000, 1B.

Pittman, Craig. "Bird may no longer be deemed threatened." *St. Petersburg Times,* January 12, 2002, 8B.

Sherman, Christopher. "Neighborhood mourns when eagles fly away." *Orlando Sentinel*, March 7, 2002, A1.

A Birder's Guide To Florida.

Associated Press. "Will the new state bird fly?" *Orlando Sentinel*, December 27, 1998, B3.

Armstrong, Eva. "The Greening of the 1999 Legislature." *The Florida Naturalist*, Second Quarter 1999, p. 8-9.

Kennedy, John. "Scrub jay could top state's pecking order." *Orlando Sentinel*, March 23, 1999, D5.

Associated Press. "Students back scrub jay but key lobbyist doesn't." *Orlando Sentinel*, March 15, 2000, D5.

-----------. "Archie Carr Refuge." *The Florida Naturalist*, Summer 1991, pg. 8.

Bryan, Dana. "Florida Audubon Society Sanctuaries." *The Florida Naturalist*, Winter 1992, p. 9-14.

-----------. "Archie Carr National Wildlife Refuge." U.S. Fish and Wildlife Service. [http://archiecarr.fws.gov/index.html]

---------. "Florida Audubon and Chapter News." *The Florida Naturalist*, Winter 1993, p. 10.

----------. "Florida Audubon Society Annual Report 1994." *The Florida Naturalist*, Summer 1995, insert.

------------. "Florida Audubon Society Annual Report 1995." *The Florida Naturalist*, Fall 1996, insert.

Gluckman, David. "Property Rights – Yours or Mine?" *The Florida Naturalist*, Spring 1990, p. 10.

--------. "State News." *The Florida Naturalist*, Summer 1997, p. 24-25.

Regaldo, Nancyann, and Erin Deady. "Planning Florida's Future." *The Florida Naturalist*, Fall 1997, p. 6-8.

-------. "John Ellis 'Jeb' Bush." Florida Department of State. [http://dhr.dos.state.fl.us/governors/jebbush.html]

Hauserman, Julie. "Bush plans looser guide for growth." *St. Petersburg Times*, October 25, 1999, A1.

Reed, Nathaniel P. "Will Florida Grow Smarter?" *The Florida Naturalist*, Spring 2000, p. 24-25.

Reed, Nathaniel Pryor. "Mr. Toad's Wild Ride: The Process to Revise Florida's Growth Management Act." News release, 1000 Friends of Florida, January 2000.

Associated Press. "Bush backs idea to gauge impact of developments." *Orlando Sentinel*, February 20, 2001, B5.

Shenot, Christine. "New ideas on growth aim at builders' wallets." *Orlando Sentinel*, January 5, 2001, A1.

Kennedy, John, and Christine Shenot. "Jammed schools go home begging." *Orlando Sentinel*, May 5, 2001, A1.

Associated Press. "Critics say DCA's policy changing landscape of Florida." *Orlando Sentinel*, May 13, 2002, D3.

Pittman, Craig. "Homestead airport plan stirs up protest." *St. Petersburg Times*, August 2, 2000, 1B.

Pittman, Craig. "Air Force blocks airport near Everglades." *St. Petersburg Times*, January 17, 2001, 1A.

Associated Press. "Air Force nixes airport proposal." *St. Petersburg Times*, December 8, 2001, 5B.

Johnson, Tim, and Curtis Morgan. "Deals block oil drilling in Everglades and Gulf." *Miami Herald*, May 30, 2002, A1.

Associated Press. "Plant wants to burn controversial fuel." *Orlando Sentinel*, February 20, 1987, D4.

Armstrong, Eva. "The 1997 Florida Legislation." *The Florida Naturalist*, Summer 1997, p. 23.

Kleindienst, Linda. "FPL loses in latest bid to use alternative fuel." *Orlando Sentinel*, June 25, 1998, D4.

Armstrong, Eva. "The 1998 Legislative Session." *The Florida Naturalist*, Spring 1998, p. 18.

Henderson, Clay. "Letter from the President." *The Florida Naturalist*, Third Quarter 1999, insert.

Rist, Karsten A. "Chairman's Report." *The Florida Naturalist*, Summer 1995, p. 2.

Bague, Irela, Communications Director, Audubon of Florida. Correspondence with author, April 22, 2002.

Alvarez, J., and L.C. Polopolus. *The Florida Sugar Industry*. Institute of Food and Agricultural Sciences, University of Florida, Gainesville, 1998.

Sitterson, J. Carlyle. *Sugar Country; The Cane Sugar Industry in the South, 1753-1950*. University of Kentucky Press, Lexington, Ky., 1953.

-----------. "Everglades Sugar." *Business Week*, February 13, 1937, p. 68.

Associated Press. "Future of Everglades is mired in the muck." *Orlando Sentinel*, August 1, 1980, 4C.

Dacy, G.H. "Tapping America's Newest Sugar Bowl." *Popular Mechanics,* June 1925, p. 915-916.

Henderson, Clay. "President's Line." *The Florida Naturalist,* Spring 1997, p. 4.

Zaneski, Cyril T. "The Philanthropists, Mary Barley and Paul Tudor Jones." *Audubon,* July-August 2001, p. 80-81.

Lee, Charles. "Everglades Restoration Moves Ahead." *The Florida Naturalist,* First Quarter 1999, p. 18.

-----------. "Florida." U.S. Census Bureau. [http://quickfacts.census.gov/qfd/states/12000.html]

Associated Press. "Sugar industry ad tries to stir opposition to 'Glades tax." (Fort Lauderdale, Fla.) *Sun-Sentinel,* September 27, 1996, 10A.

Zaneski, Cyril T. "Penny tax is on sugar industry, not consumer." *Miami Herald,* November 3, 1996, L1.

Kennedy, John. "Poll: Voters sour on proposed sugar tax." *Orlando Sentinel,* November 1, 1996, A1.

Lee, Charles. "The Everglades Vote." *The Florida Naturalist,* Spring 1997, p. 5-6.

Sargent, Robert Jr., and Ramsey Campbell. "Well bill pumps up a dispute." *Orlando Sentinel,* April 10, 2001, D1.

Lee, Charles, Senior Vice President, Audubon of Florida. Interview with author, May 7, 2002.

Henderson, Clay. "Celebrating New Challenges in Conservation." *The Florida Naturalist,* Third Quarter 1999, p. 4.

Rist, Karsten. "The Everglades ... Past, Present and Future." *ENFO,* July 1986, p. 1-11.

-----------. "The Everglades Restoration Plan: A Formula for Failure." *The Everglades Reporter,* Friends of the Everglades, Spring 2000.

King, Robert P. "Proposal to restore Everglades partly fulfills 'Marshall Plan.' " *Palm Beach Post,* April 25, 1999, 1A.

Kleindienst, Linda. "Vote leaves aquifer open to untreated water." *Orlando Sentinel,* April 17, 2001, D1.

Kennedy, John. "Tainted water won't go underground." *Orlando Sentinel,* May 1, 2001, D5.

Pittman, Craig, and Lucy Morgan. "Aquifer injection scuttled." *St. Petersburg Times,* May 1, 2001, 1A.

Ullman, Jonathan, Everglades Representative, Sierra Club Florida chapter. Interview with author, June 2002.

Hausermann, Julie, and Craig Pittman. "Law to pump millions into Everglades." *St. Petersburg Times,* May 16, 2002, 1B.

Pranty, Bill. "A New Way To Protect Bird Populations." *The Florida Naturalist,* Spring 2000, p. 22-23.

Pranty, Bill. "Important Bird Areas." Audubon of Florida. [http://www.audubon.org/bird/iba/florida/]

-----------. Earthjustice. [http://www.earthjustice.org/regional/tallahassee/]

Smith, Nancy. "Creek open again after legal battle." *Osceola Sentinel,* September 19, 1997, p. 7.

Associated Press. "Fisheating Creek, land under state ownership." *Orlando Sentinel,* December 4, 1999, D3.

-----------. Florida PEER. [http://www.peer.org/florida/]

Associated Press. "2 DEP officials take leave during agency's probe." *Orlando Sentinel,* August 13, 1999, D3.

Associated Press. "Environment chief, workers end dispute." *Orlando Sentinel,* April 14, 1999, D3.

Thomas, Jim. "Soupy Mess Continues To Plague Lake Apopka." *The Florida Naturalist,* Spring 1997, p. 12-13.

Thomas, Jim. "The Story of Lake Apopka – A Historic Review." *The Florida Naturalist,* Third Quarter 1999, p. 6-10.

-----------. Friends of Lake Apopka. [http://www.fola.org/]

Bouma, Katherine. "State admits mistakes led to bird deaths." *Orlando Sentinel,* June 10, 1999, A1.

Roy, Roger. "Feds investigate bird kill at lake." *Orlando Sentinel,* October 6, 1999, A1.

Bouma, Katherine. "Top environmental enforcer quits." *Orlando Sentinel,* November 3, 1998, D3.

Florida Department of Environmental Protection. "Order Vacating Final Orders." OGC No. 98-2600, DEP98-1479.

Shields, Gerald. "Fishing net fight lures $1.4 million." *Orlando Sentinel,* October 27, 1994, C1.

Associated Press. "Fish stocks thrive since '95 net ban." *Orlando Sentinel,* September 8, 1998, C1.

Pritchard, Peter C.H. "Net Fishing in Florida: What's Really Going On?" *The Florida Naturalist,* Fall 1993, p. 9-10.

------------. "CCA Florida – A History of Conservation." Coastal Conservation Association Florida. [http://www.cca-florida.com/chronology.htm]

Henderson, Clay. "President's Line." *The Florida Naturalist*, Fall 1995, p. 2.

Henderson, Clay. "Making Florida's Constitution A Little Greener." *The Florida Naturalist*, Fall 1997, p. 5.

Henderson, Clay. "Keeping Florida Special." *The Florida Naturalist*, Fall 1998, p. 6-7.

Henderson, Clay. "President's Line." *The Florida Naturalist,* Spring 1999, p. 4.

Krueger, Curtis. "Many proposed amendments win voters' approval." *St. Petersburg Times*, November 4, 1998, 9B.

--------. "1999 Legislative Issues: Florida Forever Coalition." News release, 1000 Friends of Florida, December 4, 1998.

--------------. "Position Statement." The Conservancy of Southwest Florida, February 26, 2002.

Rado, Diane. "Senators propose to tap land fund." *St. Petersburg Times*, March 23, 2001, 6B.

Bendick, Robert J. "It defies logic that legislature took Preservation 2000 funds." *Orlando Sentinel*, May 21, 2001, A15.

Macdonald, Laurie. Florida Director, Defenders of Wildlife. Interview with author, June 2002.

CHAPTER 10

Campbell, Ramsey, and Robert Sargent Jr. "Bottlers tap springs as state runs dry." *Orlando Sentinel*, January 20, 2002, A1.

----------. "Protecting Our Environmental Heritage: The Florida Natural Areas Inventory." *ENFO*, February 1990, p. 1-10.

Bague, Irela, Public Affairs Coordinator, Audubon of Florida, correspondence with author, April-May 2002.

Cerulean, Susan. "A new century of Audubon in Florida." *The Florida Naturalist*, Spring 2000, p. 4-17.

Logan, Tom H. "Numerical summary of species listed by state and federal agencies as endangered, threatened or otherwise categorized of concern." Florida Fish and Wildlife Conservation Commission.

[http://www.floridaconservation.org/pubs/endanger.html#nume]

-----------. "Development Opportunities." The St. Joe Company. [http://www.joe.com/develop.html]

Shenot, Christine, and Jim Stratton and Kevin Connolly. "Expressway proposal awakens sleeping giant." *Orlando Sentinel*, August 13, 2001, A1.

Hauserman, Julie. "Governor agonizes over Everglades bill." *St. Petersburg Times*, May 15, 2002, 5B.

Pittman, Craig. "Swiftmud indicates interest in aiding second desal plant." *St. Petersburg Times*, April 16, 2002, 1B.

Huntley, Helen. "Enron: The Florida connection." *St. Petersburg Times*, February 3, 2002, 4A.

Salamone, Debbie. "Lost Jewels." *Orlando Sentinel*, May 6, 2002, A1.

Salamone, Debbie. "Wither the Springs." *Orlando Sentinel*, May 5, 2002, A1.

Kennedy, John. "Bush cuts budget $107 million." *Orlando Sentinel*, June 6, 2002, B1.

Glenn, John, Membership Chair, Florida Chapter Sierra Club. Correspondence with author, May 2002.

Rice, Darden, Global Warming and Energy Organizer, Florida Chapter Sierra Club. Interview with author, May 2002.

CHAPTER 11

REED

Buckow, Ed. "Conservationist Gives Stirring Talk." *Palm Beach Post-Times*, February 18, 1967, D7.

Reed, Nathaniel. Address to meeting of The Nature Conservancy, April 27, 1968.

Albertson, Mike. "Landmark Decision Sets Pollution Guidelines." *Pensacola Journal*, January 22, 1970, 1A.

Walker, James. "State Pollution Leader Quits To Take U.S. Post." *Tampa Tribune*, April 2, 1971, 1B.

Hornig, Roberta. "River-Changing By U.S. Hit." *Washington Star*, June 4, 1971, 1B.

Dyckman, Martin. "Reed: Will He Run For Governor?" *St. Petersburg Times*, August 25, 1972, 1B.

Osolin, Charles. "Interior's Reed drops plans to challenge Chiles next year." *Miami News*, April 25, 1975, 1A.

United Press International. "Reed Eyes Governor's Race in '78." *Miami Herald*, May 27, 1976, 1B.

Hughes, Daniel S. "Ford Asks $1.5 billion for parks, refuges." *National Park Service Newsletter*, October 1976, p. 1-4.

Reed, Nathaniel, et al. Memorandum to Lt. Gen. John W. Morris, U.S. Army Corps of Engineers, January 12, 1977.

Reed, Nathaniel. "The Name of the Game Is … Keeping It Wild." *Florida Wildlife*, March-April 1977, p. 12-16.

Frye, Barbara. "South Florida Republican Reed will manage Eckerd's campaign." *St. Petersburg Times*, April 15, 1978, 2B.

Burns, Robert. "Nat Reed: The Champion of Lands Bill." *Palm Beach Post*, October 1, 1978, D1.

Associated Press. "Florida Saved In 1969?" *Palm Beach Post-Times*, December 21, 1969, D8.

Cullen, Pat. "Family Donates 600 Acres To Hobe Sound Refuge." *Palm Beach Post*, August 10, 1971, B1.

Cullen, Pat. "Reed: 25 Cents a Person To Clean Air." *Palm Beach Post-Times*, October 20, 1971, D2.

Cullen, Pat. "Wading in the Big Cypress." *Palm Beach Post*, January 6, 1972, A1.

LEE

Lee, Charles, Senior Vice President, Audubon of Florida. Interview with author, May 7, 2002.

Pittman, Craig. "Everglades deal could be unmaking of activist." *St. Petersburg Times*, April 7, 2002, 1B.

-----------. "Charles Lee Receives National Award." *The Florida Naturalist*, Fall 1996, p. 5

-----------. "Growth Management Study Commission Members – Charles Lee." Florida Department of Community Affairs. [http://www.dca.state.fl.us/growth/members/lee.htm]

Gluckman, David. Correspondence with author, May 2002.

JONES

--------. "FWC renames Hungryland area after conservationists." News release, Florida Fish and Wildlife Conservation Commission, May 29, 2002. [http://floridaconservation.org/whatsnew/hungrylandjones-st.html]

Jones, John C. Interviews with author, April 2002.

Jones, Mariana. Interviews and correspondence with author, April 2002.

-------------. "Poised for a new century: Local history, 1980-1999." *Palm Beach*

Post, December 19, 1999, 32.

King, Robert P. "Polluted runoff put back into Lake O." *Palm Beach Post*, March 31, 2001, 1A.

PENNEKAMP

Watson, Tom. Letter to John Pennekamp, May 6, 1948. John D. Pennekamp papers, University of Florida collections.

Pennekamp, John. Untitled address to Florida State Retailers Association, October 29, 1947. John D. Pennekamp papers, University of Florida collections.

Pennekamp, John. "Can South Florida Run Out of Water?" Address to annual meeting of National Audubon Society, Miami, November 9, 1963. John D. Pennekamp papers, University of Florida collections.

Pennekamp, John. Untitled address to annual meeting of Florida Institute of Park Personnel, Winter Park, Fla., October 4, 1967. John D. Pennekamp papers, University of Florida collections.

Bellamy, Jeanne. "John's Other Life – Pennekamp Style." *Miami Herald*, April 11, 1969.

------------. "High Court Rules Press Has Right To Chide Courts." *New York Times*, June 4, 1946.

Hunter, David. "He's A Cincinnatian To Remember." *Cincinnati Enquirer*, December 21, 1969, 7K.

Greene, Juanita. "John Pennekamp Signs Off After 51 Years." *Miami Herald*, January 2, 1977.

Burt, Al. "Mr. Pennekamp Visits His Park." *Miami Herald*, undated, John D. Pennekamp papers, University of Florida collections.

Hiaasen, Car. "John Pennekamp Dies at 80; Led Fight To Save Everglades." *Miami Herald*, June 18, 1978, 1A.

CARR

Ritchie, Bruce. "Carr wonders if she'll see a free Ocklawaha." *Gainesville Sun*, June 13, 1997.

Martin, Doug. "Environmentalist Marjorie Harris Carr dies Friday at 82." Gainesville Sun, October 11, 1997, 1A.

------------. "Marjorie Carr, 'Lady of Rivers,' dies at 82." *St. Petersburg Times*, October 12, 1997, 4B.

Alachua Audubon Society bulletins, various dates, Florida Defenders of the Environment papers, University of Florida collections.

Anthony, David. Interview with author.

Poole, Lesie. "Our Lady of the Rivers." *The Florida Naturalist*, Fall 1997, p. 4.

----------. "Marjorie Harris Carr." Florida Defenders of the Environment. [http://www.fladefenders.org/marjorie/]

TIPPETTS

--------. "In Memoriam, Katherine Bell Tippetts." *The Florida Naturalist*, July 1951, p. 76.

St. Petersburg and the Florida Dream, 1888-1950.

Hartzell, Scott Taylor. "Everything she did was her way of being good." *St. Petersburg Times*, March 17, 1999.

History of Pinellas County

Eastman, Susan. "Bird Woman took wing ahead of time." *St. Petersburg Times*, June 18, 1997.

Rich Paul, Manager, Florida Coastal Islands Sanctuaries, Audubon of Florida. Correspondence with author, April 2002.

----------------. "The Mockingbird." Geobopological Survey. [http://206.63.59.98/Symbols/Animals/Birds/1/Mockingbird/]

MARSHALL

Hood, Danny. "Conservationist of the Decade award taken by Art Marshall." *Palatka Daily News*, November 1, 1984.

Cloud, Bill. "Reluctant Bureaucrat Fights for Mother Nature's Rights." *Miami Herald*, December 10, 1968, D1.

Burt, Al. "Grande Dame of the Everglades." *Miami Herald*, April 4, 1982.

Kahn, Jeffery. "Light Now Shines on Biologist's Lonely Quest." Jeffery Kahn, *Palm Beach Post*, September 10, 1984, 1A.

Burt, Al. "Glades protector dies of cancer." *Miami Herald*, February 20, 1985, 1A.

Loftis, Randy. "Endowment honors 'prophetic' ecologist." *Miami Herald*, September 26, 1986, 1D.

Jones, John C. Interviews with author, April 2002.

Arthur Marshall citation from Florida Audubon Society, 1969. Arthur R. Marshall papers, University of Florida collections.

Burt, Al. "The Marshall Plan." Tropic, *Miami Herald*, Oct. 21, 1984.

McLachlin, Mary. "Refuge named for 'prophet' Art Marshall." *Palm Beach Post*, February 11, 1988, 1A.

Poor, Peggy. "A Florida ecologist suggests an old maxim for a modern problem." *Orlando Sentinel*, Aug. 23, 1970, D1.

Marshall, John A., Chief Executive Officer, The Arthur R. Marshall Foundation. Correspondence, with author, April-May 2002.

HIAASEN

White, Nick, former Editorial Page Editor, *Today*. Interview with author, April 2002.

Hiaasen, Carl. Correspondence with author, March 2002.

Hiaasen, Carl, edited by Diane Stevenson. *Kick Ass: Selected Columns of Carl Hiaasen*. University Press of Florida, Gainesville, 1999.

Hiaasen, Carl. *Team Rodent: How Disney Devours the World*. The Library of Contemporary Thought, Ballantine Publishing Group, New York, 1998.

--------. "Carl Hiaasen." [http://www.carlhiaasen.com/]

Hammond, Margo. "Carl Hiaasen: Super Satirist." St. Petersburg Times, August 29, 1993, 1D.

Pate, Nancy. "Crazy About Carl." *Orlando Sentinel*, February 13, 2002, E1.

MacDonald, Jay Lee. "Carl Hiaasen takes a bite out of crimes against the environment." BookPage.
[http://www.bookpage.com/0001bp/carl_hiaasen.html]

Schindehette, Susan. "Tree Hugger From Hell." *People*, October 21, 1991, p. 95-96.

Cheakalos, Christina. "Hurricane Hiaasen." *People*, May 15, 2000, p. 139-140.

CRUICKSHANKS

Eichhorn, Betty, Indian River Audubon Society. Interview with author, April 14, 2002.

Eichhorn, Karl, Indian River Audubon Society. Interview with author, March 27, 2002.

Cruickshank, Helen Gere, with photos by Allan D. Cruickshank. *A Paradise of Birds: When Spring Comes to Texas*. Dodd, Mead & Company, New York, 1968.

Cruickshank, Helen G., with photos by Allan D. Cruickshank. *Flight Into Sunshine*. The MacMillan Company, New York, 1948.

Cruickshank, Allan D., edited by Helen G. Cruickshank. *The Birds of Brevard County*. Florida Press Inc., Orlando, 1980.

Meitin, Don. "Land Fill Work Is Picketed; 'It's Killing the Wildlife.' " *Today*, April 21, 1968, 1A.

Danney, Linda. "He Watches the Birdie." *Today*, March 12, 1967, 1D.

Shaleuly, Margaret. "Naturalist Lived A Dozen Lives." *Today*, October 20, 1974, 1D.

---------. "River Acres Protected 'Forever.' " *Today*, Oct. 22, 1969, 1B.

Cullen, Pat. "Cocoa Beach To Pull Back on Bulkhead." *Today*, Feb. 10, 1969, 1A.

------------. "Allan D. Cruickshank, 1907-1974." Turner Learning. [http://www.turnerlearning.com/efts/species.970730/cruick.html]

Zewen, Ann. "Cruickshank, Noted Ornithologist, Author, Dies In Gainesville." *Orlando Sentinel Star*, October 12, 1974, 2A.

--------. "Allan D. Cruickshank." *Audubon Magazine*, November 1974, p. 123.

Morrison, Ken. "Allan Dudley Cruickshank, 1907-1974." *The Florida Naturalist*, December 1974, p. 25.

Gibson, Dee. "Bird Expert Dies After Long Illness." *Today*, October 12, 1974, 1B.

Devlin, John C. "Allan D. Cruickshank, 67, Dies." *New York Times*, October 12, 1974, p. 34.

Associated Press. "A photographer, protector of nature, Helen Cruickshank dies." *Orlando Sentinel*, April 6, 1994, C4.

Misselhorn, Lou. "Revered nature writer Helen Cruickshank dies." *Florida Today*, April 5, 1994, 1B.

Lancaster, Cory Jo. "Wildlife is 90-year-old's life's work." *Orlando Sentinel*, March 16, 1992, B1.

DOUGLAS

Pullen, Pam. "The Everglades Has A Staunch, Outspoken Friend." *Orlando Sentinel*, November 9, 1975, 1F.

Poole, Leslie Kemp. "Woman of the Century." *The Florida Naturalist*, Summer 1998, p. 8-9.

National Audubon Society web site [http://magazine.audubon.org/century/champion.html#CRAIGHEAD]

--------. "Marjory Stoneman Douglas: Defender of the Everglades." Friends of the Everglades. [http://www.everglades.org/msd.html]

Basse, Craig. "Grande dame of the Everglades." *St. Petersburg Times*, May 15, 1998, A1.

Fichtner, Margaria. "Guardian of the Glades dies at 108." *Miami Herald*, May 15, 1998, 1A.

Reed, Nathaniel Pryor. "Memories of Marjory Stoneman Douglas and Her Everglades Crusade." *Foresight*, Fall 1998.

Churchville, Victoria. "Crusade to preserve Everglades stresses need for political action." *Orlando Sentinel*, March 26, 1983, C5.

Klinkenberg, Jeff. "Though expected, the loss of a hero still stings." *St. Petersburg Times*, May 15, 1998, 6A.

Collie, Tim. "Voice of the river." (Fort Lauderdale, Fla.) *Sun-Sentinel*, May 15, 1998, 1A.

More than Petticoats.

Voice of the River.

------------. "The Everglades Restoration Plan: A Formula for Failure." *The Everglades Reporter*, Friends of the Everglades, Spring 2000

PARTINGTON

Partington, Bill. Interviews with author, April 2002.

Anthony, David. Interview with author, April 8, 2002.

-----------. "About Environmental Defense." Environmental Defense Fund. [http://www.environmentaldefense.org/aboutus.cfm?subnav=aboutus]

DOMMERICHS

------------. Dommerich genealogical records, Dommerich family papers, Maitland Historical Society.

----------. Photographs, Dommerich family papers, Maitland Historical Society.

-----------. "Reports of Societies." *Bird-Lore,* June 1900, p. 96-97.

----------. "Reports of Societies." *Bird-Lore,* December 1900, p. 203.

Vanderpool, Mrs. I. "Florida Society." *Bird-Lore*, September-October 1901, p. 183.

Bavar, Emily. "Famed Estate Makes Way For Homes." Florida Magazine, *Orlando Sentinel*, August 22, 1954.

Allen, Jim. "Faceless Dommerichs A Part of Maitland History." (Winter Park, Fla.) *Sun-Herald*, August 17, 1978, p. 1.

Landfried, Tracy. "The Early History of the Florida Audubon Society, 1900-1905." Florida Audubon Society papers, Maitland Historical Society.

-------. Louis F. Dommerich, *Bird-Lore*, July-August 1912, p. 258.

Blackman, Lucy Worthington. 1935. *The Florida Audubon Society 1900-1935.* Florida Audubon Society, Winter Park, Fla., 1936.

Dommerich, Clara J. Minutes of Florida Audubon Society meeting, March 2, 1900, Florida Audubon Society papers, Maitland Historical Society.

COE

-------. "Ernest Coe, Glades Park Father, Dies." *Miami Herald*, January 2, 1951, 1A.

Pratt, Theodore. "Papa of the Everglades."

Clement, Gail. "Everglades Biographies: Ernest Coe." Publication of Archival Library and Museum Materials, Florida International University. [http://everglades.fiu.edu/reclaim/bio/coe.html]

---------. "Everglades: Ernest F. Coe biography." National Park Service. [http://www.nps.gov/ever/eco/coe.htm]

The Long Frontier.

JENNINGS

Matthews, Rabun. " 'Mother of Forestry,' Mrs. Jennings, Dies." *Florida Times-Union*, April 25, 1963, p. 15.

More Than Petticoats.

May Mann Jennings, Florida's Genteel Activist.

---------. "Housing Facilities Tour: Jennings Hall." University of Florida Division of Housing. [http://www.housing.ufl.edu/housing/halls/jennings.htm]

--------. Citation from Florida Forestry Association, May Mann Jennings papers, University of Florida collections.

INDEX

Florida Defenders of the Environment 79, 82, 106, 113, 118, 120, 123, 144, 189, 197, 229, 230, 233, 240
Florida Federation of Women's Clubs 31, 35, 44, 45, 52, 215, 246
Florida Forever 158, 159, 179
Florida Public Interest Research Group
  PIRG 127, 152
Frank M. Chapman
  Frank Chapman 20, 25, 28, 33, 38

G

Gilbert Pearson 24, 36, 54
Green Swamp 82, 230
Guy Morrell Bradley
  Guy Bradley 32

H

Hal Scott 91, 111, 112, 115, 122, 175, 220
Harriett Lawrence Hemenway 24
Henry B. Whipple
  Henry Whipple 28

I

ivory-billed woodpecker 37, 63
Izaak Walton League 49, 52, 54, 83, 98, 115, 153, 220, 225

J

John James Audubon 12, 14, 21, 30, 64
John Pennekamp 46, 68, 69, 107, 130, 131, 209, 220, 236, 237
John Storer 58
Johnny Jones
  John C. Jones 87, 101, 109, 116, 123, 136, 137, 175, 220, 227, 228

K

Katherine Bell Tippetts 53, 245
Ken Morrison 88, 229, 230, 231, 241
Key deer 67, 68, 128
Kissimmee River 99, 108, 109, 123, 135, 161, 181, 217, 218, 225, 226, 239

PEER 151

R

Rachel Carson 61
Reubin Askew 82, 99, 101, 122, 135, 218, 225, 242
river of grass
    River of Grass 41, 208, 210
Rodman Dam 78, 80, 82, 123, 144, 145, 198, 232
Royal Palm State Park
    Royal Palm Hammock 35, 44, 216
Rubert J. Longstreet
    R.J. Longstreet 49, 54, 58

S

Save the Manatee Club 125, 126, 145, 146, 169, 171
scrub jay 14, 148, 149, 150
Seadade 83, 84
Sierra Club 77, 85, 90, 100, 110, 111, 113, 115, 130, 136, 137, 139, 150, 156, 161, 167, 168, 169, 170, 171, 172, 173, 175, 180, 186, 187, 192, 195, 223, 228

T

The Florida Naturalist 49, 53, 58, 62, 91, 112, 114
The Nature Conservancy 60, 88, 91, 110, 128, 134, 149, 150, 154, 168, 169, 181, 190, 192, 230, 232, 239, 243
Theodore Roosevelt 28, 30, 50
Thomas Barbour 55
Tiger Creek Preserve 89, 230, 232
Tropical Audubon Society 68, 220

W

W.E.D. Scott 21
Walt Disney World 90, 106, 117
Wekiva River 117, 118, 119, 120, 121, 125, 140, 144, 234
William Bartram 8, 9, 12, 24, 34, 65, 197
William Dutcher 29
William Fremont Blackman
    William Blackman 36